AF837623

The Audit Failures of the Wirecard Scandal

Edgar Löw · Reinhard Heyd

The Audit Failures of the Wirecard Scandal

Examining the Role of the Auditor in Regulatory Oversight

palgrave
macmillan

Edgar Löw
Frankfurt School of Finance & Management
Frankfurt, Hessen, Germany

Reinhard Heyd
Ulm, Baden-Württemberg, Germany

ISBN 978-3-031-59853-1 ISBN 978-3-031-59854-8 (eBook)
https://doi.org/10.1007/978-3-031-59854-8

© The Editor(s) (if applicable) and The Author(s), under exclusive license to Springer Nature Switzerland AG 2024

This work is subject to copyright. All rights are solely and exclusively licensed by the Publisher, whether the whole or part of the material is concerned, specifically the rights of translation, reprinting, reuse of illustrations, recitation, broadcasting, reproduction on microfilms or in any other physical way, and transmission or information storage and retrieval, electronic adaptation, computer software, or by similar or dissimilar methodology now known or hereafter developed.
The use of general descriptive names, registered names, trademarks, service marks, etc. in this publication does not imply, even in the absence of a specific statement, that such names are exempt from the relevant protective laws and regulations and therefore free for general use.
The publisher, the authors and the editors are safe to assume that the advice and information in this book are believed to be true and accurate at the date of publication. Neither the publisher nor the authors or the editors give a warranty, expressed or implied, with respect to the material contained herein or for any errors or omissions that may have been made. The publisher remains neutral with regard to jurisdictional claims in published maps and institutional affiliations.

Cover credit: Kazimierz Jurewicz/Alamy Stock Photo

This Palgrave Macmillan imprint is published by the registered company Springer Nature Switzerland AG
The registered company address is: Gewerbestrasse 11, 6330 Cham, Switzerland

If disposing of this product, please recycle the paper.

Preface

Wirecard is the biggest economic scandal in Europe since the Second World War—comparable to the Enron scandal in the USA and the Satyam Computer Services scandal in India. In around twenty years, the payment service provider went from a rather dubious start-up company to a German technology group that supposedly wanted to catch up with global companies such as Apple or Microsoft—only in a different field. Wirecard ousted Commerzbank, which was more than one hundred and fifty years old, from the DAX 30, and at one point was worth more than Deutsche Bank, which it even wanted to take over.

Suddenly, within just one week, Wirecard collapsed. Board members and senior executives were arrested or evaded arrest by fleeing. What remained was a fraud on an enormous scale—thousands of shareholders lost their savings and lawsuits were filed against Wirecard, the supervisory authorities, the management board, and the auditor.

This book is dedicated to the role of Wirecard's auditors—Ernst & Young. They audited Wirecard's consolidated financial statements over ten years and used different partners. The basis for an audit of the financial statements of a German group was the auditing standards of the Institute of Public Auditors in Germany (IDW PS) applicable in the years in question. They are usually based on the International Standards on Auditing (ISA) but are specifically adapted to German legal conditions. In addition, standards were issued in certain specialized areas in which no ISA (yet) existed. Ernst & Young has undertaken to comply with the IDW PS in its auditing practice fully.

We will demonstrate that compliance with the existing auditing standards would have meant that fraud could have been detected at a very early stage. Numerous indicators of fraud, which are listed in one of the auditing standards, were identified at Wirecard. However, this did not have a sufficient impact on Ernst & Young's risk-oriented audit approach. On the contrary, the company was often satisfied with oral statements provided by Wirecard. In our investigation, we focused on the business activities of third-party acquiring in the Asian region, which have been precisely those activities that ultimately almost did not exist but were largely invented. Ernst & Young was familiar with Wirecard's business model. Nevertheless, it was admitted that the risk situation was completely misrepresented in the Group risk reports and that the reported segment reports did not even begin to reflect reality correctly. On the contrary, numerous disclosure requirements of the International Financial Reporting Standards (IFRS) were violated without the auditor raising any objections.

We are focusing intensively on the financial years from 2015 to 2018. No consolidated financial statements were published for the 2019 financial year. We chose 2015 as the start of our investigations for various reasons. The Financial Times began this year with a series of very intensive allegations in a series of articles, first on the Internet and then in the print version. At this point at the latest, there was an additional external reason for the auditor to investigate particular allegations against Wirecard. In 2015, a huge acquisition was made, the value of which was repeatedly called into question. In the same year, the German securities regulator became active for the first time—ultimately in Wirecard's favor. And finally, a German court in Munich implied that Wirecard's consolidated financial statements had been falsified since at least 2015.

We have structured our book in such a way that we first provide a brief chronicle of Wirecard, the allegations and the demise of the company (Chapter 1). There has been a whole series of alarm signals with high relevance for the preparation of the risk-oriented audit approach by the auditor. We then provide a legal introduction to the Fundamental Principles of an Audit, which include German law and, above all, German auditing standards (Chapter 2). Two standards are of fundamental importance for the planning and execution of an audit—on the one hand, the risk-oriented audit approach and principle of materiality and, on the other, how to deal with risks of inaccuracies and violations.

The basis of every audit is knowledge of the business model and an examination of its impact on the audit planning. In the case of Wirecard, the auditor cannot be criticized for not having examined the business model carefully enough. Certain accounting consequences were discussed with him in detail and possibly even proposed by the auditor. We therefore devote a detailed discussion to the presentation of the business model against the background of the accounting effects (Chapter 3). Given that Ernst & Young knew Wirecard's business model very well, as the reader carefully goes through our book it becomes even less clear that the audit procedures were not geared toward this during the numerous years of auditing.

The fraud at Wirecard took place in Asia through business activity with third-party acquirers. The scandal resulted in 1.9 billion Euro in payment funds not being available. They were allegedly held in escrow accounts. We will therefore first deal with types of fiduciary relationships and accounting consequences and then go into the necessary audit procedures (Chapter 4). We show which audit procedures had to be carried out to ensure that the cash shown in the balance sheet actually existed. If the audit would have been provided properly, the fraud could have been discovered very quickly. We uncover the massive deficiencies in the audit procedures. We then look at the question of accounting, assuming that Wirecard had control over the assets, and consider whether they should be recognized as trade receivables or as cash and cash equivalents (Chapter 5).

Every audit firm has to pay particular attention to the audit of sales. The relevant auditing standard already explicitly mentions that revenues are particularly subject to the risk of fraud. In this respect, we show under which conditions Wirecard should have recognized gross revenues and that commissions were predominantly to be shown in the income statement in the acquirer business (Chapter 6). We conclude this analysis with the necessary audit procedures to clarify—as in the previous chapters—which paragraphs of the relevant auditing standards were violated. Without disregarding the legal requirements of the relevant auditing standards, it would have been revealed that numerous transactions did not exist at all—the fraud would have been discovered much earlier.

While the balance sheet and the income statement provide an overall overview of the asset/liability and earnings situation, the notes have the task of, on the one hand, breaking down these figures in more detail and, on the other hand, explaining them verbally. We deliberately do not want to dive into these small-scale details, since it has already been proven in the previous chapters that the overall picture is not correct. However, since the business activity in its entirety has to be conveyed to the reader of the financial statements by fulfilling two additional accounting standards under specific aspects, we address the disclosure according to these two special standards separately. This is the obligation to present and explain the company's situation across individual business areas (segments) (Chapter 7) as well as the obligation to show and make transparent the risks from business activities to which a company is exposed in a differentiated form (Chapter 8).

In full knowledge of the actual business model, the Group segment reporting presented to the reader of the financial statements was absolutely incomplete and materially incorrect. Wirecard massively violated the relevant accounting standard. The auditor should have objected to this. Instead, the addressees of the consolidated financial statements were deliberately misled—without any reaction from the auditor, which is a fundamental breach of his professional duties.

The same applies to risk reporting, which we differentiate between financial risks and other risks. The obligation to present financial risks is essentially based on an International Accounting Standard, while the other risks had to be presented largely based on a supplementary national standard. Both accounting standards were seriously breached. Once again, despite his knowledge of the business model, the auditor did not insist on reflecting the reality of Wirecard's risk situation. Instead, he allowed the actual risks not to be addressed at all in some cases and the overall risk situation of the group to be completely concealed, which again represents a massive breach of his professional duties.

At the end of an audit, the auditor is obliged to form an opinion, which is expressed in an auditor's report. The audit opinion can be issued without any objections, as was the case with Wirecard by Ernst & Young. However, it can also be qualified or refused altogether. Based on the previous chapters, we explain in a further section that there were sufficient grounds for refusing the audit opinion (Chapter 9). If the auditor's report would have been refused at an early stage, which—as we demonstrate—would have been the inevitable consequence if the audit had been carried out properly, the negative financial effects for shareholders and other investors would have been significantly less and the reputation of Germany as a financial market would have been less damaged. For the reputation of the auditing profession, the inadequate audit procedures were a catastrophe that was clearly avoidable.

In our concluding remarks (Chapter 10), we outline further developments following the discovery of the fraud. Some measures, in particular to strengthen governance, appear to make sense. As far as the role of the auditor in the Wirecard scandal is concerned, we show that the failure of Ernst & Young in the Wirecard financial statements could not have been prevented by new or stricter requirements for the auditor. Simple compliance with the existing rules and regulations and a careful audit by Ernst & Young, as is to be expected of a conscientious auditor, could have uncovered Wirecard's fraud, which had been going on for years, at an early stage. An optimistic and positive conclusion can be drawn for both young students and experienced auditors. Anyone who carries out their work seriously in the interests of the public and behaves professionally, carefully, straightforwardly, and uprightly toward the audited company does not need to worry about liability regulations.

The book is not a lurid novel that delves into the abysses of secret service activities. Instead, the numerous and very massive breaches of accounting standards on the part of Wirecard and of auditing standards on the part of Ernst & Young are demonstrated factually and it is shown at least where there is a blatant failure on the part of the auditor. We only deal with subject areas in which we can clearly demonstrate the auditor's failures. With regard to the takeover of an Indian payment company, Wirecard was heavily criticized from various sides for the extremely high purchase price, because around 90% of the assets acquired were only customer relations and goodwill and the acquired company had only been worth around 10% of the purchase price just a short time before. Personal interests of Wirecard's key personnel may have been behind this acquisition. Violations of the relevant accounting standards, IFRS 3, IFRS 10, IFRS 12, and IAS 24, cannot be identified in the consolidated financial statements. The extent to which the auditor violated his professional duties in this transaction cannot be assessed as an outsider without an insight into internal documents. Since we do not speculate, we have not addressed this issue in our book. Only the reader can judge whether the book can therefore be considered dry. We particularly recommend reading it to members of the auditing profession, students who are still very interested in the attractive and very interesting profession of auditing and all those affected by the Wirecard scandal (like shareholders and other investors) and—especially—the judges.

We use verbatim quotations in our book. Where these originate from German examination standards or German literature, we have translated them into English to the best of our knowledge and belief. Even if, strictly speaking, it is no longer a literal quotation in the academic sense, we have retained the inverted commas.

We would like to thank the two reviewers who recommended that the publisher support our idea of a factual book on the role of the auditor in the case of Wirecard and the courage of Tula Weis from the publishing house Palgrave Macmillan to realize the project with us. We would also like to thank the two employees of Palgrave Macmillan, Saranya Siva and Supraja Yegnaraman, for their technical support. Very special thanks are due to Raphael Klei. He is an alumnus of the Master in Auditing program at the Frankfurt School of Finance and Management and Mainz University of Applied Sciences, which trains future auditors. He provided us with very valuable technical support.

Frankfurt, Ulm
June 2024

Edgar Löw
Reinhard Heyd

Contents

Abbreviations

AAA	triple A, Rating category
AfD	Alternative für Deutschland
AG	Aktiengesellschaft; Stock corporation
AktG	Aktiengesetz; Stock corporation law
AO	Abgabenordnung
APAS	Abschlussprüferaufsichtsstelle, Auditor Oversight Authority
ASCG	Accounting Standards Committee of Germany
BAFA	Bundesamt für Wirtschaft und Ausfuhrkontrolle, Federal Office of Economics and Export Control
BaFin	Bundesanstalt für Finanzdienstleistungsaufsicht; Federal Financial Supervisory Authority
BC	Basis of Conclusion
BIN	Bank Identification Number
BKR	Zeitschrift für Bank- und Kapitlamarktrecht
BLZ	Berliner Zeitung
BMJV	Bundesministerium für Justiz und Verbraucherschutz, Federal Ministry of Justice and Consumer Protection
BS	Berufssatzung; Professional Statute (for Public Auditors)
CDU	Christlich Demokratische Union Deutschlands
CEO	Chief Executive Officer
CF	Conceptual Framework
cf.	confere, compare
CFO	Chief Financial Officer
CG	Corporate Governance
CG Code	Recommendations of the Government Commission German Corporate Governance Code

CSU	Christlich Soziale Union
DAX	Deutscher Aktienindex; German Stock Index
DB	Der Betrieb
DE	Deutschland; Germany
DGAP	Deutsche Gesellschaft für Auswärtige Politik; German Council on Foreign Affairs
DOI	Digital Object Identifier
dpa	Deutsche Presseagentur; German Press Agency
DRS	Deutscher Rechnungslegungsstandard; German Accounting Standard
EBIT	Earnings before Interest and Taxes
EBITDA	Earnings before Interest, Taxes, Depreciation and Amortisation
EBS	Electronic Billing Systems
ECON	European Parliament's Committee on Economic and Monetary Affairs
ed	editor
EGOV	Economic Governance Support Unit
ejbmr	European Journal of Business and Management Research
ESMA	European Securities and Market Authority
EU	European Union
EY	Ernst & Young
F.A.Z.	Frankfurter Allgemeine Zeitung
FAQ	Frequently asked questions
FBI	Federal Bureau of Investigation
FDP	Freie Demokratische Partei
FinTech	Financial Technology
FISG	Finanzmarktintegritätsstärkungsgesetz; Financial Market Integrity Strengthening Act
FREP	Financial Reporting Enforcement Panel
FT	Financial Times
FYI	For Your Information
GAAP	Generally Accepted Accounting Principles
GAS	German Accounting Standards
GmbH	Gesellschaft mit beschränkter Haftung; Limited company (Ltd.)
GoA	Grundsätze ordnungsmäßiger Abschlussprüfung, Generally Accepted Standards on Auditing
GoMoPa	Goldman Morgenstern & Partners
HGB	Handelsgesetzbuch; German Commercial Code
i.e.	exempli gratia, for example
IAS	International Accounting Standards
ibid.	ebenda; Article that has already been mentioned
ICS	Internal Control System
IDW	Institut der Wirtschaftsprüfer; Institute of Public Auditors in Germany

IDW QS	Qualitätssicherungsstandards des Instituts der Wirtschaftsprüfer; Quality Standards of the Institute of Public Auditors in Germany (Requirements for Quality Assurance in Auditing Practice)
IFRS	International Financial Reporting Standards
Inc	Incorporated
ISA	International Standards on Auditing
ISA DE	International Standards on Auditing (Fassung für Deutschland; German version)
ISO	International Organization for Standardization
IT	Information Technology
KoR	Zeitschrift für kapitalmarktorientierte und internationale Rechnungslegung
KPMG	Klynfeld Peat Marwick Goerdeler
KWG	Kreditwesengesetz; Credit law
LLC	Limited Liability Company
Ltd	Limited
MI5	Military Intelligence, Section 5 (British Secret Service)
mm	Manager Magazin
n.F.	neue Fassung; new version
NDR	Norddeutscher Rundfunk
NGZ	Neue Zeitschrift für Gesellschaftsrecht
no.	number
No.	Number
OLB	Oldenburgische Landesbank
p.	page
para	Paragraph
pdf	Portable Document Format
PH	Prüfungshinweis; Auditing Guideline
PIE	Public Interest Entity
pp.	pages
PS	Prüfungsstandards; German Standards on Auditing
PSP	Payment Service Provider
R&T	Rajah & Tann
RegE	Regierungsentwurf; Government Draft
RMS	Risk Management System
SAFE	Leibniz Institute for Financial Research
SdK	Schutzgemeinschaft für Kapitalanleger
SG/HFA	Schmalenbachgesellschaft/Hauptfachausschuss des Instituts der Wirtschaftsprüfer
SMSG	European Securities and Markets Stakeholder Group
SPD	Sozialdemokratische Partei Deutschlands
StaRUG	Corporate Stabilization and Restructuring Act
StuB	Unternehmenssteuern und Bilanzen

TecDAX	Deutscher Aktienindex für Technologiewerte
thes.	same source
TPA	Third Party Acquiring
UK	United Kingdom
US	United States
USD	United States Dollars
vol.	Volumen; volume
WA	Washington
WDR	Westdeutscher Rundfunk
WDT/WDB	Abbreviation used by EY for Wirecard
WHU	Otto Beisheim School of Management
WM	Wertpapier-Mitteilungen
WPg	Die Wirtschaftsprüfung
WP-Handbuch	Wirtschaftsprüferhandbuch
WpHG	Wertpapierhandelsgesetz
WPK	Wirtschaftsprüferkammer
WPO	Wirtschaftsprüferordnung; German Auditors' Code
ZCO	Business Referral and Commission Agreement
ZHR	Zeitschrift für das gesamte Handelsrecht und Wirtschaftsrecht
ZWIRN	Zentrum für wissenschaftliches, interdisziplinäres Risikomanagement und Nachhaltigkeit

1

Wirecard: Chronicle, Public Allegations, and the Downfall of the Company

Wirecard was founded in 1999 by Detlev Hoppenrath and Peter Herold and was a pioneer in the processing of digital payments. The company specialized in linking a credit card and the Internet by developing corresponding software as an interface between credit card companies, online merchants, and the merchants' customers. The company initially became known for processing payments for online gambling and porn sites. "In the early phase of e-commerce, European gambling sites accounted for a high proportion of payments processed via the Internet, and by 2004, it was probably almost 50 per cent of all real-time transactions," admitted Markus Braun, the long-standing CEO. "In this respect, Wirecard was a mirror of the overall market at the time." Later, the share of gambling in payment processing fell to less than ten percent.[1]

Detlev Hoppenrath became the first Chairman of Wirecard, and Peter Herold acted as Chairman of the Supervisory Board for one year after the company was founded. Hoppenrath hired Jan Marsalek back in 2000. He had developed online stores and a cell phone payment application at his previous employer. A major project by Marsalek to reprogram the entire platform failed and is said to have cost around DM 2 billion, jeopardizing Wirecard's existence at the time. KPMG was then commissioned to support the project. KPMG sent Markus Braun as a consultant, hired by Wirecard as Chief Technology Officer shortly afterwards. In May of the following year, i.e., in 2001,

[1] Hesse (April 30, 2016): Finanzmärkte: Die Schlacht um Wirecard - Wette auf den Absturz (D. Spiegel, ed.); Der Spiegel (18/2016), pp. 65–67.

© The Author(s), under exclusive license to Springer Nature Switzerland AG 2024

E. Löw and R. Heyd, *The Audit Failures of the Wirecard Scandal*,
https://doi.org/10.1007/978-3-031-59854-8_1

the previous CEO, Hoppenrath, moved to the Supervisory Board, and Wirecard relocated its Headquarters to Aschheim. After some turbulence, which almost led to insolvency,[2] Hoppenrath resigned from the Supervisory Board in October of the same year. Wirecard was taken over by Electronic Billing Systems (EBS) in January 2002. Between 2002 and 2004, the company was reorganized and listed on the stock exchange as Wirecard AG.[3]

To go public, Wirecard used a company called InfoGenie, which had been listed since 2000. A subsidiary of EBS acquired more than 25% of InfoGenie's shares in March 2002. InfoGenie's shares expired on the stock exchange and were supposed to be delisted. However, the courts prohibited Deutsche Börse from doing so. In December 2004, it was decided to contribute Wirecard to InfoGenie as of 1 January 2005, in return for a contribution in kind. InfoGenie was renamed Wire Card, which became Wirecard in June 2006. In this way, Wirecard became a listed company, and Markus Braun became Chairman of the Management Board (CEO). In January 2006, Wirecard acquired a bank and developed into a full-service payment company providing software and systems.[4] Wirecard was admitted to the TecDAX in 2006. "Wirecard´s rapid rise in the German stock market was due to a perception that Wirecard services were growing worldwide, particularly in Asia."[5]

The first allegations of irregularities in Wirecard's balance sheet were made as early as 2008.[6] Markus Straub, Chairman of the German Protective Community for Investors (shareholders' association, Schutzgemeinschaft für Kapitalanleger (SdK)), made vehement allegations at Wirecard's Annual

---

[2] Cf. Betz/Kim: Economic regulation and corporate governance: The case of Wirecard Institute for policy models, Seattle, WA, USA, Department of International Business, Keimyung University, Keimyung University, Daegu, South Korea Modern Economy, 2021, 12, pp. 1386–1423, https://www.scirp.org/journal/me, p. 1387.

[3] See Hesse (April 30, 2016): Finanzmärkte: Die Schlacht um Wirecard – Wette auf den Absturz (D. Spiegel, ed.); Der Spiegel (18/2016), pp. 65–67.

[4] See McCrum (June 25, 2020): Wirecard: The timeline (T. F. Times, ed.); retrieved on July 23, 2020 from https://www.ft.com/content/284fb1ad-ddc0-45df-a075-0709b36868db. Cf. Orlandi: The Wirecard case: Challenges for German and European supervision, working paper Luiss University Rome, Department of Economics and Finance, Chair of Market Law and Regulation, Coordinator Prof. Paola Lucantoni, Advisor Prof. Mirella Pellegrini, Academic Year 2020/2021.

[5] Cf. Betz/Kim: Economic regulation and corporate governance: The case of Wirecard Institute for policy models, Seattle, WA, USA, Department of International Business, Keimyung University, Keimyung University, Daegu, South Korea Modern Economy, 2021, 12, pp. 1386–1423, https://www.scirp.org/journal/me, p. 1388.

[6] See Krüger (July 23, 2020): EY, was soll das? FAQ on the Wirecard scandal (t. V. GmbH, ed.); retrieved on July 29, 2020 from https://taz.de/FAQ-zum-Wirecard-Skandal/!5695456/?goMobile2=159408000000. See also Möllers: The Wirecard accounting scandal in Germany, and how the financial industry failed to spot it; The International Lawyer, vol. 54, no. 3, 2021, pp. 325–360, 328.

General Meeting on 24 June 2008.[7] The Management Board and Supervisory Board of Wirecard were accused of incomplete and misleading consolidated financial statements for 2007 in various key points.[8] Furthermore, the earnings situation of the banking division was not transparent. Wirecard was concealing income from the processing of online betting transactions.[9] Furthermore, the SdK threatened to file criminal charges for falsification of the balance sheet, which is why an action for annulment was filed with the Munich Regional Court against the resolutions of the Annual General Meeting.[10]

As a result, the auditing firm Ernst & Young (EY) was commissioned by Wirecard to conduct a special audit, and it subsequently replaced a small Munich-based auditing firm that had previously acted as a group auditor for Wirecard.[11] During the audit, it became known that the Head of SdK had already bet on a sharp decrease in Wirecard's share price weeks earlier using derivatives.[12] Fund managers from Sal. Oppenheim also bet on falling share prices. As Wirecard's shares lost almost 70% of their value, Wirecard filed criminal charges for market manipulation and insider trading.[13] In this way, Wirecard immediately took itself out of the public eye.

Since 2009, Wirecard has concluded numerous contracts with companies in financial difficulties to buy their customers for its payment services.[14] The business activities were restructured, and half a billion Euro was raised from investors to finance the high expenditure. According to the Financial Times, there had been an apparent mismatch in the assets and liabilities reported

---

[7] Hammer (November 21, 2008): Streit um Wirecard: Aktionärsschützer im Zwielicht (Zeit online, ed.); retrieved on July 25, 2020 from https://www.zeit.de/online/2008/30/querdax-wirecard/komplettansicht#comments.

[8] Cf. None (July 24, 2008): Straub stolpert über Insidergeschäfte. Wirecard-Affäre (Z. Online, ed.); retrieved on July 23, 2020 from https://www.zeit.de/online/2008/31/sdk-ruecktritt-straub.

[9] See Hammer (November 21, 2008): Streit um Wirecard: Aktionärsschützer im Zwielicht (Z. online, ed.); retrieved on July 25, 2020 from https://www.zeit.de/online/2008/30/querdax-wirecard/komplettansicht#comments.

[10] Cf. Jahn (July 21, 2008): Anlegerschützer unter Verdacht (F.A.Z., ed.); retrieved on July 24, 2020 from https://www.faz.net/aktuell/finanzen/aktien/kursmanipulation-anlegerschuetzer-unter-verdacht-1665356.html#void; see also Hesse (April 30, 2016): Finanzmärkte: Die Schlacht um Wirecard - Wette auf den Absturz (D. Spiegel, ed.); Der Spiegel (18/2016), pp. 65–67.

[11] See McCrum (June 25, 2020): Wirecard: The timeline (T. F. Times, ed.); retrieved on July 23, 2020 from https://www.ft.com/content/284fb1ad-ddc0-45df-a075-0709b36868db.

[12] See Hammer (November 21, 2008): Streit um Wirecard: Aktionärsschützer im Zwielicht (Z. online, ed.); retrieved on July 25, 2020 from https://www.zeit.de/online/2008/30/querdax-wirecard/komplettansicht#comments.

[13] See Hammer (November 21, 2008): Streit um Wirecard: Aktionärsschützer im Zwielicht (Z. online, ed.); retrieved on July 25, 2020 from https://www.zeit.de/online/2008/30/querdax-wirecard/komplettansicht#comments.

[14] See here and in the following McCrum (2015); retrieved on July 28, 2020.

by Wirecard for the payments business from 2009 to 2015. While Wirecard did not disclose the totals, they were evident from the adjustments to the published accounts.[15] The nature of the growth and the high value of intangible assets of 670 million Euro reported on the balance sheet have already raised questions.[16]

In 2010, Jan Marsalek was appointed Chief Operating Officer. In the same year, new allegations arose against Wirecard.[17] The financial news service GoMoPa.net (Goldman Morgenstern & Partners) published a critical report on the online payment service provider Wirecard. It stated that, according to documents from the US Federal Bureau of Investigation (FBI), the company had allegedly transferred 5.7 million USD to the real estate agent Michael Olaf Schütt in Florida on behalf of the English real estate company "Bluetool Limited" in the previous year.[18] However, the money was not intended for real estate transactions but to pay out illegal winnings from illegal gambling in online casinos. Schütt pleaded guilty in the trial. The indictment stated that the deposits were made via Mastercard and Visacard, for which Wirecard had the status of acquirer, and were ultimately processed via Wirecard Bank.[19] Due to this announcement, Wirecard shares fell by more than 30% in one day.

Wirecard obtained an investigation into market manipulation directed against the Heads of the financial news service GoMoPa.net, Klaus Maurischat, and Mark Vornkahl.[20] According to the press spokesman of the

---

[15] See McCrum (July 23, 2015): Wirecard: adjust your perspective (part 1). House of Wirecard series (F. Times, ed.); retrieved on July 28, 2020 from https://ftalphaville.ft.com/2015/07/23/2131270/wirecard-adjust-your-perspective-part-1/; Cf. McCrum (July 23, 2015): Wirecard: adjust your perspective (part 2). House of Wirecard series (F. Times, ed.); retrieved on July 28, 2020 from https://ftalphaville.ft.com/2015/07/23/2134015/wirecard-adjust-your-perspective-part-2/.

[16] See McCrum (2015); retrieved on July 28, 2020.

[17] See McCrum (June 25, 2020): Wirecard: The timeline (T. F. Times, ed.); retrieved on July 23, 2020 from https://www.ft.com/content/284fb1ad-ddc0-45df-a075-0709b36868db.

[18] Cf. here and in the following GoMoPa.net. (October 26, 2012): Staatsanwalt stellt Wirecard-Ermittlung gegen GoMoPa-Chefs ein. Press Release (G. -G. Partners, ed.); retrieved on July 16, 2020 from https://www.gomopa.net/Pressemitteilungen.html?id=1052&meldung=Staatsanwalt-stellt-Wirecard-Ermittlung-gegen-GoMoPa-Chefs-ein&__cf_chl_jschl_tk__=38a6b6b538be7b1e4e220b017ee212d260b55b1f-1595325949-0-ASbKuF4TqxEa04XiU6PRJwWTGjoYaVpqaTlgtsJMMwVzgUNR48dWjol.

[19] See here and in the following McCrum (February 25, 2016): Shares in fintech darling plunge on critical report (F. Times, ed.); retrieved July 28, 2020 from https://www.ft.com/content/0706763a-dadf-11e5-a72f-1e7744c66818.

[20] Cf. here and in the following GoMoPa.net. (October 26, 2012): Staatsanwalt stellt Wirecard-Ermittlung gegen GoMoPa-Chefs ein. Press Release (G. -G. Partners, ed.); retrieved on July 16, 2020 from https://www.gomopa.net/Pressemitteilungen.html?id=1052&meldung=Staatsanwalt-stellt-Wirecard-Ermittlung-gegen-GoMoPa-Chefs-ein&__cf_chl_jschl_tk__=38a6b6b538be7b1e4e220b017ee212d260b55b1f-1595325949-0-ASbKuF4TqxEa04XiU6PRJwWTGjoYaVpqaTlgtsJMMwVzgUNR48dWjol.

Munich I public prosecutor's office, the proceedings were discontinued on 12 October 2012, on suspicion of an offence under the German Securities Trading Act (WpHG) due to a lack of evidence. After intensive investigations by the public prosecutor's office, it was established that the intelligence service neither had been commissioned by a third party nor had it received money or any other benefit from the allegation and the subsequent share crash.

From 2011 to 2014, things became somewhat quieter around Wirecard, with offensive allegations. The company raised several million Euros from its shareholders during these years. It used these funds to buy up (obscure) payment companies in Asia with specially structured deals.[21] The starting point was Singapore, which eventually became the headquarters of the region. The company's rapid growth attracted more and more investors.

Subsequently, based on research by NDR, WDR, and Süddeutsche Zeitung, the Munich I public prosecutor's office assumes that those responsible at Wirecard had already decided in 2014 to inflate the consolidated balance sheet with faked income artificially and to report funds allegedly held in escrow accounts in the 2015 balance sheet.[22]

With a series of articles called House of Wirecard (alluding to the series House of Cards) in the FT Alphaville blog of the Financial Times (FT), the then 37-year-old journalist Dan McCrum and Singapore correspondent Stefania Palma pointed out inconsistencies in Wirecard's balance sheet from 2015 onwards.[23] The Financial Times began publishing its series of articles on 27 April 2015, in which questions about inconsistencies in the Wirecard Group's accounts were continuously raised—also based on information provided by whistleblowers.[24] In 2015, the FT declared that the most significant allegation was that the balance sheet had a hole of 250 million Euro.[25]

---

21 See here and in the following McCrum (June 25, 2020): Wirecard: The timeline (T. F. Times, ed.); retrieved on July 23, 2020 from https://www.ft.com/content/284fb1ad-ddc0-45df-a075-0709b36868db.

22 See Niedersachsen, N. 1. (2. Juli 2020): OLB gab Wirecard-Chef offenbar Millionen-Kredit (N. Rundfunk, Hrsg.) Oldenburg; retrieved on August 11, 2020 from https://www.ndr.de/nachrichten/niedersachsen/oldenburg_ostfriesland/OLB-gab-Wirecard-Chef-offenbar-Millionen-Kredit,wirecard104.html; cf. Strunz (July 2, 2020): Bilanzen über Jahre aufgebläht? Wirecard-Skandal (A.-a. / . tagesschau.de, ed.); retrieved on July 27, 2020 from https://www.tagesschau.de/investigativ/ndr/wirecard-149.html.

23 Ten articles in 2015 and two in 2016. Cf. ESMA: p. 66. For the chronology of the years 2015 to July 2020, see very detailed, ESMA: pp. 38–42 and Annex 3.

24 See here and in the following McCrum (June 25, 2020): Wirecard: The timeline (T. F. Times, ed.); retrieved on July 23, 2020 from https://www.ft.com/content/284fb1ad-ddc0-45df-a075-0709b36868db.

25 Cf. Orlandi: The Wirecard case: Challenges for German and European supervision, working paper Luiss University Rome, Department of Economics and Finance, Chair of Market Law and Regulation, Coordinator Prof. Paola Lucantoni, Advisor Prof. Mirella Pellegrini, Academic Year 2020/2021, p. 55.

Wirecard responded with letters from the British law firm "Schillings" and commissioned FTI Consulting in London to manage external public relations.[26]

In the third quarter of the year, in October 2015, Wirecard announced the acquisition of the Indian payment company "GI Retail" with a total value of 340 million Euro—Wirecard's largest deal to date.[27] One year earlier, the value of the acquired companies was only approximately 46 million Euro. "Wirecard had taken over the Indian GI retail company up to 340 million Euro which is 49 times the earnings before tax and 280 times the annual profit in 2015."[28] "According to the 2015 annual financial report, the purchase price for the Indian business represented around 11% of the total assets of Wirecard, the related goodwill and customers relations represented 11% (almost more than 90% of the assets recognised in the India business were goodwill and customer relations)."[29] Nevertheless, CEO Braun defended the acquisition with the underlying growth opportunities offered in India. GI Retail is one of the leading payment transaction providers there. In this respect, the acquisitions are not too costly, as even loss-making Indian payment providers have valuations of one billion Euro.[30] Wirecard did not see it as a problem that employees, whom Wirecard had taken over as managing directors in the course of the GI Retail purchase, had previously worked with someone who had been warned about illegal gambling. The Reserve Bank of India had previously checked both. In addition, each takeover's past and future business development is extensively reviewed, and the auditors check the corresponding balance sheet items annually.[31] Therefore, the alleged inflated prices for acquisitions and the companies' worthlessness were inaccurate.

[26] See McCrum (October 15, 2019): Wirecard's suspect accounting practices revealed (T. F. Times, ed.). London; retrieved on July 23, 2020 from https://www.ft.com/content/19c6be2a-ee67-11e9-bfa4-b25f11f42901. Cf. Peemöller: Bilanzanalytische Aufarbeitung des Wirecard-Bilanzbetrugs, Fallstudie zur Bilanzfälschung und Erklärungsansätze zu deren Nichterkennung, Zeitschrift für internationale und kapitalmarktorientierte Rechnungslegung, (KoR) 2021, pp. 89–94, here p. 89.

[27] See here and in the following McCrum (November 2015): Rupee do: What is Wirecard buying? House of Wirecard series (F. Times, ed.); retrieved on July 28, 2020 from https://ftalphaville.ft.com/2015/11/12/2144182/rupee-do-what-is-wirecard-buying/; see Storbeck/McCrum (October 3, 2018). Wirecard's meteoric rise prompts questions (F. Times, ed.). Aschheim-London. Retrieved on July 28, 2020 from https://www.ft.com/content/d080c3fc-c561-11e8-8670-c5353379f7c2.

[28] ESMA: p. 73, see also p. 44.

[29] ESMA: pp. 73–74.

[30] See Karami: Das kollektive Kontrollversagen - ein Fall für die Lehrbücher; Karami (ed.), Skandalfall Wirecard: Eine wissenschaftlich-fundierte interdisziplinäre Analyse, Wiesbaden 2022, pp. 1–85, here p. 15.

[31] See Hesse (April 30, 2016): Finanzmärkte: Die Schlacht um Wirecard – Wette auf den Absturz (D. Spiegel, ed.); Der Spiegel (18/2016), pp. 65–67.

J Capital Research, a US company specializing in publishing research reports on listed companies focusing on overvalued companies, revealed that Wirecard's activities in the Asian region were far lower than claimed.[32] In its report on 30 October 2015, J Capital Research also made strong allegations: "Having found little evidence that Wirecard has any volume of business, we visited five of the subsidiaries in Southeast Asia. Only one of the premises had a reasonably credible presence; even that one appeared much smaller than disclosures suggest. We could find no company at two of the listed locations, although there were unrelated companies with similar names."[33] "Wirecard's purchase prices for companies on which it provides valuation detail appear to be based on the target company's "customer relationship" value, but that value does not seem to be based on the number of customers acquired: some of the acquisitions are of companies providing a technology platform that is unlikely to deal directly with individual customers. Others seem to be tiny companies with few customers. This is physical evidence that the balance sheet is bloated with phantom assets. Wirecard's goodwill and intangibles ballooned to a nearly combined 50% of revenue by 2014, with no explanation."[34] "Wirecard says it derives its growth from outside Europe. The ex-European portion of the business has grown from 9.1% of total transactions in Q1 2012 to 24.3% in Q2 2015. The implied growth rate of transactions is 47% for Europe over the 2.5 years and 372% for ex-Europe. Our analysis of the last three years of earnings revealed that less than 10% of Wirecard's growth is organic, and the rest has been generated through acquisitions. To achieve these growth rates, Wirecard tells investors, it needs to acquire customer relationships in Asia by buying companies at inflated valuations. While Wirecard claims that the acquisitions enable it to boost payments activities in the region, it does not appear to have sufficient on-the-ground resources to offer value in payments clearing."[35] Wirecard replied that this report was only produced because short sellers wanted to profit from falling share prices and had paid for the report to be produced.

---

32 See here and in the following McCrum (June 25, 2020): Wirecard: The timeline (T. F. Times, ed.); retrieved on July 23, 2020 from https://www.ft.com/content/284fb1ad-ddc0-45df-a075-0709b36868db.

33 https://www.jcapitalresearch.com/uploads/2/0/0/3/20032477/2015_10_30_wirecard_initiation_global_shorts.pdf, executive summary.

34 https://www.jcapitalresearch.com/uploads/2/0/0/3/20032477/2015_10_30_wirecard_initiation_global_shorts.pdf, pp. 28–29.

35 https://www.jcapitalresearch.com/uploads/2/0/0/3/20032477/2015_10_30_wirecard_initiation_global_shorts.pdf, p. 29.

In February 2016, FT reporter McCrum first reported on a damning, comprehensive 100-page report, the "Zatarra Papers".[36] Investors and short sellers Fraser Perring and Matt Earl were ultimately behind Zatarra. Four reports were published in quick succession under the code name Zatarra. In these reports, hedge funds—speculating on falling share prices as short sellers—accused Wirecard of money laundering and balance sheet manipulation and outlined a confusing group structure through which dubious payments were concealed. It was also stated that Wirecard was buying companies in Asia at significantly inflated conditions. It was suspected that leading persons at Wirecard (parts of the company management and former managers) may have taken a share of the transaction price for their purposes.[37]

Short sellers usually identify supposedly overvalued companies and sell shares in the company that they have borrowed from other investors for a fee.[38] They speculate on being able to buy the shares at a lower price than they sold them short, i.e., without owning them. The price difference minus the lending fee is their profit. Short sellers who wait for the price to adjust to the supposedly economically correct value have to be distinguished from those who disseminate damaging information about the company they are analyzing. In these cases, the dissemination of information often leads to the (expected) price loss. "The motivation of any short selling ban is of utmost importance in order to avoid that substantial doubts of market participants about the companies' (financial) credibility are ignored, and that companies which do not deserve so are illegitimately protected."[39]

The authorities may only prohibit such short selling in an emergency—in the event of a threat to financial stability or market confidence, for

---

[36] Cf. ESMA: p. 134.

[37] Cf. Möllers: The Wirecard accounting scandal in Germany, and how the financial industry failed to spot it; The International Lawyer, vol. 54, no. 3, 2021, pp. 325–360, 328.

[38] Regarding market manipulation by short selling see Langenbucher/Leuz/Krahnen/Jan/Pelizzon/ (2020): What are the wider supervisory implications of the Wirecard case? SAFE White Paper, No. 74, ISBN 978-92-846-7442-8, Leibniz Institute for Financial Research SAFE, Frankfurt a. M., https://doi.org/10.2861/936827; this Version is available at:http://hdl.handle.net/10419/226215, p. 12. See further Bayram/Meier: Marktmanipulation durch Leerverkaufsattacken; Zeitschrift für Bank- und Kapitalmarktrecht (BKR) 2018, pp. 55–63, Möllers: Marktmanipulationen durch Leerverkaufsattacken und irreführende Finanzanalysen; Neue Zeitschrift für Gesellschaftsrecht (NGZ) 2018, pp. 649–658, Mülbert: Rechtsschutzlücken bei Short Seller-Attacken – und wenn ja, welche?; Zeitschrift für das gesamte Handelsrecht und Wirtschaftsrecht (ZHR) 2018, pp. 105–113 and Poelzig: Shortseller-Attacken im Aufsichts- und Zivilrecht; Zeitschrift für das gesamte Handelsrecht und Wirtschaftsrecht (ZHR) 2020, pp. 697–760, see also Karami: Das kollektive Kontrollversagen – ein Fall für die Lehrbücher; Karami (ed.): Skandalfall Wirecard: Eine wissenschaftlich-fundierte interdisziplinäre Analyse, Wiesbaden 2022, pp. 1–85, here pp. 28–29.

[39] SMSG: p. 14.

example, during deliberate market manipulation.[40] "It should be noted that shortsellers, which in academic papers are often considered as "informed traders", play an important role, as they are cosidered to be critical voices to detect fraud (just as whistleblowers, journalists, other market participants, and investor and consumer representatives). … BaFin's choice of the short selling tool can be critically questioned."[41]

Wirecard has denied all allegations of fraud regarding the allegations in the Zatarra report,[42] stating that the allegations are defamatory and completely untrue.[43] "We believe that this report was distributed to impact our share price negatively. We have taken legal action."[44]

In addition, the Financial Times received internal documents from members of Wirecard's finance department. The documents concerned Wirecard's third-party acquiring (TPA) business. The leaked document describes an (alleged) Al Alam deal and the monitoring of customer relationships.[45] The documents list payments from 34 major customers totaling 350 million Euro that were processed via Al Alam on behalf of Wirecard.[46] However, there were clear indications that many of these transactions could not have taken place. When contacted by the FT, 15 of the 34 customers stated that

---

40 See Langenbucher/Leuz/Krahnen/Jan/Pelizzon (2020): What are the wider supervisory implications of the Wirecard case? SAFE White Paper, No. 74, ISBN 978-92-846-7442-8, Leibniz Institute for Financial Research SAFE, Frankfurt a. M., https://doi.org/10.2861/936827, this Version is available at:http://hdl.handle.net/10419/226215, p. 12.

41 SMSG: p. 14.

42 Cf. Jo/Hsu/Llanos-Popolizio/Vergara-Vega: Corporate governance and financial fraud of Wirecard; European Journal of Business and Management Research www.ejbmr.org, http://dx.doi.org/10.24018/ejbmr.2021.6.2.708, vol. 6, no. 2, March 2021, pp. 102–103.

43 Cf. Wirecard AG, t. (March 16, 2016): Wirecard statement. Statement (Wirecard AG, ed.); retrieved July 25, 2020 from https://ir.wirecard.de/websites/wirecard/German/5110/nachrichtendetail.html?newsID=1642675&fromID=5000; cf. Handelsblatt Online. (February 22, 2017): Aktien von Wirecard brechen ein. According to "Manager Magazin" Report (WirtschaftsWoche, ed.); retrieved on July 20, 2020 from https://www.wiwo.de/unternehmen/it/nach-manager-magazin-bericht-aktien-von-wirecard-brechen-ein/19429738.html.

44 Handelsblatt Online (February 22, 2017): Aktien von Wirecard brechen ein. According to "Manager Magazin" Report (WirtschaftsWoche, ed.); retrieved on July 20, 2020 from https://www.wiwo.de/unternehmen/it/nach-manager-magazin-bericht-aktien-von-wirecard-brechen-ein/19429738.html.

45 See here and in the following Wirecard AG, w. (December 31, 2016): Monitoring Customer Relationships. Spreadsheet. Financial Times; retrieved on July 23, 2020 from https://www.ft.com/content/19c6be2a-ee67-11e9-bfa4-b25f11f42901; Wirecard AG, x. (December 31, 2017): Q4 2017 Monitoring CR_internal. Financial Times; retrieved on July 23, 2020 from https://www.ft.com/content/19c6be2a-ee67-11e9-ebfa4-b25f11f42901.

46 See here and in the following McCrum (June 25, 2020): Wirecard: The timeline (T. F. Times, ed.); retrieved on July 23, 2020, from https://www.ft.com/content/284fb1ad-ddc0-45df-a075-0709b36868db; see McCrum/Palma (October 18, 2019): Wirecard: The unanswered questions (F. Times, ed.). London-Singapore; retrieved on July 28, 2020 from https://www.ft.com/content/f4a89186-f0eb-11e9-ad1e-4367d8281195; McCrum/Storbeck (October 16, 2019): Wirecard faces calls from analysts for information on its accounting (F. Times, ed.). London-Frankfurt; retrieved on July 28, 2020 from https://www.ft.com/content/04706e68-f029-11e9-ad1e-4367d8281195.

they had never heard of Al Alam. Eight of these companies closed their business activity in 2017 when their names appeared next to the monthly financial data for transactions,[47] six ignored the requests and made no statements, and the remaining five of the alleged clients could not be traced, so there could have been no contact between them and the FT. According to the Financial Times, the business activity accounted for around half of earnings before interest, tax, depreciation, and amortization (EBITDA) in 2016. According to the FT, the revenue generated with one of the TPA partners had flowed through two subsidiaries whose financial statements had not been audited by the auditor of the consolidated financial statements.

In response to the criticism of the Al Alam business, Wirecard published a statement in which the company commented on the allegations in more detail in an ad hoc announcement. It states that using independent partners such as Al Alam is a "common approach in the industry." Wirecard also stated: "The 34 company names cited by the Financial Times relate to labels of customer clusters created for reporting and reconciliation purposes, each containing hundreds of individual genuine merchants. The Financial Times' conclusions are therefore incorrect."[48] Al Alam commented on what happened, saying that they operated "in full compliance with all applicable laws, rules, and regulations" and were "not involved in any alleged process to falsify revenues or profits at Wirecard."[49] "The group auditor Ernst & Young GmbH Germany has confirmed that all legal and professional audit requirements have been and will be fully complied with."[50] Wirecard asserted that the FT had only relied on fabricated documents.[51] At the same time,

---

[47] See McCrum/Palma (October 18, 2019): Wirecard: The unanswered questions (F. Times, ed.). London-Singapore; retrieved on July 28, 2020, from https://www.ft.com/content/f4a89186-f0eb-11e9-ad1e-4367d8281195; McCrum/Storbeck (October 16, 2019): Wirecard faces calls from analysts for information on its accounting (F. Times, ed.). London-Frankfurt; retrieved on July 28, 2020 from https://www.ft.com/content/04706e68-f029-11e9-ad1e-4367d8281195. See also ESMA: p. 43.

[48] See McCrum/Palma (October 18, 2019): Wirecard: The unanswered questions (F. Times, ed.). London-Singapore; retrieved on July 28, 2020 from https://www.ft.com/content/f4a89186-f0eb-11e9-ad1e-4367d8281195; McCrum/Storbeck (October 16, 2019): Wirecard faces calls from analysts for information on its accounting (F. Times, ed.). London-Frankfurt; retrieved on July 28, 2020 from https://www.ft.com/content/04706e68-f029-11e9-ad1e-4367d8281195.

[49] See here and in the following McCrum (June 25, 2020): Wirecard: The timeline (T. F. Times, ed.); retrieved on July 23, 2020 from https://www.ft.com/content/284fb1ad-ddc0-45df-a075-0709b3 6868db.

[50] See Aktionär, D. (October 16, 2019): Wirecard: So äußert sich das Unternehmen (D. Aktionär, ed.); retrieved on July 24, 2020 from https://www.deraktionaer.de/artikel/aktien/wirecard-so-aeussert-sich-das-unternehmen-20192275.html; cf. McCrum/Palma (October 18, 2019): Wirecard: The unanswered questions (F. Times, ed.). London-Singapore; retrieved on July 28, 2020 from https://www.ft.com/content/f4a89186-f0eb-11e9-ad1e-4367d8281195.

[51] See here and in the following McCrum (June 25, 2020): Wirecard: The timeline (T. F. Times, ed.); retrieved on July 23, 2020 from https://www.ft.com/content/284fb1ad-ddc0-45df-a075-0709b3 6868db.

Wirecard sued the Financial Times before a German civil court. According to Wirecard, the FT had misused company secrets, and Wirecard demanded compensation.

The Financial Times' House of Wirecard series in 2015 marked the beginning of the announcements by the German Federal Financial Supervisory Authority (Bundesanstalt für Finanzdienstleistungsaufsicht, BaFin) and the public prosecutor's office in the Wirecard case. However, Wirecard was not investigated. The financial gap of 250 million Euro noted by the FT and the allegedly overpriced purchase of the Indian payment companies amounting to 340 million Euro were not considered. According to the Reuters news service, the spectacular share price collapse at payment processor Wirecard in 2016 had a criminal background in the opinion of the public prosecutor's office.[52] However, it was not Wirecard that was targeted by public authorities, but the counterparties, as the unsubstantiated allegations of fraud against Wirecard were a case of market manipulation, according to a spokeswoman for the Munich public prosecutor's office.[53] The authorities have completed their investigation and applied to the Munich District Court for a penalty order against the publisher of the Wirecard analysis distributed on the Internet, Fraser Perring, one of the two publishers of the Zatarra report.[54] According to the Financial Market Authority, it is rare for the public prosecutor's office to find evidence of a criminal offense following suspicious price movements. 40% of all prosecutions come to nothing because initial suspicions are not confirmed.

For outsiders, it is easy to suspect that the German Federal Financial Supervisory Authority (BaFin) that BaFin wanted to protect Wirecard, because even in 2016, after Wirecard denied all allegations against the Al Alam deal and Zatarra, BaFin investigated Zatarra (and others) for alleged market manipulation[55] on suspicion of price manipulation and insider trading.[56] Accordingly, a spokeswoman for the authority stated: "We routinely look

---

52 See here and in the following Poltz (December 10, 2018): Ermittler sehen Manipulation mit Wirecard-Aktien als erwiesen an (R. -i. News Agency, ed.). Munich; retrieved on July 20, 2020 from https://de.reuters.com/article/deutschland-wirecard-zatarra-idDEKBN1O91TG.

53 Cf also Hennrichs: Finanzmarktintegritätsstärkungsgesetz (FISG) – die „richtigen Antworten auf Wirecard"? Der Betrieb (DB), 2021 pp. 368–279, 268.

54 See Karami: Das kollektive Kontrollversagen - ein Fall für die Lehrbücher; Karami (ed.): Skandalfall Wirecard: Eine wissenschaftlich-fundierte interdisziplinäre Analyse, Wiesbaden 2022, pp. 1–85, here p. 9.

55 See McCrum (June 25, 2020): Wirecard: The timeline (T. F. Times, ed.); retrieved on July 23, 2020 from https://www.ft.com/content/284fb1ad-ddc0-45df-a075-0709b36868db.

56 See Hesse (April 30, 2016): Finanzmärkte: Die Schlacht um Wirecard - Wette auf den Absturz (D. Spiegel, ed.); Der Spiegel (18/2016), pp. 65–67.

at the events surrounding Wirecard concerning possible market manipulation through incorrect or misleading information."[57] Neither BaFin nor the British and American authorities wanted to comment further—not on Wirecard or Zatarra.[58]

The spreadsheets leaked just one year later, in July 2017,[59] which were shared by Wirecard executives and titled "Overview Third Party Acquirer," as well as several other Excel files, contain data records stating that Al Alam was responsible for a turnover of 265 million Euro in 2016. This corresponded to a quarter of Wirecard's global annual turnover, meaning that the 4.2 billion Euro in payments processed through the Al Alam business in 2016 generated more profit for Wirecard than the rest of its transactions.[60] The documents also show that Al Alam's profits were channeled through subsidiaries in Dubai and Ireland, neither of which published financial statements.[61]

Also in 2017, Zatarra published a new dossier with allegations against Wirecard concerning money laundering. In it, Zatarra also accuses Wirecard of defrauding the credit card companies Mastercard and Visacard by concealing the origin of risky payments processed by Wirecard that was made by credit card.[62] While Mastercard did not comment, a Visa Europe spokesperson stated: "We investigate and take seriously any alleged breach of our operational rules designed to protect the integrity of our payment system."

Another allegation by Zatarra in 2017 related to the acquisition of GI Retail in 2015. The allegation, which other parties had already made, was (once again) that Wirecard had paid far too high prices for acquisitions and justified these with supposedly valuable, dubious customer relationships.

---

[57] Cf. mm-newsdesk. (February 24, 2016): Aktie bricht nach dubioser Studie ein - Short-Attacke gegen Wirecard? (m. magazin, ed., & rei/Reuters, editor); retrieved on July 21, 2020 from https://www.manager-magazin.de/finanzen/artikel/wirecard-dubiose-studie-reisst-aktie-in-die-tiefe-a-1079111.html.

[58] See Hesse (April 30, 2016): Finanzmärkte: Die Schlacht um Wirecard - Wette auf den Absturz (D. Spiegel, ed.); Der Spiegel (18/2016), pp. 65–67.

[59] Cf. Betz/Kim: Economic Regulation and Corporate Governance: The Case of Wirecard Institute for Policy Models, Seattle, WA, USA, Department of International Business, Keimyung University, Keimyung University, Daegu, South Korea Modern Economy, 2021, 12, pp. 1386–1423, https://www.scirp.org/journal/me.

[60] See McCrum (June 25, 2020): Wirecard: The timeline (T. F. Times, ed.); retrieved on July 23, 2020 from https://www.ft.com/content/284fb1ad-ddc0-45df-a075-0709b36868db. It appears that the FREP received corresponding documentation via a whistleblower on 29 September 2016, see ESMA: pp. 67, 86.

[61] See McCrum (October 15, 2019): The Wirecard documents, explained. House of Wirecard series (F. Times, ed.); retrieved on July 28, 2020 from https://ftalphaville.ft.com/2019/10/14/1571059326000/The-Wirecard-documents--explained/.

[62] See here and in the following Hesse (April 30, 2016): Finanzmärkte: Die Schlacht um Wirecard - Wette auf den Absturz (D. Spiegel, ed.); Der Spiegel (18/2016), pp. 65–67.

In reality, the underlying companies were worthless. Quintel Financial, an information provider specializing in litigation support, also investigated the transactions of this mysterious deal and stated: "We examined the balance sheets of the acquired companies and found various indications that there were irregularities in the valuation," says Al-Majali. "We found it unusual that Wirecard wants to take over a company for 280 times the reported profit."

Following the Zatarra allegations against Wirecard, a European private investigation agency took action against more than just the Financial Times.[63] Journalists, researchers, hedge funds, and short sellers who were critical of the Wirecard Group received "spear phishing" emails with PDF attachments through a year-long hacking campaign. According to press reports, 28 private investigators worked for Wirecard in the UK, including former MI5 and military personnel and several lawyers from a prestigious law firm. "Given the extent to which Wirecard and the individuals behind it have tried to silence us with cyber-attacks and bribery, it was right to remain anonymous," said Zatarra, justifying that the allegations were made from anonymity.[64] Only later did it become known that Matt Earl and Fraser Perring had been hiding behind the alias "Zatarra." They had written the report together but wanted to remain anonymous due to the personal risk.[65] However, the authorities they cooperated with knew Zatarra's identity and protected the individuals as requested.[66]

In 2017, BaFin carried out several audits.[67] From 3 June to 21 July 2017, the financial supervisory authority conducted a special audit at Wirecard Bank lasting almost two months, which is said to have focused on the lending business.[68] Almost two years later, in mid-2019, the supervisors followed up with another special audit focusing on money laundering. BaFin therefore had two special audits carried out just 24 months apart.

---

63 See here and in the following McCrum (October 15, 2019): Wirecard's suspect accounting practices revealed (T. F. Times, ed.). London; retrieved on July 23, 2020 from https://www.ft.com/content/19c6be2a-ee67-11e9-bfa4-b25f11f42901.

64 See Hesse (April 30, 2016): Finanzmärkte: Die Schlacht um Wirecard - Wette auf den Absturz (D. Spiegel, ed.); Der Spiegel (18/2016), pp. 65–67.

65 See Murphy (December 11, 2019): Wirecard critics targeted in London spy operation (F. Times, ed.); retrieved on July 28, 2020 from https://www.ft.com/content/d94c938e-1a84-11ea-97df-cc63de1d73f4.

66 See Hesse (April 30, 2016): Finanzmärkte: Die Schlacht um Wirecard - Wette auf den Absturz (D. Spiegel, ed.); Der Spiegel (18/2016), pp. 65–67.

67 See Seidenstuecker/Uhlig (May 12, 2020): BaFin nimmt Wirecard an mehreren Fronten ins Visier. Unternehmensnachrichten (Reuters, ed.). Frankfurt. Retrieved on August 1, 2020 from https://de.reuters.com/article/deutschland-bafin-wirecard-idDEKBN22O14D.

68 See here and in the following Kirchner (July 14, 2020): Bafin führte bei Wirecard Bank große Sonderprüfung durch. Exclusively (finanz-szene.de, ed.); retrieved on August 1, 2020 from https://finanz-szene.de/payments/bafin-fuehrte-bei-der-wirecard-bank-grosse-sonderpruefung-durch/.

In 2018, whistleblowers Dan McCrum and Stefania Palma from the FT drew attention to alarming events in Singapore.[69] Wirecard was accused of fabricating documents and falsifying invoices and contracts by employees at its Asian headquarters, including a Wirecard executive. It was also alleged that the company's management and the German authorities were aware of this.

The forged and backdated contracts had been used for a series of suspicious transactions that raised doubts about the integrity of the accounts at one of Europe's rare technology success stories.[70] An internal presentation described potentially fraudulent cash flows at Wirecard worth 20 billion Euro. The Financial Times had seen the presentation of 7 May 2018, titled "Project Tiger Summary," and other documents as part of an investigation into Edo Kurniawan's transactions and possible violations of Singapore laws, including account forgery and money laundering.

In March 2018, Wirecard's lawyers launched an internal investigation against three members of its finance department on suspicion of "round-tripping," which refers to the fraudulent sending of funds to India via third parties.[71] The law firm Rajah & Tann (R & T) was commissioned to conduct a separate internal investigation. Singapore's Public Prosecution Service explained that eight Wirecard subsidiaries were investigated as it was suspected that document forgery, money laundering, and round-tripping had already occurred between 2014 and 2018.[72] Two of the subsidiaries mentioned were the Indian heavyweight companies: "Hermes iTickets" and "GI Technology," which were acquired in October 2015 by taking over the payment business of "GI Retail" at a high value of 340 million Euro.

R & T submitted a 31-page preliminary report on 4 May 2018.[73] It included numerous allegations such as the "falsification of accounts" and grounds for suspicion of "fraud, criminal breach of trust, corruption and/

[69] See here and in the following Golod (July 11, 2020): So hat Dan McCrum den Wirecard-Skandal aufgedeckt (Z. Rundfunk, ed.); retrieved on July 27, 2020 from https://www.ndr.de/fernsehen/sendungen/zapp/So-hat-Dan-McCrum-Wirecard-Skandal-aufgedeckt,wirecard110.html; see Zapp (producer) & NDR (director): So hat Dan McCrum den Wirecard-Skandal aufgedeckt [movie]; retrieved on July 27, 2020 from https://www.ndr.de/fernsehen/sendungen/zapp/So-hat-Dan-McCrum-Wirecard-Skandal-aufgedeckt,wirecard110.html; see also Karami: Das kollektive Kontrollversagen - ein Fall für die Lehrbücher; Karami (ed.): Skandalfall Wirecard: Eine wissenschaftlich-fundierte interdisziplinäre Analyse, Wiesbaden 2022, pp. 1–85, here pp. 17, 26.

[70] See here and in the following McCrum/Palma (January 30, 2019): Executive at Wirecard suspected of using forged contracts (F. Times, ed.). Singapore; retrieved on July 27, 2020 from https://www.ft.com/content/03a5e318-2479-11e9-8ce6-5db4543da632.

[71] See McCrum (June 25, 2020): Wirecard: The timeline (T. F. Times, ed.); retrieved on July 23, 2020 from https://www.ft.com/content/284fb1ad-ddc0-45df-a075-0709b36868db.

[72] See here and in the following McCrum (2019); retrieved on July 28, 2020.

[73] See here and in the following McCrum/Palma (February 7, 2019): Wirecard: Inside an accounting scandal. Singapore; retrieved on July 23, 2020 from https://www.ft.com/content/d51a012e-1d6f-11e9-b126-46fc3ad87c65.

or money laundering." The report also stated: "We can draw strong and irrefutable conclusions from the documentary evidence. At least several accounting irregularities took the form of falsified agreements. At best, the purpose of these deliberate acts may be limited to the false creation of revenue without misappropriation of funds." Wirecard then told the FT that, according to R & T's preliminary report, the allegations were unfounded, and no regulations had been breached.[74] Although Wirecard's Management Board put it this way, the report did not speak in Wirecard's favor at all, which is why the share price plummeted at this point.

In October 2018, whistleblowers again contacted the FT to say that the internal investigation in Singapore against Wirecard had been closed.[75] Wirecard convinced its investors that there had only been another false attack.[76] According to McCrum, all analysts believed Wirecard because the auditors had nothing to complain about. This was probably also why the supervisory authorities did not act. On the other hand, the Munich public prosecutor's office initiated investigations against the Financial Times journalists for constant damage to Wirecard's reputation. As a result, McCrum was insulted by the Internet community and labelled a criminal.[77]

The Dubai-based Wirecard subsidiary, CardSystems Middle East, is now prominent in the Wirecard Group structure. According to the Financial Times, the company contributed almost a third of Wirecard's turnover in 2018. Its share of total annual profit was even higher at 60% or 237 million Euro.

In the fall of 2018, Wirecard replaced Commerzbank in the DAX 30 index.

In 2019, Fahmi Quadir, founder of the New York hedge fund Safkhet Capital, forwarded information to BaFin in which Wirecard was accused of criminal activities, particularly money laundering. However, according to her statements, BaFin did not follow up on this information.

---

[74] See McCrum/Palma (February 07, 2019): Wirecard: Inside an accounting scandal. Singapore; retrieved on July 23, 2020 from https://www.ft.com/content/d51a012e-1d6f-11e9-b126-46fc3ad87c65.

[75] Cf. McCrum (June 25, 2020): Wirecard: The timeline (T. F. Times, ed.); retrieved on July 23, 2020 from https://www.ft.com/content/284fb1ad-ddc0-45df-a075-0709b36868db.

[76] See here and in the following see McCrum (June 25, 2020): Wirecard: The timeline (T. F. Times, ed.); retrieved on July 23, 2020 from https://www.ft.com/content/284fb1ad-ddc0-45df-a075-0709b36868db.

[77] See Golod (July 11, 2020): So hat Dan McCrum den Wirecard-Skandal aufgedeckt (Z. Rundfunk, ed.); retrieved July 27, 2020 from https://www.ndr.de/fernsehen/sendungen/zapp/So-hat-Dan-McCrum-Wirecard-Skandal-aufgedeckt,wirecard110.html; cf. Zapp (producer), & NDR (director) (2020): So hat Dan McCrum den Wirecard-Skandal aufgedeckt [movie]; retrieved on July 27, 2020 from https://www.ndr.de/fernsehen/sendungen/zapp/So-hat-Dan-McCrum-Wirecard-Skandal-aufgedeckt,wirecard110.html.

Also in 2019, right at the beginning of the year, the Financial Times published its first story on the previous year's investigation in Singapore. The reporting was preceded by a meeting in Singapore in October 2018 with the then-Head of Wirecard's Asia legal department and later whistleblower, Pav Gill, who had unsuccessfully complained internally about fraudulent accounting. From the documents presented, McCrum could see how Wirecard managers had falsified invoices and faked payment flows. According to the documents, many merchants who (allegedly) generated significant sales for Wirecard via third-party partners did not exist at all. When the FT tried to visit some of these Wirecard partners in the Philippines, it only discovered a retired sailor and his family, who were told that an international payment business was allegedly based in their house. Allegedly, agreements with three partner companies in the Philippines, Singapore, and Dubai were responsible for most of the group's global profits. On 29 March 2019, 24 April 2019, and 20 May 2019, Dan McCrum and Stefania Palma substantiated their allegations.[78]

In response to this news, Braun declared the figures inaccurate in a press conference and announced that he would sue the FT. He explained: "Everything has been checked, and the auditor is obliged to go into all the important relationships and partnerships. I think we can comfort you today that everything that has been bought forward in the last two months is fully reflected here, and we have a clear and strong result."[79]

In addition, Wirecard filed a lawsuit against the Singapore authorities and challenged the criminal investigation when the local prosecutors classified five Wirecard employees and eight Asian subsidiaries as suspects.

When the Financial Times asked Wirecard about its relationship with its Dubai partner in the summer of that year, Wirecard claimed, based on an allegedly existing tape recording, that the FT had colluded with short sellers. The Handelsblatt then reported on Wirecard's allegations. The FT published documents showing that Wirecard's profits in Dubai and Dublin had been fraudulently increased and that the customers did not exist.

Wirecard attempted to correct the public image caused by the negative reporting—successfully for a long time. On 15 February 2019, Senior Public Prosecutor Hildegard Bäumer-Hösl received a message from Wirecard's lawyer. Wirecard claimed that the financial news agency Bloomberg was attempting to blackmail the company. Wirecard was told to pay six million

[78] Cf. ESMA: p. 4.

[79] See Storbeck/McCrum (April 25, 2019): Wirecard seeks to put scandal behind it with results (F. Times, ed.). Frankfurt-London; retrieved on July 28, 2020 from https://www.ft.com/content/9f6b4f70-671f-11e9-9adc-98bf1d35a056.

Euro. Otherwise, Bloomberg would report negatively about Wirecard, like the Financial Times. Wirecard eventually sued the FT for "misuse of trade secrets" about the January and February articles.

Against the backdrop of the previous years and the emergence of mysterious documents in connection with the Al Alam deal, the Munich public prosecutor's office told the FT that it had not initiated any investigations against Wirecard or its employees for possible accounting irregularities.[80] However, the public prosecutor's office has been investigating suspected market manipulation concerning the company's share price fluctuations for several months. It stated that this "investigation is directed against unknown persons" and is still ongoing. "We are, therefore, unfortunately unable to disclose any further details," said a spokesperson.

Following a criminal complaint from an investor, the public prosecutor's office in Munich I initiated preliminary proceedings against McCrum for "offenses under the German Securities Trading Act."[81] Dan McCrum and Stefania Palma were caught in the crossfire of BaFin and the public prosecutor's office.

Following the publication of the Financial Times article with the story about the investigations in Singapore, BaFin began an investigation into the FT on charges of market manipulation.[82] The reporters were officially suspected of colluding with short sellers to profit from a manipulated Wirecard share price.

On 18 February 2019, BaFin issued a general ruling based on Article 20 of Regulation (EU) No. 236/2012 ("Short Selling Regulation") "Prohibition on establishing and increasing net short positions in Wirecard AG shares." "The EU Short Selling Regulation 236/2012 was published in March 2012 as a response to the global financial crisis of 2008–2009. The regulation puts a special focus on short selling activities and created regulatory tools to restrict short selling either in exceptional circumstances or in the case of a significant decrease in share price."[83] Articles 18–21 of the Short Selling

[80] See here and in the following McCrum/Storbeck (October 16, 2019): Wirecard faces calls from analysts for information on its accounting (F. Times, ed.). London-Frankfurt; retrieved on July 28, 2020 from https://www.ft.com/content/04706e68-f029-11e9-ad1e-4367d8281195.

[81] See Stenzel (July 6, 2020): Wie ein Journalist Wirecard auffliegen ließ. Hintergrund (Augsburger Allgemeine, ed.); retrieved on July 27, 2020 from https://www.augsburger-allgemeine.de/wirtschaft/Wie-ein-Journalist-Wirecard-auffliegen-liess-id57684581.html.

[82] See McCrum (June 25, 2020): Wirecard: The timeline (T. F. Times, ed.); retrieved on July 23, 2020 from https://www.ft.com/content/284fb1ad-ddc0-45df-a075-0709b36868db.

[83] SMSG: p. 13.

Regulation provide special intervention measures for the competent authorities.[84] In exceptional situations that seriously threaten financial stability or market confidence in a Member State or the Union, the competent authorities should be able to take flexible measures to prevent a disorderly fall in prices.[85]

"Since the EU Short Selling Regulation entered into force, prohibitions and restrictions on short selling had only been imposed on struggling banks in Italy and Portugal for just a few trading days. In the Wirecard case, the two months short selling prohibition was triggered in January 2019 after BaFin's observation of negative press reports, a rise of net short positions and a price decline of Wirecard shares by 40 percent."[86] The announcement of the two-month short selling ban referred to Wirecard's "importance to the economy" and the "serious threat to market confidence" after the share price fell below 100 Euro. BaFin justified its order: "Currently, unfavorable events or developments have occurred that seriously threaten market confidence in Germany. Massive uncertainties have been observed in the financial markets in recent days. This has been triggered in particular by the price development of Wirecard AG shares in recent weeks. This refers to the reports by the Financial Times on Wirecard, in which, according to the financial supervisory authority, net short positions in Wirecard shares have increased. "The net short positions are held by various holders, in particular from abroad, also below the publication threshold," the authority said. With its decision, BaFin created a precedent that certainly caused discussion. The German Bundesbank did not support the short selling ban.[87] Nevertheless, BaFin Director Elisabeth Roegele issued it because the Bundesbank is responsible for the financial system's stability but not for market confidence in terms of investor protection. Even though BaFin emphasized that it was not concerned with protecting an individual company but with creating confidence in a functioning market,[88] it has positioned itself one-sidedly in favor of Wirecard.

---

[84] Cf. Langenbucher/Leuz/Krahnen/Jan/Pelizzon (2020): What are the wider supervisory implications of the Wirecard case? SAFE White Paper, No. 74, ISBN 978-92-846-7442-8, Leibniz Institute for Financial Research SAFE, Frankfurt a. M., https://doi.org/10.2861/936827, p. 12; this Version is available at http://hdl.handle.net/10419/226215, and Möllers: The Wirecard accounting scandal in Germany, and how the financial industry failed to spot it; The International Lawyer, vol. 54, no. 3, 2021, pp. 325–360.

[85] See further Mülbert/Sajnovits: Short-Seller-Attacken 2.0: der Fall Wirecard; Zeitschrift für Bank und Kapitalmarktrecht (BKR) 2019, pp. 313–323, especially pp. 315–316.

[86] SMSG: p. 13.

[87] Cf. SMSG: p. 13.

[88] See Nienhaus (February 21, 2019): Warum schützt die Finanzaufsicht das Unternehmen? (D. Zeit, ed.) Die Zeit (No. 9/2019); retrieved on 27 July 2020 from https://www.zeit.de/2019/09/wirecard-finanzaufsicht-bafin-schutz-unternehmen-kursschwankungen?print.

"BaFin's choice of the short selling tool can be critically questioned. Instead of using the circuit breaker mechanism foreseen in article 23 of the EU Short Selling Regulation (with a pre-defined threshold (e.g. a fall in value of 10% or more in the case of a liquid share) and with a limited duration of two trading days), BaFin applied in the Wirecard case the empowerment foreseen in article 20 of the EU Short Selling Regulation."[89]

When the tech investor Softbank put much pressure on the Supervisory Board and demanded a clarification of the allegations, the Supervisory Board of Wirecard commissioned a special forensic audit by KPMG on 21 October 2019, to clarify the allegations of balance sheet manipulation.[90] "The Management Board and Supervisory Board of Wirecard have decided to commission the auditing firm KPMG with an independent investigation to comprehensively and independently clarify all allegations raised by the British newspaper "Financial Times." The investigation is to begin immediately. KPMG will submit an investigation report in due course and is solely responsible to the Supervisory Board."[91] "KPMG has unrestricted access to all information at all levels of the Group. The result of this report will be published. Thomas Eichelmann, Chairman of the Audit Committee of the Supervisory Board and former CFO of Deutsche Börse AG will accompany the investigation on the Wirecard side." Braun continued: "I am convinced that the independent investigation will strengthen confidence in our successful and fast-growing business."[92] And Wulf Matthias, Chairman of the Supervisory Board, added: "We have full confidence in the audit procedures and their results to date. We assume that the new independent audit will finally put an end to all further speculation."

In the special audit report, in which KPMG presented the results of a six-month special audit in 2019,[93] the auditors complained about Wirecard's

[89] SMSG: p. 14.

[90] Cf. BLZ (Berliner Zeitung), & Reuters. (July 16, 2020): Wirecard: Manager will auspacken (B. Zeitung, ed.); retrieved on July 29, 2020 from https://www.berliner-zeitung.de/wirtschaft-verantwortung/wirecard-manager-will-auspacken-li.93575.

[91] Wirecard AG, p. (October 21, 2019): Wirecard AG beauftragt unabhängige Prüfung. DGAP-News (Wirecard AG, ed.); retrieved on July 25, 2020 from https://ir.wirecard.de/websites/wirecard/German/5110/nachrichtendetail.html?newsID=1838277&fromID=5000; see KPMG Report: retrieved on February 27, 2024 from https://www.wirecard.com/uploads/Bericht_Sonderpruefung_KPMG.pdf, p. 1. see McCrum/Storbeck (May 5, 2020): How the paper trail went cold in KPMG's special audit of Wirecard. Wirecard AG (F. Times, ed.). London-Frankfurt; retrieved on July 28, 2020 from https://www.ft.com/content/cc64ac71-9232-4815-b2df-41c46a73a5f0.

[92] Wirecard AG, p. (October 21, 2019): Wirecard AG beauftragt unabhängige Prüfung. DGAP-News (Wirecard AG, ed.); retrieved on July 25, 2020 from https://ir.wirecard.de/websites/wirecard/German/5110/nachrichtendetail.html?newsID=1838277&fromID=5000; cf. KPMG Report: p. 1.

[93] See McCrum/Storbeck (May 5, 2020): How the paper trail went cold in KPMG's special audit of Wirecard; Wirecard AG (F. Times, ed.). London-Frankfurt; retrieved on July 28, 2020 from https://www.ft.com/content/cc64ac71-9232-4815-b2df-41c46a73a5f0.

lack of document supply.[94] Wirecard did not provide some of the documents requested during the investigation or only provided them several months after they were requested.[95] In this respect, the published KPMG report states that from 17 April 2020 to 24 April 2020, documents and evidence not previously provided were (now) provided by the company. Also, further documents were provided by EY on 23 April 2020.[96] Nevertheless, the delay made it necessary to postpone the reporting date. Furthermore, KPMG states that it has not (or no longer) investigated the authenticity of the documents provided as of 17 April 2020. Numerous documents were only available in the form of a copy or scan. Therefore, the auditing firm could not assess the authenticity of these versions.

The share fell drastically following the special audit report by KPMG, which was published on 28 April, 2020, after the report was highlighted and critically scrutinized by many media outlets.[97] The Handelsblatt Morning Brief of 29 April 2020 also examined the KMPG report and, among other things, critically examined the work of Wirecard's auditor in this context: "The DAX company Wirecard perfectly fulfilled its role as the biggest yo-yo share of all time yesterday. The share lost 24.1 per cent or almost 32 Euro following the publication of a special audit by KPMG, which was supposed to bring great relief from all the pain. Although no evidence was found for the falsification of the balance sheet repeatedly insinuated by the Financial Times, all kinds of weaknesses in the system were exposed, which alarmed investors. For example, the collaboration with third-party partners – and thus the turnover in countries where Wirecard does not have a banking license – could not be fully clarified. The Socratic statement "I know that I know nothing" became an "obstacle to investigation" at KPMG. Third-party partners had shown little willingness to cooperate. Wirecard had also failed to provide requested documents or only provided them late."

On 16 June 2020, the Philippine banks informed the auditor that the documents, which allegedly contained cash amounting to 1.9 billion Euro in escrow accounts, were incorrect. The auditor then refused to issue an unqualified audit opinion for 2019—after having issued unqualified audit

---

94 See here and in the following Hoefer/Engemann (April 28, 2020): Sonderprüfung bei Wirecard lässt Fragen unbeantwortet (General-Anzeiger, ed.); retrieved on July 27, 2020 from https://ga.de/news/wirtschaft/ueberregional/sonderpruefung-bei-wirecard-laesst-fragen-unbeantwortet_aid-50283803.

95 See Karami: Das kollektive Kontrollversagen - ein Fall für die Lehrbücher; Karami (ed.): Skandalfall Wirecard: Eine wissenschaftlich-fundierte interdisziplinäre Analyse, Wiesbaden 2022, pp. 1–85, here pp. 33–35.

96 See here and in the following KPMG Report: pp. 7–10.

97 See here and in the following Gschrei (May 15, 2020): Kurskapriolen der Wirecard-Aktie und die EY-Testate 2017 und 2018. Wirtschaftsprüfung in den Medien. (w. e.-V. Wirtschaftsprüfung, ed.) Munich; retrieved on July 30, 2020 from https://www.wp-net.com/Pressemitteilungen.html.

opinions from 2009 to 2018. Wirecard feared several banks could terminate loans totaling around 2 billion Euro if an audited balance sheet could not be presented. Trading in Wirecard shares was temporarily suspended.

BaFin decided (at least) six weeks after the KPMG investigation report's publication to place Wirecard under its supervision. It examined the special audit report by KPMG and took a closer look at the statements made by the payment service provider before the report was published.[98] The Financial Supervisory Authority examined whether Wirecard had made misleading statements in advance.

The company itself announced in an ad hoc announcement on 22 June 2020 that "the credit balances in the bank escrow account amounting to 1.9 billion Euro (in all probability) do not exist."[99] This figure corresponds to around a quarter of the balance sheet total and two-thirds of the turnover of the unaudited 2019 Consolidated Financial Statements. The share price then plummeted by more than two-thirds.

On 25 June 2020, the management filed for insolvency at the Munich Local Court due to imminent insolvency and over-indebtedness.[100]

---

98 See here and below dpa-AFX. (November 20, 2019): Wirecard-Aktie sackt ab: Kein Testat für singapurische Wirecard-Tochter - Wirecard sieht keine Unregelmäßigkeiten (finanzen.net, ed.). Düsseldorf; retrieved on July 27, 2020 from https://www.finanzen.net/nachricht/aktien/jahresabschluss-2017-wirecard-aktie-sackt-ab-kein-testat-fuer-singapurische-wirecard-tochter-wirecard-sieht-keine-unregelmaessigkeiten-8240195.

99 See Wirecard u. (June 3, 2020): Wirecard AG zur aktuellen Situation des Unternehmens. Stellungnahme (Wirecard AG, ed.); https://ir.wirecard.com/websites/wirecard/English/5110/news-detail.html?newsID=1985593&fromID=5000, retrieved on July 27, 2020.

100 See Wirecard 2020: Application for opening of insolvency proceedings https://ir.wirecard.com/websites/wirecard/English/5110/news-detail.html?newsID=1988247&fromID=1000, retrieved on July 27, 2020.

2

Fundamental Principles of an Audit

2.1 Legal Basis of an Audit and Duties of the Auditor

The legal basis for auditing financial statements for companies based in Germany is set out in the German Commercial Code (HGB). Section 316 HGB regulates which companies are subject to an audit, and Section 317 HGB regulates the scope of the audit, i.e., the audit objects. Per Section 316 (1) HGB, medium-sized and large capital companies are obliged to have their annual financial statements and management reports audited. Capital market-oriented companies that are not required to prepare consolidated financial statements are required to have their annual financial statements audited, including a cash flow statement, a statement of changes in equity and (formulated as an option) a segment reporting as well as a management report, and listed corporations are generally required to be audited regardless of their size and legal form. In addition, the existence and effectiveness of a prescribed risk early warning system by Section 91 (2) AktG have to be audited for these companies in accordance with Section 317 (4) HGB.

If the accounting entity is the parent company of a group, groups with parent companies in the legal form of a corporation that are not capital market-oriented and for which specific exemption provisions (by Section 291 HGB to Section 293 HGB) do not apply, Section 316 (2) HGB requires an audit of the consolidated financial statements, including a consolidated cash flow statement, a consolidated statement of changes in equity, and (formulated as an option) a consolidated segment report and a group management report.

© The Author(s), under exclusive license to Springer Nature Switzerland AG 2024
E. Löw and R. Heyd, *The Audit Failures of the Wirecard Scandal*,
https://doi.org/10.1007/978-3-031-59854-8_2

However, if the corporation is capital market-oriented, the audit obligation extends to all components of consolidated financial statements in accordance with IFRS, which have to include a consolidated statement of comprehensive income and a consolidated segment report, plus the group management report in accordance with Section 315 HGB, which capital market-oriented companies are also obliged to prepare following Section 315e HGB, even if they prepare their accounts under IFRS.

Section 317 (1) HGB stipulates that the audit of the annual financial statements has to include the accounting records. The objective of the audit of the annual financial statements and the consolidated financial statements is, by Section 317 (1) HGB, to determine whether the statutory provisions have been observed. In accordance with Section 317 (1), the statutory obligation requires to conduct an audit in such a way that inaccuracies and violations of statutory provisions that have a material effect on the presentation of the true and fair view are identified in the course of a conscientious professional auditing practice. Section 317 (3) HGB clarifies that the group auditor is obliged to also audit the annual financial statements combined with the consolidated financial statements and the reconciliations to the consolidated financial statements about their compliance with legal requirements. Special requirements are placed on the auditor if the annual financial statements were not audited by the auditor itself but by other auditors. Section 317 (3) HGB requires the group auditor to review and document the other auditor's work.

When conducting an audit, the auditor has to apply those international auditing standards that the European Commission has adopted, following a specific procedure by Section 317 (5) HGB.

Consolidated financial statements of capital market-oriented companies have to be prepared under IFRS insofar as these have been endorsed by the EU and in accordance with the supplementary German statutory provisions applicable under Section 315e (1) HGB. IFRS 7.31 to IFRS 7.42 require detailed reporting on the nature and extent of risks arising from financial instruments. IFRS does not provide for a more extensive risk and opportunity report, as is required as part of the (group) management report under German law (Sections 289, 315, 315a HGB), nor does it provide for a comprehensive (group) management report. As a result, Section 315e (1) HGB requires capital market-oriented companies to prepare a group management report in accordance with the requirements of Section 315 HGB in addition to the consolidated financial statements under IFRS.

In accordance with Section 315 (2) No. 1a HGB, this group management report has to also address the group's risk management objectives and methods and, by No. 1b HGB, certain market risks and default risks. In this respect, there is a partial overlap with the requirements under IFRS 7. To avoid duplication of disclosure requirements in the (consolidated) notes under IFRS and in the group management report under HGB, a cross-reference is often found in practice within the (consolidated) notes, in which reference is made to the fact that the disclosure requirements under IFRS 7 are found in full in the (consolidated) management report. Outsourcing to the (group) management report without a corresponding note would result in the consolidated financial statements not being fully compliant with the IFRS. The Accounting Standards Committee of Germany (ASCG) is responsible for the content of the group management report (to be prepared in accordance with HGB).

By Section 342 (1) HGB, the ASCG is tasked, among other things, with developing principles for group accounting. Suppose the ASCG has drawn up corresponding accounting recommendations, which have been published by the Federal Ministry of Justice and Consumer Protection (BMJV). In that case, they acquire the status of Generally Accepted Accounting Principles (GAAP) in accordance with Section 342 (2) HGB. Concerning the group management report, the ASCG has used its authority to develop GAAP with the publication of GAS 20 and its announcement by the BMJV.

The interpretation of both categories of standards, the IFRS provisions, and the German Accounting Standards have to comply with general legal principles of subsumption. The teleological interpretation of the legal provision is of particular importance, i.e., based on the purpose of the standard. For IFRS, this arises from IAS 1.9,[1] which requires providing useful information for a wide range of users, particularly equity and debt investors.[2] The "true and fair view" is the guideline, benchmark, and limitation of the information in the financial statements. According to a ruling by the Higher Regional Court of Frankfurt am Main on 4 February 2019 (at the latest), an objective concept of error is decisive when assessing the conformity of consolidated financial statements with standards. The accounting company and the auditor are bound by the ruling of the Higher Regional Court of Frankfurt am Main as the court of last instance in the context of enforcement proceedings.[3]

[1] See also Conceptual FrameworkConceptual Framework (CF): para. 12.

[2] See Conceptual FrameworkConceptual Framework (CF): para. 10.

[3] See Karami: Das kollektive Kontrollversagen - ein Fall für die Lehrbücher; Karami (ed.): Skandalfall Wirecard: Eine wissenschaftlich-fundierte interdisziplinäre Analyse, Wiesbaden 2022, pp. 1–85, here p. 21.

2.2 Generally Accepted Standards on Auditing

In addition to the accounting regulations, the related formal legal standards and Generally Accepted Standards on Auditing (Grundsätze ordnungsmäßiger Abschlussprüfung, GoA) are also relevant for auditing financial statements. Both categories of standards are closely linked to European law. The European law include the Statutory Audit Directive (Directive 2006/43/EC), transformed into German national law, and the Statutory Audit Regulation (Directive 537/2014 EU), directly applicable law within the EU.

The GoA are rules on the type and scope of audit services to be provided for the annual financial statements. They relate to the audit objective and the process of achieving it, namely, issuing an audit opinion with the required audit assurance. The purpose of the audit of the annual financial statements is to assess whether the annual financial statements as the subject of the audit comply in all material respects with the specified accounting standards. This is intended to increase the credibility of the financial statement information. To fulfill this expectation, the auditor is obliged to apply all relevant auditing standards during the audit—issued by the Institute of Public Auditors in Germany (Institut der Wirtschaftsprüfer, IDW). The German Standards on Auditing (Prüfungsstandards, PS) are based on the International Standards on Auditing but consider the legal environment of Germany. By IDW PS 200 para. 17 and IDW PS 210 para. 14, a critical mindset toward the company that will be audited has to be taken as a fundamental basis.

There are various sources for the relevant auditing standards.[4] They originate from legislators, professional organizations, individual audit firms, or other sources such as case law or specialist literature. A distinction is, therefore, necessary to be made between statutory, professional, company, and other standards.

Legal norms are laws, EU regulations, EU directives, and their transformation into national law. Professional organizations specify the legal regulations with their pronouncements. This applies, for example, to the professional statutes (Berufssatzung, BS) of the German Chamber of Public Accountants (Wirtschaftsprüferkammer, WPK) concerning the German Auditors' Code (Wirtschaftsprüferordnung, WPO). In this respect, the BS represents a sub-legal standard. The pronouncements of the Institute of Public Auditors in Germany (IDW) can be divided into auditing standards, explanatory audit instructions, and International Standards on Auditing DE (ISA DE)

[4] See Marten/Quick/Ruhnke: Wirtschaftsprüfung, 6th, revised edition, Stuttgart 2020, p. 167.

concerning the audit of financial statements. The latter represent International Standards on Auditing, which have been modified to take into account the national characteristics of the German legal system (therefore, DE). The IDW's Information Technology Committee pronouncements deal with auditing topics focusing on IT. Internal guidelines, as operational procedural regulations, control the audit conduct at the level of the individual audit firms. Other sources of standards include case law and expert and specialist literature.

The degree of binding force and the binding effect of the individual sources of standards for the audit can vary. Audit standards that are codified in formal laws are to be complied with.[5] Violations of formal legal audit standards are sanctioned as violations of the law. The BS does not have a status-forming but a status-filling character. As a public corporation, the WPK is authorized to issue binding standards. It concretizes the provisions of the WPO. The professional statutes correspond to the laws regarding the degree of obligation.

Pronouncements of the Institute of Public Auditors in Germany (IDW pronouncements) are not statutory standards and have no sanctioned binding force. However, Section 43 (1) sentence 1 WPO requires every auditor to exercise the profession conscientiously. This undefined legal term is specified in Section 4 (1) BS—among other things, with the postulate that the relevant professional regulations for the profession have to be observed. These are in the Auditing Standards of the IDW (IDW PS) and the IDW Auditing Guidelines (IDW Prüfungshinweise, IDW PH). IDW membership is voluntary for auditors and auditing firms. However, IDW members undertake to comply with the IDW PS in accordance with Section 4 (9) of the IDW statutes. This self-obligation to comply with the IDW standards as an expression of conscientious professional practice, as required by Section 43 (1) sentence 1 WPO, leads to a de facto obligation to apply them. If an IDW member deviates from the IDW standards by exception, he is required to justify his deviation in court in case of doubt. IDW PH are guidelines that explain the IDW PS and are, therefore, less binding than IDW PS.

GoA are the auditing principles the IDW established, specified in the auditing standards and instructions. They are to be applied when auditing financial statements, regardless of whether they were prepared by national or international standards.[6] The GoA are either the German translation of the International Standards on Auditing (ISA), marked ISA (DE), or national

---

[5] Cf. in more detail Marten/Quick/Ruhnke: Wirtschaftsprüfung, 6th, revised edition, Stuttgart 2020, pp. 173–183.

[6] See Graumann: Wirtschaftliches Prüfungswesen, 7th revised edition, Herne 2023, p. 205.

modifications of the ISA on individual aspects to make them compatible with German law. Finally, they can also be independent IDW PS. They are published if either very extensive modifications of the ISA would be necessary so that recourse to the ISA seems hardly possible or there is no ISA on the relevant topic.

In line with the timing of an audit, the GoA relate to the individual audit steps from the acceptance of the engagement, audit planning, the performance of risk assessments and the response to assessed risks of error, the audit procedures to obtain audit evidence and the subsequent formation of an opinion, the accompanying documentation, and communication requirements through to reporting in the auditor's report.

Upon acceptance of the engagement, the scope of the audit, the audit fee, and, if applicable, the focal points and extensions of the audit engagement are agreed upon in writing. An engagement confirmation letter always contains the requirement to ensure that the auditor has access to the company's documents, information, and data and the obligation to submit a declaration of completeness.[7] A reference to the legally prescribed minimum audit scope and reporting on the audit is possible. Before accepting the engagement, the auditor is obliged to define his strategy and planning (the audit program). This requires a preliminary assessment of the audit risk, whereby the main risk areas are to be identified, and the potential of the audit firm to audit the audit objects for error risks has to be assessed. In particular, the resources to be used by the audit firm for the audit engagement are necessary to be planned regarding material, time, and personnel. Audit results and third-party judgments have to be included in the resource planning. To accept an engagement, determine the audit strategy, and prepare the planning, the audit manager has to obtain knowledge of the business activities, the economic environment, and the internal control system of the company to be audited.

The auditor has to state the auditing principles applied both in the auditor's report (Section 321 (3) sentence 2 HGB) and in the auditor's opinion (Section 322 (1) sentence 2, (1a) HGB). The auditor thus undertakes to conscientiously apply these auditing principles, including the professional duties under Section 57 WPO, and is liable to pay damages to the corporation or an affiliated company for intentional or negligent breaches of duty (Section 323 (1) sentences 1 and 3 HGB).

[7] See Almeling/Flick/Scharr: Abschlussprüfung klipp und klar, Wiesbaden 2020, p. 7.

2.3 Risk-Oriented Audit Approach and Principle of Materiality

The main risk for auditors is that they overlook a material error in the annual or consolidated financial statements and issue an unqualified opinion as part of the audit opinion on the financial statements.[8] "Misstatements are deemed material if they could individually or collectively influence economic decisions that investors make based on financial statements. These risks may reduce investor confidence or cause reputational damage and may have legal consequences."[9] If a material error subsequently becomes known, the auditor faces the risk of damage to its reputation, the risk of sanctions being imposed by enforcement bodies such as the WPK or the Auditor Oversight Authority (Abschlussprüferaufsichtsstelle, APAS), or the risk of liability in the event of an obligation to pay damages.[10] Risks of error are partly inherent, like the matter, i.e., in the susceptibility of the annual financial statement information to be audited for errors as inherent risks.[11] These include[12]:

- The economic facts to be recognized in the financial statements are complex.
- Business transactions are unique or one-off, and the company has no established routines.
- Issues require a high degree of estimation.
- Mass transactions are processed automatically, and changes or individual characteristics may not be adequately considered.

The application of the risk-oriented audit approach by IDW PS 261 n.F. requires the identification and assessment of the risks of error in the audit objects to obtain sufficient and appropriate audit evidence as a basis for the audit opinion (IDW PS 300 n.F. para. 4). To this end, the auditor is obliged to identify and assess the inherent risks in the business model as a whole as

---

[8] See Almeling/Flick/Scharr: Abschlussprüfung klipp und klar, Wiesbaden 2020, p. 6.

[9] Beerbaum: The future of audit after the Wirecard Accounting scandal—Proposal for a change in the payment model, working paper Aalto University School of Business, Department of Accounting, Helsinki, Finland; https://ssrn.com/abstract=3934773, p. 7 and Beerbaum: The future of audit after the Wirecard Accounting scandal—Consideration of the „Wambach Report", Working Paper Aalto University School of Business, Department of Accounting, Helsinki, Finland, June 2022, p. 7.

[10] See Karami: Das kollektive Kontrollversagen - ein Fall für die Lehrbücher; Karami (ed.): Skandalfall Wirecard: Eine wissenschaftlich-fundierte interdisziplinäre Analyse, Wiesbaden 2022, pp. 1–85, here p. 10.

[11] See Almeling/Flick/Scharr: Abschlussprüfung klipp und klar, Wiesbaden 2020, p. 7.

[12] The following four examples are explicitly referred to by Almeling/Flick/Scharr: Abschlussprüfung klipp und klar, Wiesbaden 2020, p. 7.

well as in the individual audit areas (susceptibility to errors in an audit area) and the control risks, i.e., the risk that material errors are not prevented or detected and corrected by the client's internal control system, by IDW PS 230.

To this end, it is necessary to understand the company and its legal and economic framework.[13] This includes the business environment, particularly the partners with whom the company is linked, the company's business relationship, the company's characteristics, objectives, and strategies, and the associated business risks. The auditor also has to ensure that he has sufficient resources and knowledge to conduct the audit.[14] The required profile of the audit team members may include knowledge of the industry and the regulatory environment.[15] The auditors are responsible for ensuring the team members have sufficient practical experience, mainly because they are familiar with the professional rules.[16] In this respect, Section 47 BS requires sufficient personnel and time resources. Furthermore, the auditor has to measure and monitor economic success. The company's objectives, strategies, and business risks are to be assessed. "For example, developing a new market may involve potential business risks, such as liability risks ... or an inaccurate assessment of market potential."[17] Finally, the auditor needs an understanding of the accounting-related internal control system.[18]

Risks of error have to be assessed, and the risks of material misstatement are required to be addressed through appropriate audit procedures. The audit procedures are to be closely linked to the previously identified risks. The risk-oriented audit approach requires the reason, scope, and intensity of the audit procedures to be based on assessing the risks of error concerning the draft financial statements submitted (business risk-oriented audit).

To determine whether the financial statements comply with the requirements, the auditor independently performs risk assessment and structural, functional, and substantive audit procedures with professional diligence as part of a risk-oriented audit approach to obtain reasonable assurance about whether the financial statements are free from material misstatement. In this

---

[13] See, for example, Marten/Quick/Ruhnke: Wirtschaftsprüfung, 6th, revised edition, Stuttgart 2020, pp. 379–391, 474–477, 492. See also IDW PS 261 n.F. para. 13–18.

[14] See IDW (ed.): WP-Handbuch, 17th edition, Düsseldorf 2020, p. 1512.

[15] Cf. IDW (ed.): WP-Handbuch, 17th edition, Düsseldorf 2020, p. 1526. Cf. in more detail Graumann: Wirtschaftliches Prüfungswesen, 7th revised edition, Herne 2023, p. 346.

[16] See IDW (ed.): WP-Handbuch, 17th edition, Düsseldorf 2020, pp. 1512–1513, 1522 and clearly emphasizing, p. 1533.

[17] IDW (ed.): WP-Handbuch, 17th edition, Düsseldorf 2020, p. 1534.

[18] See Karami: Das kollektive Kontrollversagen - ein Fall für die Lehrbücher; Karami (ed.): Skandalfall Wirecard: Eine wissenschaftlich-fundierte interdisziplinäre Analyse, Wiesbaden 2022, pp. 1–85 here p. 39.

respect, in addition to the risk of errors in the financial statement documents (IDW PS 261 n.F.), the materiality of a possible misstatement for the overall statement of the annual or consolidated financial statements (IDW PS 250 n.F.) has always to be examined.

The content of the professional practice of auditors concerning the selection and scope of their audit procedures is set out in the IDW auditing standards. By IDW PS 210 para. 14, the audit of financial statements are to be planned and performed with a critical mindset towards the audited company, its legal representatives, employees, and the supervisory body. The audit of the financial statements is generally not a full audit but a sample audit (IDW PS 200 para. 19). However, this does not exclude the possibility that a specific audit matter has to be audited in total, for example, if it involves specific risks. Therefore, the audit strategy, planning, and execution have to be determined based on the audit risk identified and assessed before the start of the audit. According to IDW PS 200 para. 20, this requires

- knowledge of the business activities and the economic and legal environment (see also IDW PS 230),
- expectations about possible errors, and
- assessment of the effectiveness of the accounting-related internal control system.

The assessment of knowledge of the business activities and the economic environment by IDW PS 230 para. 6 includes, in particular, a risk assessment and identification of potential problem areas (inherent and control risks), effective and appropriate audit planning and audit performance, including determining materiality limits and evaluating audit evidence and its informative value.[19]

Inherent risks are the susceptibility of the annual financial statement information to be audited to errors that occur, which are material in themselves or together with errors in other audit areas and are determined without taking the internal control system into account (IDW PS 261 n.F. para. 6). Control risks are the danger that errors that are material about an audit area are not prevented or detected and corrected by the company's internal control system. If the internal control system is ineffective or only partially effective, the control risks are high. If the internal control system is effective, the control

[19] See Graumann: Wirtschaftliches Prüfungswesen, 7th revised edition, Herne 2023, p. 240.

risks are relatively low (IDW PS 261 n.F. para. 6). There is an inextricable link.[20]

Other important company-specific knowledge includes knowledge about the corporate culture and company organization as well as staffing, financing methods, and the organization of accounting and IT systems. The corporate culture is so important for the auditor to assess because it can directly impact employees' behavior about error avoidance or the open addressing of errors, for example.[21]

In addition, analytical audit procedures are to be performed before the start of an audit. These are plausibility assessments of ratios and trends (IDW PS 312 para. 5). Relationships between a company's audit-relevant data and other data should be identified, and conspicuous deviations should be determined. If significant deviations or peculiarities are identified, special attention has to be paid to these in the subsequent audit. This can go as far as defining key audit areas. In this sense, preparatory analytical audit procedures, as part of the audit planning, make it possible to set priorities for the subsequent audit. This benefits both risk-oriented and efficient audit execution.

During the audit, the auditor is required to collect and evaluate sufficient audit evidence quantitatively and qualitatively. The audit evidence has to be sufficient and appropriate so that the audit findings can be made with reasonable assurance. This requires a search until there is no doubt about the authenticity of the audit evidence (authenticity, credibility, certainty, reliability, truth), by IDW PS 300 para. A5, increasing the quantity cannot necessarily compensate for a lack of quality of audit evidence.[22]

As the audit opinion relates to confirming with reasonable assurance that the financial statements are free of material misstatements and errors, the materiality criterion of the audit field is of particular importance for the overall statement in addition to the audit risk assessment.[23] Materiality assessments are to be made in accordance with IDW PS 250 as amended.

According to IDW PS 250 para. 5, accounting information is to be regarded as material if it can reasonably be expected that its misstatement (including its omission) will influence the economic decisions of the users of the financial statements taken based on the financial reporting, individually or as a whole. In the audit of financial statements, the concept of materiality, according to IDW PS 250 para. 6, states that "the audit of the annual

[20] On the importance of the internal control system, see Marten/Quick/Ruhnke: Wirtschaftsprüfung, 6th, revised edition, Stuttgart 2020, pp. 397–399.

[21] Almeling/Flick/Scharr: Abschlussprüfung klipp und klar, Wiesbaden 2020, p. 23.

[22] See also Graumann: Wirtschaftliches Prüfungswesen, 7th revised edition, Herne 2023, p. 300.

[23] See Marten/Quick/Ruhnke: Wirtschaftsprüfung, 6th, revised edition, Stuttgart 2020, p. 320.

financial statements and the management report … has to be designed to obtain reasonable assurance about whether the misstatements are likely to affect the significance of the financial statements for the users of the financial statements due to their size or materiality." IDW PS 250 para. 17 points out that the assessment of materiality and audit risk may change at the time of the evaluation of the results of the audit procedures compared to the original assessment in the audit planning as a result of changed circumstances or new findings by the auditor, whereupon the criterion of materiality has to be adjusted by IDW PS 250 para. 18. In this respect, the audit of the financial statements is obliged to be geared toward "detecting with reasonable assurance misstatements which, due to their magnitude (quantitative) or significance (qualitative), have an impact on the informative value of the financial statements for the users of the financial statements and are, therefore, material."[24]

2.4 Risks of Inaccuracies and Violations

Section 317 (1) sentence 3 HGB requires the auditor to conduct his audit to identify inaccuracies and violations that have a material impact on the presentation of the net assets, financial position, and results of operations with reasonable assurance when exercising his profession conscientiously. In accordance with Section 43 (4) WPO and IDW PS 200 para. 17, the auditor is required to maintain a critical mindset in this regard. The audit of financial statements does not constitute an audit of misappropriation. Nevertheless, the auditor is not allowed to rely on the credibility of the company's legal representatives and the accuracy of their statements. Instead, the auditor has to obtain evidence of their statements and assess them independently.

The terms in Section 317 HGB, namely inaccuracy and violation, can also be described as errors in accounting and fraud or fraudulent acts.[25] In the auditing standards, both are subsumed under irregularity. The difference between the two terms is that inaccuracies, i.e., errors, occur unintentionally, while violations, i.e., fraud or fraudulent acts, are carried out intentionally. Fraud includes deception (also or only) in the financial statements, damage to assets, or law violations.[26]

---

[24] IDW (ed.): WP-Handbuch, 17th edition, Düsseldorf 2020, p. 1603, also p. 1601 contains explicit reference to qualitative and (alternatively) quantitative characteristics.

[25] See IDW (ed.): WP-Handbuch, 17th edition, Düsseldorf 2020, p. 1629.

[26] See Almeling/Flick/Scharr: Abschlussprüfung klipp und klar, Wiesbaden 2020, p. 33.

"Fraudulent acts and other breaches of standards are undoubtedly one of the key problem areas in auditing."[27] Fraud is facilitated by a confluence of three critical factors known as the fraud triangle: opportunity, motivation, and justification.[28] Opportunity to commit fraud means that there is an opportunity to circumvent controls. In this respect, missing or ineffective controls favor the opportunity to commit fraud. "In particular, it can be easy for management to circumvent or override controls."[29] An incentive, i.e., a motivation, can often be justified with personal, financial, or activity-related (sham) arguments. In addition to these two characteristics, the fraudster has an internal justification. This is based on his personality traits, attitudes, and values.

IDW PS 210 deals exclusively with irregularities (inaccuracies and violations). IDW PS 210 para. 35 contains a detailed list of indicators for which there is an increased risk of fraud, including (verbatim and in excerpts)

- Doubts about the integrity or competence of management
  - o the control of the management body by one or a few persons without the existence of an effective supervisory body,
  - o opaque organizational structures,
  - o lack of willingness to improve the internal control system,
  - o permanent understaffing of the accounting department.
- Critical business situations
  - o … over-expanding business activities,
  - o high-risk sources of income …,
  - o dependence on a small number of suppliers or customers.
- Unusual business
  - o transactions with a material impact on profits …,
  - o complicated transactions or unusual accounting treatment of transactions,
  - o transactions with related parties,
  - o excessive expenses for agency commissions about the service received ….

[27] Marten/Quick/Ruhnke: Wirtschaftsprüfung, 6th, revised edition, Stuttgart 2020, p. 580.

[28] See, for example, Institute of Public Auditors in Germany (IDW) (ed.): WP-Handbuch, 17th edition, Düsseldorf 2020, p. 1628, in detail Graumann: Wirtschaftliches Prüfungswesen, 7th revised edition, Herne 2023, pp. 216–232 or Marten/Quick/Ruhnke: Wirtschaftsprüfung, 6th revised edition, Stuttgart 2020, p. 585.

[29] Almeling/Flick/Scharr: Abschlussprüfung klipp und klar, Wiesbaden 2020, p. 35. See IDW PS 210 para. 43.

- Difficulties in obtaining audit evidence, such as
  - o inadequate posting or documentation of business transactions,
  - o high number of differences between the accounting results and third-party confirmations,
  - o evasive or difficult-to-understand information provided by management in response to the auditor's inquiries.
- Other circumstances, such as
  - o insufficient effectiveness of internal auditing.

In connection with fraud risks, IDW PS 210 para. 36 requires the auditor to obtain a basic understanding of the legal framework in which the company to be audited operates, including an assessment of the extent to which the company complies with these standards. "The auditor has a positive search responsibility concerning the detection of fraud."[30] IDW PS 210 para. 38 requires: "The auditor has to identify and assess risks of material misstatement due to violations at the financial statement level and the level of individual statements relating to certain types of transactions, account balances, and financial statement information.[31] These risks always represent significant risks. This means that the auditor is required to gain an understanding of the relevant control measures." IDW PS 210 para. 39 explicitly refers to deception, which often results from the overstatement of revenue, for example, by booking fictitious revenue. Therefore, IDW PS 210 para. 39 states: "The auditor has to, therefore, assume that there may be risks of misstatements in connection with revenue recognition and determine which types of revenue and transactions affecting profit or loss or (other) statements in the financial statements may be susceptible to such risks. These risks of material misstatement due to non-compliance should also be treated as significant risks."

Potential fraud issues have to be taken into account both in the audit planning and in the performance of the audit. In the early the audit planning stage, the auditor is obliged to identify and assess the risks of irregularities based on their findings to meet the requirements of IDW PS 210 so that the audit procedures are geared toward this. "During the audit performance, internal team discussions should always take place in which all members of the audit team specifically address the issue of fraud. The basis for this can be

---

[30] Marten/Quick/Ruhnke: Wirtschaftsprüfung, 6th, revised edition, Stuttgart 2020, p. 584, whereby the terms "auditor" and "positive search responsibility" are emphasized.

[31] See also Farr: Wirecard und seine Folgen für die Abschlussprüfung, Aufdeckung doloser Handlungen nach ISA (DE) 240; Die Wirtschaftsprüfung (WPg) 2021, pp. 66–74, 69.

collecting knowledge about any unusual events and other possible indications of fraud."[32] Considerations should include, among other things, what opportunities the legal representatives and other managers have to violate legal regulations and conceal accounting manipulations,[33] but also what factors within and outside the company could provide motivation or opportunity for violations or indicate corresponding attitudes on the part of the legal representatives, other managers or other persons.[34] Specialists (e.g., for forensic audits) should be involved in the discussions if necessary.[35] In this respect, the auditor has to "always consider the possibility that violations could be committed, regardless of their previous experience with the client."[36]

The Auditor's Manual (WP Handbuch, WP Handbook) published by the IDW contains a long list of potential indications of violations of laws and regulations concerning IDW PS 210 para. 25, including (selected examples are reproduced verbatim below)[37]:

- investigations by supervisory organizations (e.g., BaFin), enforcement bodies (e.g., German Financial Reporting Enforcement Panel—FREP), and authorities (e.g., tax authorities or the Federal Office of Economics and Export Control [BAFA]),
- payments to business partners in countries that are considered susceptible to corruption or subject to international sanctions, according to Transparency International,
- sales commissions or agency fees that appear excessive in comparison with those usually paid by the company or in the industry concerned or in comparison with the services received,

[32] Almeling/Flick/Scharr: Abschlussprüfung klipp und klar, Wiesbaden 2020, pp. 35–36. See also in detail IDW (ed.): WP-Handbuch, 17th edition, Düsseldorf 2020, p. 1630.

[33] Thus expressly IDW (ed.): WP-Handbuch, 17th edition, Düsseldorf 2020, p. 1631.

[34] See explicitly IDW (ed.): WP-Handbuch, 17th edition, Düsseldorf 2020, p. 1632.

[35] This is the recommendation of cf. IDW (ed.): WP-Handbuch, 17th edition, Düsseldorf 2020, p. 1638.

[36] Marten/Quick/Ruhnke: Wirtschaftsprüfung, 6th, revised edition, Stuttgart 2020, p. 584.

[37] See IDW (ed.): WP-Handbuch: 17th edition, Düsseldorf 2020, p. 1639. Zeranski/Sancak: Does the 'Wirecard AG' Case Address FinTech Crises? working paper, ZWIRN Zentrum für wissenschaftliches, interdisziplinäres Risikomanagement und Nachhaltigkeit, working paper ZWP/2020/2, October 17, 2020, p. 5: "Financial data and reports, information from whistleblowers, complaints by clients or partners, reasonable and supported comments of financial commentators of the media or press, public statements of publicly held companies, audit trails, holistic check of business models, plausibility assessment of business profitability, and many others, are important sources of information for financial supervisors. Moreover, there are internationally accepted red flags. For example, weak corporate governance structure, extraordinary financial or stock performance without supporting fundamentals, problems with audit firms, questionable balance sheet or income statement items, unrealistic rate of returns, and growth rates are some of the significant red flags for both market participants and financial supervisors."

- information systems which, by accident or design, do not allow for adequate verification or evidence,
- unauthorized or incorrectly recorded business transactions,
- negative media coverage.

If there are indications of fraud, IDW 210 para. 58 requires the auditor to assess the circumstances and effects on the financial reporting. "Making sure that early providers of information will be heard by the relevant parties and be taken seriously is crucial (…). Such information can take various forms, e.g. critical reports by analysts and short sellers, negative press reports, and whistleblowing from within the firm as well as outside business partners, or in some cases from the auditor."[38] "If there are no indications to the contrary, it has to be assumed that the suspected irregularity is not a one-off event. Insofar as a possible influence on the correctness of the financial statements is to be assumed, the auditor is required to obtain additional information" (IDW PS 210 para. 59). There is, therefore, an extended audit obligation.[39] Under no circumstances may the auditor be satisfied with unresolved risks, remaining doubts about the reliability of audit evidence, or unverifiable information about the legality of the financial statements without these assessments influencing the audit opinion. If significant questions of doubt arise regarding the audit result, professional advice has to be obtained using a consultation per Section 39 (3) BS. According to IDW QS 1 para. 142, a consultation discusses complex or controversial technical, professional, or other doubtful issues with competent persons within (or outside) the audit firm.[40] In addition, reporting obligations are triggered to the level of management that is hierarchically above the level at which the breach is suspected. If necessary, legal advice is to be obtained from the auditor.

According to IDW PS 210 para. 72, a duty to qualify or refuse the audit opinion with an obligation to provide reasons arises if the company prevents the auditor from conducting investigations to uncover possible

[38] Langenbucher/Leuz/Krahnen/Jan/Pelizzon (2020): What are the wider supervisory implications of the Wirecard case? SAFE White Paper, No. 74, ISBN 978-92-846-7442-8, Leibniz Institute for Financial Research SAFE, Frankfurt a. M., https://doi.org/10.2861/936827, p. 11; this Version is available at:http://hdl.handle.net/10419/226215.

[39] See Graumann: Wirtschaftliches Prüfungswesen, 7th revised edition, Herne 2023, p. 228, which also refers to the involvement of legal counsel or other experts.

[40] Cf. in detail Graumann: Wirtschaftliches Prüfungswesen, 7th revised edition, Herne 2023, pp. 87–88.

fraud. According to IDW PS 210 para. 72, "consequences for the auditor's report … may also be necessary if the auditor is prevented from determining whether a misstatement or a breach exists due to circumstances for which the company is not responsible."

3

Wirecard Business Model

Due to the obligation to apply a risk-oriented audit approach, Wirecard's business model is necessary to first be presented and analyzed regarding its inherent risks. The risk and control system implemented within the Wirecard Group, particularly about the accounting process, is required to be included in the considerations for the actual audit procedure.

"Even when Wirecard was already a stock market darling and about to enter the DAX, the details of its business model remained nebulous even for experts."[1] Wirecard's main business activities are in the field of electronic payment processing.[2] "Wirecard is part of the payment industry as a service

[1] Jakubeit: The Wirecard scandal and the role of BaFin, A case for unifying capital markets supervision in the European Union, working paper 5/2021, Luiss School of European Political Economy Rome, March 22, 2021, p. 9.

[2] Cf. ESMA: p. 33. SMSG states on page 4: "It described itself as a global technology group that facilitates electronic payment. It was classified neither as a payment institution nor as a financial holding, but as a technology company – and was therefore not subject to direct supervision of the German Federal Financial Supervisory Authority (BaFin)."

See also Jo/Hsu/Llanos-Popolizio/Vergara-Vega: Corporate governance and financial fraud of Wirecard; European Journal of Business and Management Research www.ejbmr.org, http://dx.doi.org/10.24018/ejbmr.2021.6.2.708, vol. 6, no. 2, March 2021, p. 98, see also Navaretti/Calzolari/Pozzolo: What are wider supervisory implications of the Wirecard case? Study Requested by the ECON committee, Economic Governance Support Unit (EGOV), Directorate-General for Internal Policies, PE 651.384—October 2020, http://www.europarl.europa.eu/supporting-analyses, p. 12; see also Orlandi: The Wirecard case: Challenges for German and European supervision; working paper Luiss University Rome, Department of Economics and Finance, Chair of Market Law and Regulation, Coordinator Prof. Paola Lucantoni, Advisor Prof. Mirella Pellegrini, Academic Year 2020/2021, pp. 42, 43–44 as well as Zeranski/Sancak: Does the 'Wirecard AG'Case Address FinTech Crises?; working paper, ZWIRN Zentrum für wissenschaftliches, interdisziplinäres Risikomanagement und Nachhaltigkeit; working paper ZWP/2020/2, 17 October 2020, p. 7: "Wirecard AG was offering its customers electronic payment transaction and risk management solutions and issuing and processing

© The Author(s), under exclusive license to Springer Nature Switzerland AG 2024

E. Löw and R. Heyd, *The Audit Failures of the Wirecard Scandal*,
https://doi.org/10.1007/978-3-031-59854-8_3

provider in the area of electronic payment processing. The business model of the industry is to enable transactions to be completed between customers and retailers with the aid of secure and simple payment processes. Transactions between customers and retailers can be processed via every sales channel in real time with the aid of credit card networks or alternative payment processes such as direct debit, invoice and hire purchase of e-wallets. Alongside consumers, retailers and credit card networks or providers of alternative payment systems, this process involves above all payment service providers (PSP), payment processors and card issuing institutions.

The competition and the interrelationships in the industry can be illustrated in simplified form using the four party model. Credit card companies or alternative types of payment provide secure networks or solutions for electronic transactions. Customer want to simply and securely conclude their transactions in real time and possess for this purpose a card product from a card issuing institution (issuer) or use an alternative payment method. It is important for retailers to offer their target groups their favoured type of payment and to keep the number of cancelled purchases and payment defaults as low as possible. In order to process transactions via card networks and distribute money to the retailer's account, the retailer requires an acquirer. A payment service provider is responsible for the technical processing of electronic payments and supplements these services mostly with risk management and fraud prevention solutions."[3]

This makes it possible to identify the following parties involved in a transaction processed via electronic payment services.

of physical and virtual cards. It connected to more than 200 international payment networks (banks, payment solutions, card networks), which resulted in 34,000 customers from various industries, and offered its services in over 100 transaction currencies."

[3] Wirecard: Annual Report 2015, p. 50. Almost identical descriptions of the business model can also be found in the annual reports of subsequent years. On the business model, see also Peemöller: Bilanzanalytische Aufarbeitung des Wirecard-Bilanzbetrugs, Fallstudie zur Bilanzfälschung und Erklärungsansätze zu deren Nichterkennung; Zeitschrift für internationale und kapitalmarktorientierte Rechnunglegung (KoR), 2021, pp. 89–94, here p. 89.

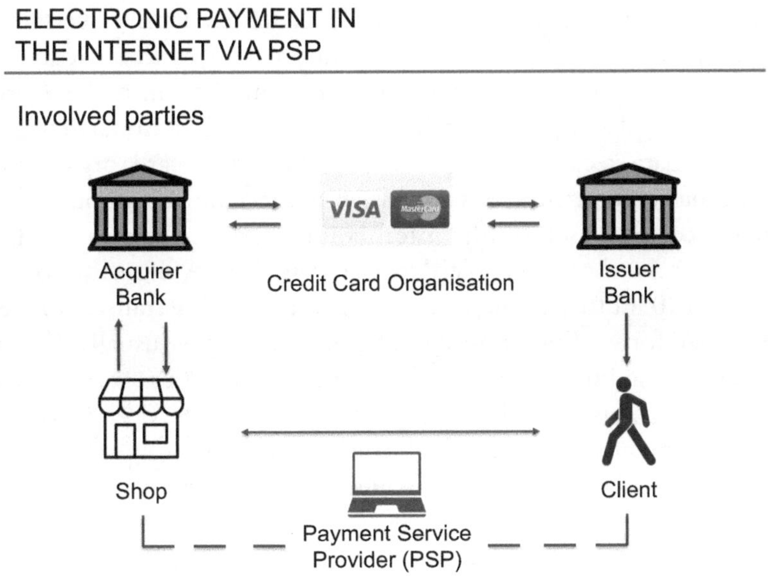

A customer purchases a product in an online store (Client). This business maintains an account with a bank called the acquirer bank (Acquirer Bank).[4] The term is explained from the perspective of the credit card company.[5] The credit card company focuses on the fact that the payment is processed via its credit card. By accepting that the transaction is processed monetarily via the credit card in question, the online merchant's bank acquires a payment transaction from the card company's perspective, which leads to commission payments for the card organization. The payment is ultimately debited from the customer's account. As this bank has issued the credit card to the customer, it is referred to as the issuer bank (Issuer Bank).[6]

The unique feature of online retail is the cross-connection between the customer and the store. While a card reader is installed between the customer and the store in brick-and-mortar retail, which performs certain functions such as verifying the customer and transforming other risk-reducing information, online retail has no such device. This function is performed by the

[4] Cf. ESMA: p. 34.

[5] See Jakubeit: The Wirecard scandal and the role of BaFin, A case for unifying capital markets supervision in the European Union; working paper 5/2021, Luiss School of European Political Economy Rome, March 22, 2021, p. 12.

[6] Cf. ESMA: p. 34.

payment service provider (PSP).[7] A PSP, therefore, receives certain information that a customer leaves behind when paying with a credit card on the Internet. The customer enters this payment data into the merchant's computer when placing an order. This information is summarized in a data record. The data record is forwarded to the credit card organization by the PSP. Finally, the customer's bank debits the required amount from the customer's account based on the information generated and forwarded. The PSP's function is, therefore, solely to transmit data. A monthly fixed fee of around 20–100 Euro per merchant connection and a transaction fee of a few cents per forwarding (routing) of a data record is usually charged for the corresponding business activity.[8] "Central to the Wirecard Group's business model are transaction-based fees for the use of services in the area of electronic payment processing. End-to-end solutions along the entire value chain are offered both for payment and acquiring services and for issuing solutions."[9]

At the beginning of its business activities, Wirecard paid particular attention to the high-risk area of adult entertainment, which includes eroticism, pornography, and unregulated gambling.[10] "Providers from this sector are unattractive as customers for the major banks, as there is a high risk of chargebacks by the end customer in this business area. This arises, for example, when customers lose a bet on the Internet, visit an erotic website, and claim that a third party has concluded the corresponding contract under their name without their knowledge. The big banks are trying to avoid the background processes associated with chargebacks. Wirecard has closed the resulting gap in the offering."[11]

---

[7] Cf. ESMA: p. 34.

[8] According to the testimony of an expert on digital payments in the Committee of Inquiry of the German Bundestag. Cf. Deutscher Bundestag: Beschlussempfehlung und Bericht des 3. Untersuchungsausschusses der 19. Wahlperiode gemäß Artikel 44 des Grundgesetzes, 22 June 2021, Drucksache 19/30900 (hereinafter cited as Committee of Inquiry), p. 179.

[9] Wirecard: Annual Report 2015, p. 60.

[10] See Committee of Inquiry: p. 179.

[11] Committee of Inquiry: p. 179.

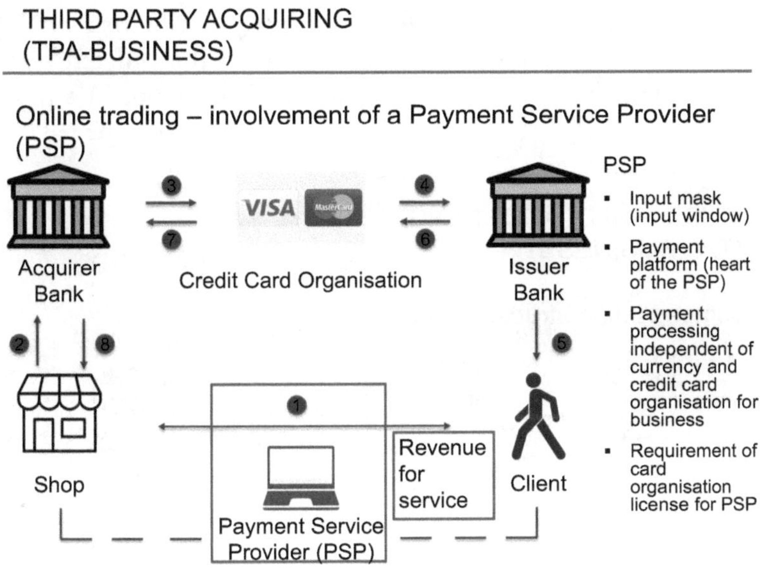

The transport route of the goods, which runs from the store directly to the customer, is completely separated from the payment. In this respect, the flow of information and the actual payment process have to be distinguished. The customer requests to purchase a product (1). The store forwards the information on how the payment will be made to the acquirer bank (2). This, in turn, involves the credit card organization to process the transaction. Initially, it is only a question of the flow of information, i.e., whether the credit card is generally covered (3). For this purpose, the credit card organization connects with the issuer bank (4). The actual payment flow is exactly the opposite. The issuer bank debits the customer's account (5) and forwards the payment to the credit card organization (6). The payment flow from the credit card organization finds its way to the acquiring bank (7), which credits the corresponding amount to the transaction's account (8).

The acquirer provides the merchant access to the payment systems of the credit card organizations and is responsible for forwarding the payment flow between the merchant and the relevant credit card organization. Thus, when the acquirer has received information from the PSP that a customer has paid on the Internet with a credit card, the acquirer requests the funds from the customer's credit card organization and forwards the amount to the merchant (retaining a fee for its service). The entire transfer of information and payment processing takes place in real time. Two parties require a banking license for payment processing: the acquirer bank and the issuer bank.

The acquirer is also responsible for assuming a specific risk when paying with a credit card. If a merchant fails to deliver the ordered goods, the customer demands his money back. If the merchant is not in a position to make the return transfer, the acquirer is obliged to take over the payment and forward it to the customer.

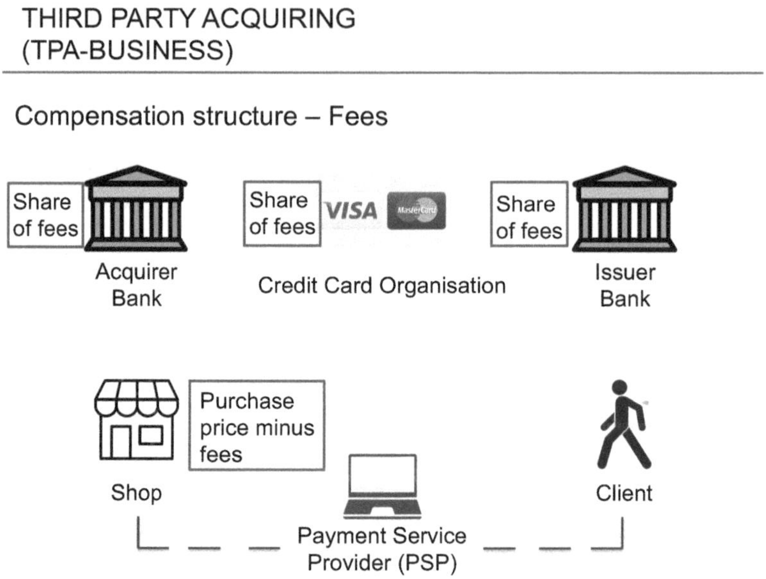

The parties involved are remunerated via commissions. The retailer does not receive the total purchase price, but the purchase price less than the commission (due amount). Commissions are due for the PSP, for example. The service essentially consists of the development and availability of an input screen and the payment platform, the heart of the PSP. In this respect, the PSP guarantees payment processing for the online merchant regardless of the currency and the card organization involved. However, this requires the PSP to have a license from the relevant credit card organization. "As an innovative partner for global credit card companies, Wirecard possesses the required licences from Visa Europe (in future Visa Inc.), MasterCard and others including Unionpay, Amex, DinersClub, JCB, Discover International and UATP."[12]

Further commission is paid to the acquirer bank and the issuer bank. The acquirer receives the commission for its service and the assumption of liability if a certain merchant who does not deliver the goods ordered from

[12] Wirecard: Annual Report 2015, p. 52.

him cannot pay the customer's payment reclaim.[13] As security for a potential customer reclaim, the acquirer bank immediately withholds a portion of the purchase price due to the merchant. The amount of the retained security depends on the merchant's risk. In the event of a loss, it is unlikely that the risk-adjusted security will not cover the repayment to the customer. The remaining default risk that is not covered by the retained collateral is very low.

It seems attractive to expand the PSP business model. The function of the acquirer bank could be replaced for the flow of information between the online merchant and the credit card organization—and, if possible, for the payment flow. A banking license is required if payment processing is also to be taken over. "Wirecard Bank AG has a full German banking license and can also offer banking services to customers in addition to acquiring and issuing solutions."[14] Wirecard was able to issue cash cards itself thanks to its banking license.[15]

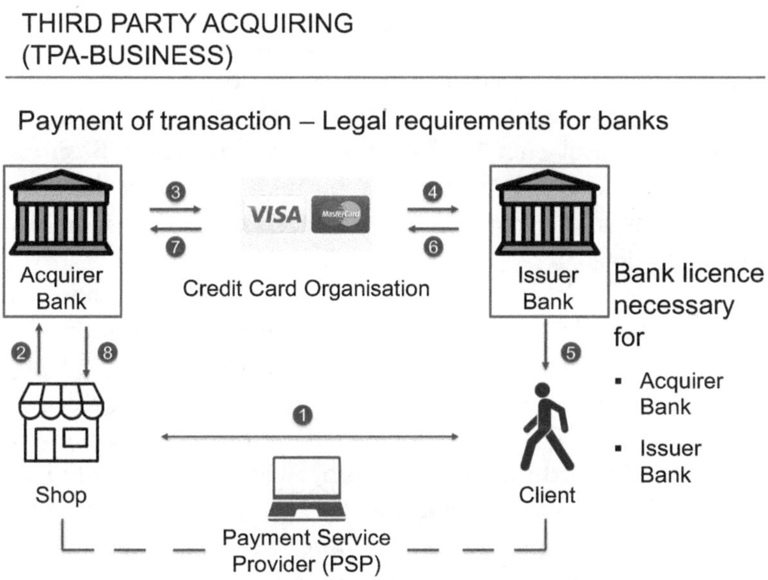

"The major share of consolidated revenues is generated on the basis of business relations with providers of merchandise or services on the Internet

[13] See Jakubeit: The Wirecard scandal and the role of BaFin, A case for unifying capital markets supervision in the European Union; working paper 5/2021, Luiss School of European Political Economy Rome, March 22, 2021, p. 12.

[14] Wirecard: Annual Report 2015, p. 52.

[15] See Committee of Inquiry: p. 180.

who outsource their electronic payment processes to Wirecard AG."[16] In this part of the business model, Wirecard offers the entire value chain of the payment business, namely as a PSP and as an acquiring bank (via Wirecard Bank). Wirecard also had many customers from the high-risk sector in the acquiring business, which (apart from adult entertainment) also included airlines.[17] "From the credit card organization's point of view, airline transactions are risky because the bookings have long lead times, and smaller airlines, in particular, often file for insolvency. Since the acquirer initially assumes the liability risk for chargebacks on behalf of the merchant, the acquirer runs the risk of being left with the costs in the event of mass cancellations due to airline insolvency."[18]

The Wirecard Bank provided another service.[19] "The problem for many new online retailers is that they are not initially considered creditworthy by the major banks. On the one hand, they would not be issued a company credit card. Secondly, they are also not accepted for getting credit cards. The latter means that a bank agrees to carry out acquiring for transactions initiated by a customer with a credit card on the website of the young merchant in question. The problem is related to the fact that the merchant bank, as the acquirer, is liable for chargebacks in case of doubt, especially in the event of the merchant's insolvency. If the bank cannot assess the business model of a new merchant correctly, this risk is too high for it. On the other hand, the merchant may first have to advance the costs of producing its goods and needs money to do so."[20]

The Wirecard Bank provided young companies with loans, corporate credit cards, and credit card acceptance but charged significantly higher fees than big banks. "Wirecard had the advantage that it was a bank and a payment service provider via another subsidiary. This provided it with more precise information about the merchant's daily turnover, giving it a better picture of its creditworthiness. On the other hand, a bank only has insight into the previous year's balance sheets. As an acquirer, the Wirecard Bank also had access to the merchant's revenue volume and could retain this as collateral for the loan granted."[21] Wirecard charged a setup fee for this business

[16] Wirecard: Annual Report 2015, p. 61.

[17] See Committee of Inquiry: p. 180.

[18] Committee of Inquiry: p. 180.

[19] Cf. Beerbaum Dirk, Jani Jignesh: Satyam versus Wirecard—A case study research on two accounting corporate scandals; Journal of Applied Research in the Digital Economy, February 2021, p. 14.

[20] Committee of Inquiry: p. 180.

[21] Committee of Inquiry: p. 181.

activity and interest on the loans granted.[22] This is not an activity in traditional payment transactions but the granting of a loan—which is a typical banking transaction.

Even though Wirecard Bank had a banking license in principle, this did not apply to all countries where the Group was active.[23] "Cooperation with local banks will be expanded in future to offer retailers acquiring services."[24] "Through partnerships with local and regional financial service providers, Wirecard AG is able to expand its network of financial services beyond Europe and thus operate in non-European markets as a full-service provider for locally active retailers and also for companies with international activities."[25]

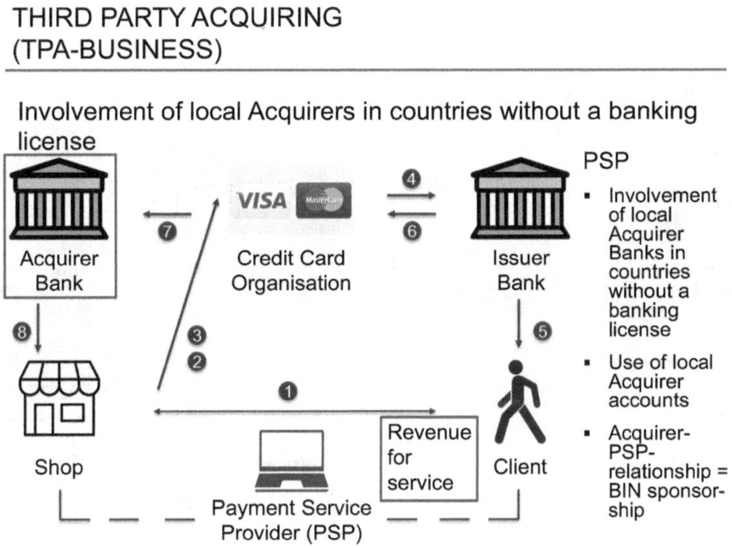

The business model can, therefore, be viewed in a differentiated manner. Where Wirecard did not have a banking license, only the information flow

---

[22] See Committee of Inquiry: p. 181.

[23] Cf. ESMA: p. 35 and Navaretti/Calzolari/Pozzolo: What are wider supervisory implications of the Wirecard case? Study Requested by the ECON committee, Economic Governance Support Unit (EGOV), Directorate-General for Internal Policies, PE 651.384—October 2020, http://www.europarl.europa.eu/supporting-analyses, p. 12 as well as Orlandi: The Wirecard case: Challenges for German and European supervision, working paper Luiss University Rome, Department of Economics and Finance, Chair of Market Law and Regulation, Coordinator Prof. Paola Lucantoni, Advisor Prof. Mirella Pellegrini, Academic Year 2020/2021, p. 44 and Zeranski/Sancak: Does the 'Wirecard AG' Case Address FinTech Crises?, working paper, ZWIRN Zentrum für wissenschaftliches, interdisziplinäres Risikomanagement und Nachhaltigkeit; working paper ZWP/2020/2, October 17, 2020, p. 7.

[24] Wirecard: Annual Report 2015, p. 52.

[25] Wirecard: Annual Report 2015, p. 64.

was separated and taken over. At the same time, payment processing was carried out via local acquirer banks whose accounts were used.[26] The relationship between the acquirer bank and the PSP is called BIN sponsorship, where BIN stands for Bank Identification Number. Therefore, a bank is accepted by a credit card organization for payment processing.

Suppose an acquirer bank is also the house bank of the online merchant. In that case, there is no information about all transactions of this online merchant at the PSP, but only about those processed simultaneously via the PSP's platform. It is, therefore, only possible to monitor the transactions if the PSP uses the acquirer bank.

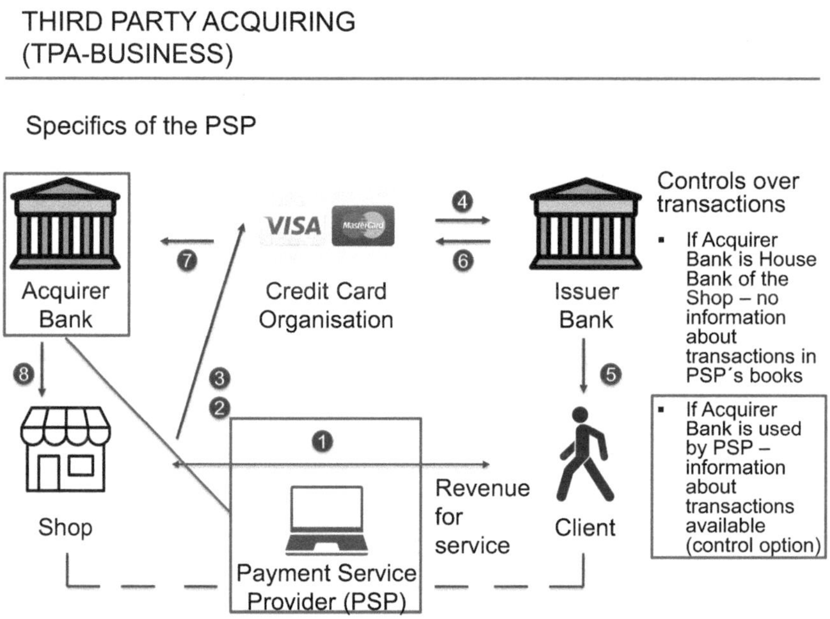

This results in three types of acquirer banks. The acquirer bank can also be the online merchant's house bank. The PSP lacks information about all merchant transactions in this case, but the commission is still paid. Secondly, the acquirer bank is also the PSP. However, this requires the PSP to have a banking license. The advantage lies in relatively high commission payments. Finally, there is the case where the PSP uses the acquirer bank itself. In this case, the PSP has information on transactions. However, only a medium

[26] Cf. Jo/Hsu//Llanos-Popolizio/Vergara-Vega: Corporate Governance and Financial Fraud of Wirecard; European Journal of Business and Management Research www.ejbmr.org, http://dx.doi.org/10.24018/ejbmr.2021.6.2.708, vol. 6, no. 2, March 2021, pp. 98, 100.

commission is earned in these cases because a share is paid to the acquirer bank.

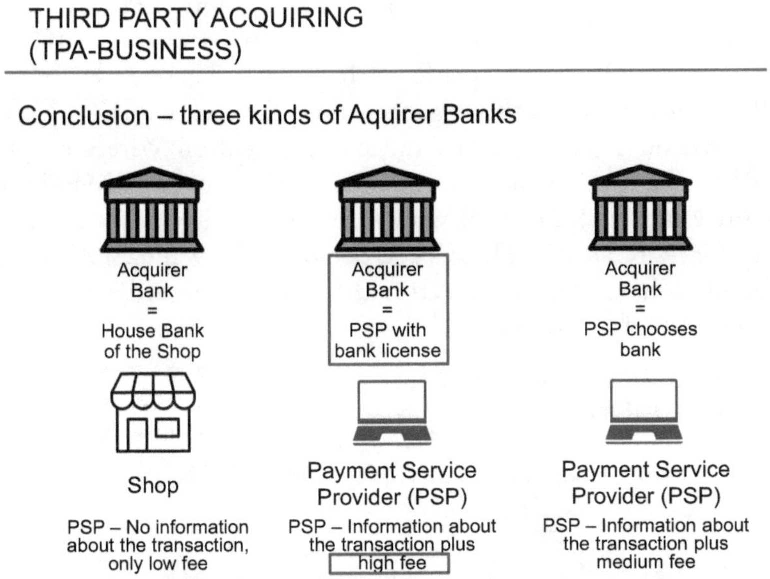

Wirecard operated the PSP business via three Wirecard Group companies, Wirecard UK and Dublin Ltd, Dublin, Wirecard Technologies GmbH, Aschheim, and Wirecard Middle East FZ-LLC, Dubai, UAE.

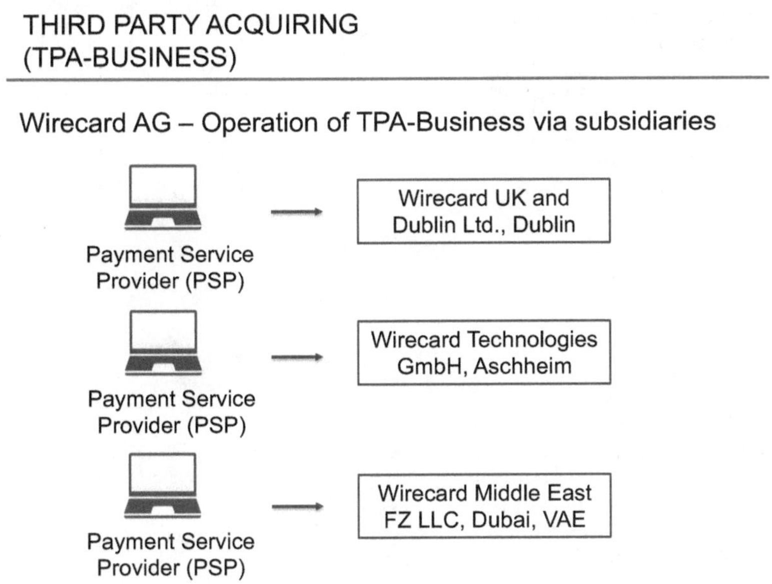

Wirecard has also concluded contracts with three third-party partners, whereby these (independent) third-party partners have taken over payment processing and acquiring.[27] These were Al Alam Solution Provider FZ-LLC, Dubai, until 2017. Wirecard acquired Al Alam on 1 January 1 2018 and has (only) operated on Wirecard's platform since 2019. The second acquirer was Senjo Payments Asia Pte. Ltd, Singapore, until the end of 2017, which Wirecard acquired on 1 January 2018 and has operated on Wirecard's platform since 2019. The third acquirer was PayEasy Solutions Inc., Manila, Philippines—since the 2018 financial year. All three acted as acquirers, i.e., BIN sponsors, for Wirecard.[28] "These TPA, Senjo, PayEasy and Al Alam in 2016 were found to have contributed around 95% of Wirecard′s EBITDA and more than 50% of its revenues."[29]

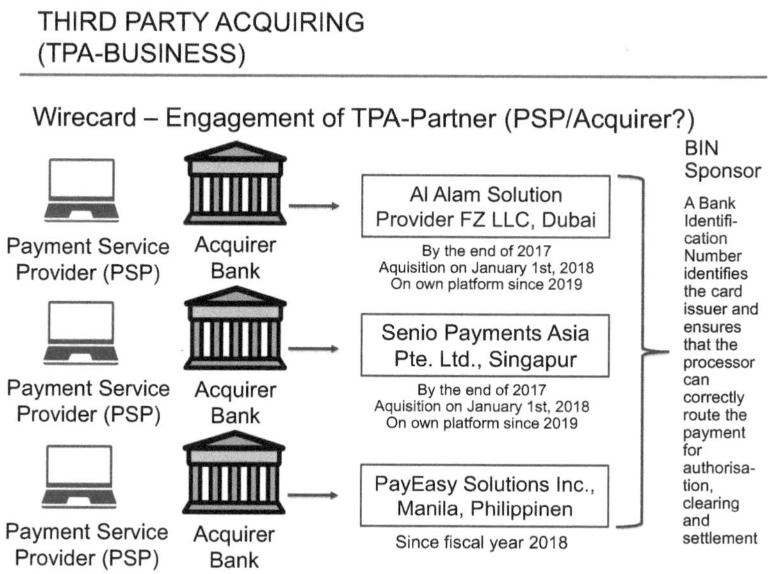

[27] For more information on accounting rumors regarding the activities with Al Alam, see Löw/Kunzweiler: Wirecard - Bilanzierungsgerüchte, BaFin-Meldungen und Niederschlag in den Konzernabschlüssen, Berlin 2021, in particular, pp. 20–24.

[28] Cf. Löw/Kunzweiler: Wirecard - Bilanzierungsgerüchte, BaFin-Meldungen und Niederschlag in den Konzernabschlüssen, Berlin 2021, in particular, pp. 20–24.

[29] Orlandi: The Wirecard case: Challenges for German and European supervision; working paper Luiss University Rome, Department of Economics and Finance, Chair of Market Law and Regulation, Coordinator Prof. Paola Lucantoni, Advisor Prof. Mirella Pellegrini, Academic Year 2020/2021, p. 45.

The TPA business is based on the fact that the regulations of credit card organizations differ in the jurisdictions of different countries. Therefore, the licenses for acquiring and issuing cards to customers are country specific.[30] Usually, this is not a problem for Internet transactions because merchants sell their goods predominantly to customers in a particular region.

"In contrast to this, the merchants Wirecard prefers to address in the digital goods sector are, by definition, international merchants, as digital services are not subject to any hurdles such as the shipping of goods, shipping costs, or customs barriers. Therefore, it does not matter to the merchant where his customer is in this area. Therefore, such international merchants face the problem that, due to the regional structure of payment service providers, they need to connect their sales page to many different service providers with different interfaces."[31] Wirecard offered these merchants a PSP and acquiring that was valid worldwide. "This meant that the merchant only had one contract and one settlement with Wirecard. Wirecard then "routed" transactions in or from regions for which it did not have its license to a cooperating regional acquirer, which then forwarded them to the system of the desired card organization."[32]

In this respect, Wirecard brokered customers to business partners (TPA partners, third-party acquirers) who processed credit card transactions as payment service providers with connections to various acquirer banks and charged Wirecard companies processing fees. The Wirecard companies did not process these transactions in the TPA business.

The processing fees were invoiced to the credit card customers by the TPA partners and recognized as revenue by the Wirecard companies. At the same time, the TPA partners received claims to commissions from the Wirecard companies for the processing services provided. The Wirecard companies recognized these commissions as the cost of materials (cost of sales). The difference between the sales revenues (credit card processing fees) and the cost of materials (processing commissions) represented gross profit in the

---

[30] Cf. Jakubeit: The Wirecard scandal and the role of BaFin, A case for unifying capital markets supervision in the European Union; working paper 5/2021, LUISS School of European Political Economy Rome, March 22, 2021, p. 12.

[31] Committee of Inquiry: p. 181.

[32] Committee of Inquiry: p. 181.

Wirecard companies' income statement and, at the same time, formed a (net) receivable from the TPA partners, as these had collected the credit card fees from the credit card customers for the Wirecard companies. For the TPA companies, this amount represents a (net) liability to the Wirecard companies. "In 2019, the TPA business accounted for half of Wirecard's total transaction volume – between 2016 and 2018, the share was even higher."[33]

Concerning payment processing, the interim result is that Wirecard operated the so-called third-party acquiring (TPA business) via subsidiaries. An audit of these business activities is therefore not possible at the level of the parent company (Wirecard AG) but via the annual financial statements of these subsidiaries and at the group level for the consolidated financial statements. Wirecard was not a PSP until the end of 2017, but it used Al Alam and Senjo, which were only transferred to Wirecard's platform in 2019, and PayEasy directly on its platform from 2018. In this respect, Wirecard also acted as an intermediary for merchants to (third-party) PSP through subsidiaries without operating and acquiring itself. After all, Wirecard's TPA partners were not acquirers in the true sense of the word but merely PSP. Without the TPA business, Wirecard would not have reported a profit, but it would have reported a loss since 2015.[34]

---

[33] Rinker: Vorwürfe wegen Bilanzmanipulationen gegen Wirecard, Darstellung ausgewählter Sachverhalte aus dem KPMG-Untersuchungsbericht; WP Praxis 2020, S. 293–297; WP Praxis, 2020, pp. 293–297, here p. 294.

[34] Cf. Jakubeit: The Wirecard scandal and the role of BaFin, A case for unifying capital markets supervision in the European Union; working paper 5/2021, Luiss School of European Political Economy Rome, March 22, 2021, p. 11. See also Jo/Hsu/Llanos-Popolizio/Vergara-Vega: Corporate Governance and Financial Fraud of Wirecard; European Journal of Business and Management Research www.ejbmr.org, http://dx.doi.org/10.24018/ejbmr.2021.6.2.708, vol. 6, no. 2, March 2021, p. 100 and Navaretti/Calzolari/Pozzolo: What are wider supervisory implications of the Wirecard case?; Study requested by the ECON committee, Economic Governance Support Unit (EGOV), Directorate-General for Internal Policies, PE 651.384—October 2020, http://www.europarl.europa.eu/supporting-analyses, p. 12.

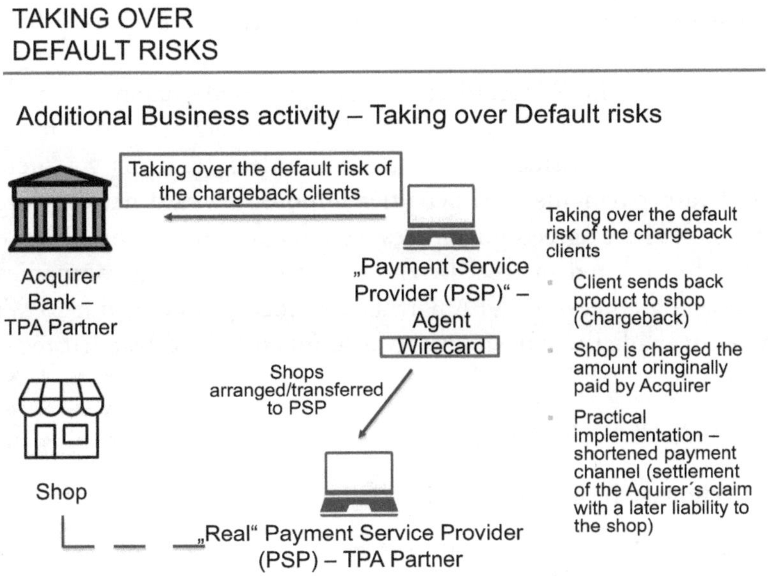

Wirecard has entered into further business activity, namely the assumption of default risks for so-called chargeback receivables. Chargeback claims result from the customer returning the goods to the online retailer. Online purchases are often followed by a (possibly partial) transaction reversal. While the customer returns the goods directly to the store, the payment method is the reverse of the original transaction. In this respect, the merchant is debited by the acquirer's bank. In principle, there is a risk that the merchant does not have sufficient funds, meaning that the corresponding amount is not transferred back. In practical terms, however, the acquirer bank's claim is offset against a future liability of the online merchant from a later transaction with another customer. In effect, this is a kind of abbreviated payment method.

In principle, this transaction bears relatively low risk. The acquirer may retain a portion of its liabilities to the online merchant in advance for future chargeback claims. This effectively provides advanced protection. In this respect, the merchant receives the purchase price reduced by the commission and a partial amount less, which is retained to secure chargeback claims. Due to the shortened payment channel, there is a (second) protection of the acquirer by the merchant. In this business model, Wirecard assumes the risk that the acquirer has to pay the card company but does not pay because, for example, an intermediary merchant does not pay. While the acquirer provides the merchant with double protection in principle, Wirecard grants the credit card company a financial guarantee for the default of this acquirer and the risk of penalty payments by this acquirer to the card organization (known as fines).

In this respect, the Wirecard companies provided guarantees to the TPA partners for any financial losses that the TPA partners may incur from transactions with the brokered credit card customers (defaults by merchants, reversal of card payments, and penalties imposed by card network organizations, etc.).[35] These agreed guarantees were secured by the provision of cash collateral administered in trust by the respective Wirecard companies.[36] To secure these guarantees, the TPA partners retained payments due to Wirecard companies or made these payments to accounts managed by a trustee (escrow accounts).

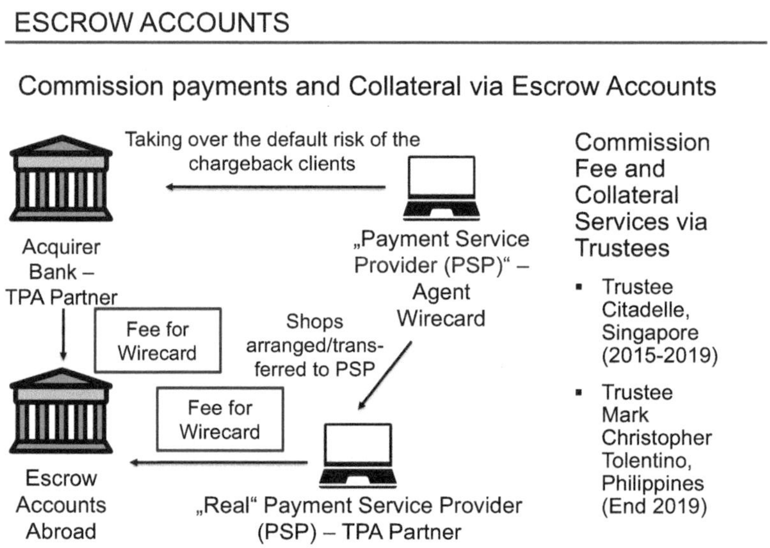

Due to the multiple advance hedging, the default risk for Wirecard is very low economically. In this respect, the question arises as to why Wirecard is needed as a low-risk guarantor. It is particularly striking that Wirecard had to deposit cash collateral for this purpose, which is said to have amounted to 100 million Euro in 2015 and 1.9 billion Euro in 2020. If the default risk is assumed to be 1 cent per 100 Euro, the cash collateral deposited would correspond to a very high transaction volume of 19 trillion Euro in 2020.

---

[35] See KPMG Report: p. 15.

[36] See KPMG Report: p. 15.

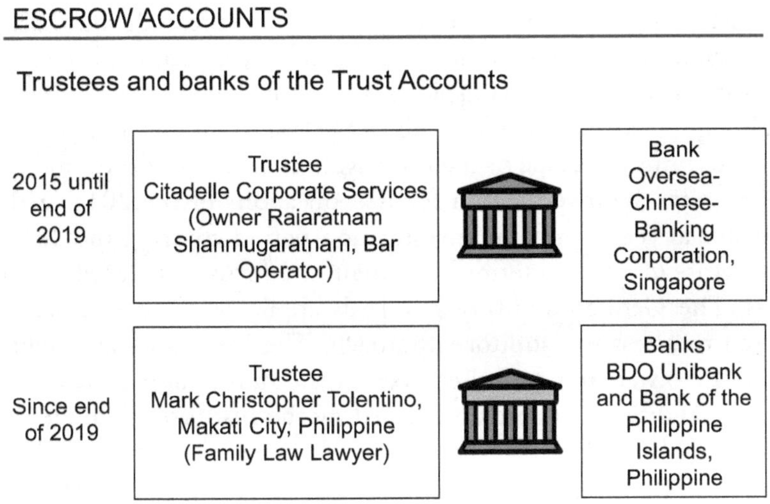

Wirecard provided security, which transferred the commission income to which it was entitled, comparable to an abbreviated payment method, to fiduciary accounts in Singapore and the Philippines.[37] From 2015 to 2019, the trustees were Citadelle Corporate Services with the owner Rajaratnam Shanmugaratnam, a bar operator. He lacked the license for (financial) trust business required under national regulations. Since the end of 2019, Mark Christopher Tolentino, Makati City, Philippines, a lawyer specializing in family law, has acted as trustee. The banks used were the Oversea-Chinese-Banking Corporation in Singapore, BDO Unibank, and the Bank of the Philippine Islands in the Philippines.

On 4 March 2021, a German Bundestag Committee of Inquiry appointed the auditing firm Rödl & Partner as the investigating agent. Their activities were carried out at the offices of the auditor, Ernst & Young (EY), in Berlin from 15 March 2021, up to and including 15 April 2021. The investigations resulted in a "Report on the findings of the investigation mandate to support the work of the German Bundestag's 3rd Parliamentary Committee of Inquiry (of the 19th electoral term)." The German press published the "Wambach Report" under the name of the Managing Director of Rödl & Partner. The report is of central importance, as the four audit partners investigating were granted insight into the auditor's working papers, which otherwise remain hidden from the public. In the working papers, the

[37] Cf. Orlandi: The Wirecard case: Challenges for German and European supervision; working paper Luiss University Rome, Department of Economics and Finance, Chair of Market Law and Regulation, Coordinator Prof. Paola Lucantoni, Advisor Prof. Mirella Pellegrini, Academic Year 2020/2021, p. 45.

auditor details the audit measures carried out and the audit findings. Auditors have direct access to internal company information as part of their work, so they can usually identify conspicuous issues earlier than the public. When determining the scope of Rödl & Partner's (Wambach's) investigation, it was necessary to limit the scope of the investigation in terms of time and content. In this respect, the investigation focused on audits of the 2014, 2015, and 2016 financial years, with the investigation period covering the 2014–2018 financial years in total. In terms of content, the focus was placed on the TPA business. The German auditing standards applicable in the respective year were used to assess the auditor's approach. The International Standards on Auditing (ISA) were not consulted because the auditor also explicitly referred only to the auditing standards published by the Institute of Public Auditors in Germany (IDW PS).

The Wambach Report concludes that the auditor has (demonstrably) dealt intensively with the TPA business model. It bases this conclusion on an auditor's working paper 2015 entitled "Third-party acquiring process & substantive audit procedures." It states

> ... Wirecard (WD) has transferred the payment processing for some Wirecard customers (also merchants) to third-party acquirers. The background to the transfer is that certain customer groups (providers of websites for Adult Services/Emotional Content (Pornography/Dating), Gambling/Gaming, Multi-Level-Marketing, Pharmacy and Health & Beauty) are no longer to be processed via Wirecard's payment processing platform or there is no acquiring/banking license on the part of Wirecard Bank AG for the merchants' territories of residence. The third-party acquirer acts as an outsourcing service provider from Wirecard's perspective.

PayEasy then acts as a payment service provider for this customer, i.e., it would primarily handle the technical processing of the payment ... take over the technical processing of the payment. The payment service would be provided by a (third-party) acquiring bank commissioned by PayEasy. The third-party acquirer is, therefore, responsible for the technical payment processing (payment service provider; PSP). The corresponding payment processing is carried out by a bank commissioned by the third-party acquirer (acquiring bank). However, Wirecard remains responsible for the customer. The services provided by Wirecard include:

- key contact for the customer and management of the customer relationship,
- partner for all questions relating to the payment processing system and the structuring of the payment processing for customers from a strategic perspective (strategy partner),
- assumption of liability risks: Wirecard continues to bear the main residual risks from the payment processing of customers.

Wirecard has a service agreement with the third-party acquirer ("Business Referral and Commission Agreement"); see ZCO-220.

> Customers have a contract directly with the third-party acquirer, but Wirecard was involved in the negotiations. There is no contract between Wirecard and the customer. However, the third-party acquirer has concluded the contract with the customer "with the approval" of Wirecard, whereby the customer also assumes that Wirecard will provide the services explained above.
>
> FYI – Wirecard also does not want a direct contract between Wirecard and the customer for reputational reasons.
>
> FYI – the supervision of PSP and acquiring banks by VISA is organized regionally, it should be noted that supervision is more "generous" for adult content, especially in the Asian region (especially concerning the question of how much volume from merchants from the "high brand risk segment" may be processed per acquirer and how to react to chargebacks, e.g. by imposing fines); this is another reason why settlement by the WDT/WDB is partly ruled out and requires Wirecard to appoint a PSP who is based in a corresponding region with less strict visa supervision.

Because—if Wirecard were to permanently bill too many customers from the "high brand risk segment", there would be a risk that Wirecard would lose its VISA license…."[38]

The Wambach Report states that many of the statements in the working paper "Third-party Acquiring Process & Substantive Audit Procedures" can also be found in a "Concurrence Memorandum dated 03.03.2016."[39]

The contracts with the three business partners in the TPA business were available to the auditor. They noted that all three contracts were worded identically. According to these contracts, Wirecard was entitled to a commission

---

[38] Rödl & Partner: Wirecard Investigation Committee, Report on the results of the investigation mandate to support the work of the 3rd Parliamentary Investigation Committee (of the 19th electoral term) of the German Bundestag (hereinafter cited as Wambach Report), p. 14.

[39] See Wambach Report: p. 14.

for referring customers (merchants) to the acquirers. The TPA partner was required to report the commission claims monthly (Wirecard does not issue an invoice based on the brokered transactions). In addition, the TPA partner was obliged to pay the commission with a time difference of six to nine months. The commission payment should be made to accounts named by the contracting parties (i.e., not Wirecard as the commission recipient).[40]

According to the Wambach Report, the audit working papers refer to collateral. Wirecard had deposited cash collaterals with the third-party acquirer. In the case of Al Alam, for example, it was initially 10 million Euro. Later, this figure rose to 20 million Euro. The cash collaterals could be adjusted.[41]

Wirecard released the third-party acquirers from liability and loss risks. Only errors in the technical processing caused by the TPA partner were excluded from this. In addition, Wirecard had to provide further security (collateral). The security was determined as a twelve-month rolling security according to the transaction volume of services with a long-term risk exposure. Subscription models were used as an example. The rolling 12-month security retention amounts to 33% of the transaction volume attributable to prepayments, which in the example are fees for the subscription in question.

In this respect, the TPA agreements had specific features compared to industry practice, requiring Wirecard to provide extensive additional collateral, namely cash collaterals and rolling collateral retentions.

In an audit in which the auditor deals with the client's business model, such unusual business practices should come to light. The reasons for a deviation from standard industry practice should be questioned.

However, the auditor did not further address the extent to which the collateral provided by Wirecard was in line with the market.[42] Although the auditor dealt with Wirecard's business model in principle, it probably did not scrutinize special features in the contracts in the TPA business with an industry-unusual shifting of (additional) collateral to Wirecard and did not investigate these further. This is all the less explainable as the auditor itself is said to have pointed out in the working papers that "no liability risks for Wirecard were identified by management in 2014, 2015, 2016, 2017 and 2018."[43] The self-evident contradiction of providing high-security deposits for only very low risks was ignored entirely.

---

[40] See Wambach Report: p. 14.

[41] See Wambach Report: p. 14.

[42] See Wambach Report: p. 15.

[43] Wambach Report: p. 16 with reference to the auditor's working papers for the relevant years.

The following findings emerge from the sub-areas of the business model. According to its descriptions, Wirecard was active as a PSP. Sales revenues or commission income are typically generated for these services, which are to be examined according to the type of activity. It is surprising that this activity probably did not initially operate on its own payment platform. Instead, third parties were involved, claiming a share of the total commissions generated by a transaction. The parent company did not operate the business activity but via three subsidiaries. Wirecard nevertheless acted as PSP.

In certain countries, Wirecard was able to act as an acquirer bank. In these countries, relatively high commissions are expected to be generated for Wirecard's other business models.

However, if Wirecard itself could not act as an acquirer bank because Wirecard only had its own banking license in some countries, the business activity would not have been carried out itself. The Wirecard companies referred customers to business partners (TPA partners, third-party acquirers) who processed credit card transactions as payment service providers with connections to various acquirer banks and charged Wirecard companies processing fees for this. This business activity can, therefore, only be examined in detail at the individual subsidiaries.

Furthermore, escrow accounts were used to process transactions in the TPA business, which is generally the standard market practice for hedging chargeback risk.[44] However, the business model was implemented with only three different business partners, which from the outset entails an operational risk, namely if one of the partners defaults, and secondly, a credit risk, which relates to the trustee on the one hand and the trustee banks on the other. Finally, the question arises as to why Wirecard had seemingly little influence, as on the one hand, the activity can in principle be carried out without fiduciary accounts. On the other, the banks were selected without Wirecard's involvement. In any case, these are not globally active banks with first-class credit ratings. Furthermore, the income ratio from this business model to total income is to be questioned. The involvement of TPA partners deprives Wirecard of part of the potential total commission, and, in addition, cash collateral was required to be deposited for reversals, which at least ties up liquidity but ultimately reduces income. Nevertheless, this activity is said to have been highly profitable.

This raises numerous questions about the fiduciary relationship. Once a decision has been made on the accounting treatment of the fiduciary transactions, it is necessary to first question whether Wirecard has even become the

[44] See Committee of Inquiry: p. 182.

beneficial owner of the balances in the fiduciary accounts and the numerous audit procedures to be performed by the auditor in the overall context have been identified, the issue—assuming beneficial ownership at Wirecard—is the type of asset to be recognized. This raises the question of whether the asset is a trade receivable or a cash or cash equivalent under IFRS. The asset then determines the subsequent measurement. Cash tends to be recognized at nominal value, while (non-current) receivables are tested for impairment (loan loss provision).

The recognition of sales revenue and commissions is closely related to asset allocation to cash and cash equivalents or receivables, on either a gross or net basis. Again, the accounting is followed by appropriate checks.

All audit activities are also influenced by whether the company has an effective internal risk control system. The less reliable this is considered, the more extensive the company's audit procedures have to be.

4

Fiduciary Relationships

4.1 Types of Fiduciary Relationships and Accounting Consequences

The accounting treatment of an asset under the German Commercial Code (Handelsgesetzbuch, HGB) in financial statements is based on beneficial ownership,[1] whereby the beneficial owner is deemed to be the company which exercises actual control over an asset and can, therefore, permanently exclude the civil law owner from having any economic influence over the asset. The interpretation usually references Section 39 (2) AO (from German tax law) or Section 246 (1) sentence 2 HGB. Under IFRS, an asset's existence and accounting attribution are based on the Conceptual Framework (CF) of the IFRS. According to CF 4.4(b), an asset is a resource controlled by an entity as a result of a past event from which an inflow of economic benefits is expected in the future. It is, therefore, of central importance in fiduciary relationships whether the company can control an asset. The legal nature of the fiduciary relationship has to be taken into account. From a legal perspective, a distinction is made between fiduciary and authorization trusts.[2]

---

[1] See Marten: Die Prüfung von Treuhandkonten im Rahmen der Abschlussprüfung; Der Betrieb (DB), 2020, pp. 1465–1469, here p. 1465.

[2] See Marten: Die Prüfung von Treuhandkonten im Rahmen der Abschlussprüfung; Der Betrieb (DB), 2020, pp. 1465–1469, here p. 1465. Justenhoven/Meyer: § 246; Beck'scher Bilanzkommentar, 13. edition Munich 2022, section 246, para. 10, 14.

© The Author(s), under exclusive license to Springer Nature Switzerland AG 2024
E. Löw and R. Heyd, *The Audit Failures of the Wirecard Scandal*,
https://doi.org/10.1007/978-3-031-59854-8_4

In a fiduciary trust, the trustee acquires full legal ownership of an asset from the settlor (or from a third party for the settlor's account).[3] "Based on the trust agreement, the trustee may exercise the acquired right to the trust property in his name, but not in his interest."[4] In the case of a fiduciary trust, the accounting treatment depends on how the fiduciary agreement is specifically structured, which depends on the individual case. According to the literature, if the agreement and the actual circumstances are such that beneficial ownership is attributable to the settlor, the settlor accounts for the trust.[5] The extent to which other views in the literature can be followed can be left open. In any case, a transfer of the interpretation to financial statements per IFRS has to be based on the possibility of control, which falls back on the review of beneficial ownership.

In the case of an authorization trust, the trustee is only authorized to dispose of the trust property in his name or to establish, change, or revoke rights to it. If this authorization is exercised, it is always for the account of the settlor. The authorization trust is, therefore, very similar to the fiduciary trust. The difference, however, is that in the case of the authorization trust, there is no transfer of ownership under civil law to the trustee. The settlor, not the trustee, also prepares the balance sheet for the authorization trust.[6] Even more clearly than in the case of the fiduciary trust, beneficial ownership remains with the settlor.

It is, therefore, of decisive importance for Wirecard to know whether it can be assumed that Wirecard has beneficial ownership of the escrow accounts. Only then is it an asset that can be capitalized in Wirecard's Consolidated Financial Statements. Given the constellation, this may well be questionable.

Various transactions are posted to the escrow accounts. They were used in the TPA business. Wirecard used subsidiaries to refer customers to TPA business partners. On the one hand, Wirecard is entitled to a commission from the credit card organization, on the other hand, Wirecard has to pay commissions to the TPA partners for their services. These payments were not processed via a freely available bank account but posted to escrow accounts. Furthermore, the business activity of assuming default risks for chargeback

---

[3] See Justenhoven/Meyer: § 246; Beck'scher Bilanzkommentar, 13. edition Munich 2022. section 246, para. 10.

[4] Justenhoven/Meyer: § 246; Beck'scher Bilanzkommentar, 13. edition Munich 2022. section 246, para. 10.

[5] See Justenhoven/Meyer: § 246; Beck'scher Bilanzkommentar, 13. edition Munich 2022, section 246, para. 11.

[6] See Justenhoven/Meyer: § 246; Beck'scher Bilanzkommentar, 13. edition Munich 2022 section 246, para. 15.

receivables was processed via these escrow accounts. Wirecard received a guarantee commission for the assumption of guarantees but, simultaneously, had to deposit cash collateral for returns (chargebacks) and possible penalties (fines).

The question on the party to capitalize the trust relationship as an asset depends on who the trustor is. Two cases are conceivable for the present constellation.

- The trustors are the Wirecard companies. In this case, Wirecard has undertaken to transfer the cash collateral (trust property) to the escrow accounts and to hold them for the occurrence of loss events. However, the actual settlement took place in that the TPA companies did not transfer amounts from their net debt to the Wirecard companies (sales revenues to be passed on (credit card processing fees) less commission income claimed) to freely available accounts of the Wirecard companies, but to escrow accounts that serve as collateral for the guarantee claims of the TPA companies and the guarantee obligations of the Wirecard companies. According to the overall appearance, this is a "fiduciary trust." In this case, the Wirecard companies are the beneficial owners of the trust property (cash collateral) and have to capitalize it in their balance sheets. This appears to be the interpretation on which Wirecard has prepared its accounts.
- The trustors are the TPA partners. In this case, the TPA partners transfer the trust property to the trustee with the provision that it is only paid out to the Wirecard companies once the guarantee obligations of the Wirecard companies have been fulfilled. In this case, the payments of the TPA partners have not (yet) been transferred to the Wirecard companies' sphere of control. The TPA companies then have to capitalize the payments. The Wirecard companies capitalize a receivable from the TPA companies until the trustee transfers the cash amounts to an account freely available to the Wirecard companies for payment at the instruction of the TPA partners as trustors if the liability risks no longer exist or if the risks for which a guarantee by the Wirecard companies exists have occurred and have been covered from the cash collateral held in the escrow accounts.

Wirecard initially knows neither the TPA partners' additions to the escrow accounts nor the utilizations to cover risks. The TPA partners make all withdrawals from the escrow account balances and subsequently communicate via screenshot to the Wirecard companies, which use the figures as a basis for booking. They cannot be allocated to individual customers or customer groups but are broken down into different and incomprehensible aggregations. As a result, Wirecard knew neither the customers whose risks Wirecard had to cover by providing collateral nor the risks incurred that were covered by the credit balances on the Wirecard accounts.

"The trust agreement from December 2015 stipulated that the account would not be managed in the name of Wirecard but by the trustee."[7] However, if TPA partners and trustees—and not Wirecard—use the escrow accounts as bank accounts and no sufficient evidence of customers or individual transactions can be found at Wirecard and its group companies, the additions to the escrow accounts by the TPA partners cannot be checked for plausibility by Wirecard via sales, as the contracts contain neither the sales categories nor the commission rates nor the percentages to be transferred from the commissions to escrow accounts. Wirecard's minor influence is also evident in that the TPA business partners were responsible not only for appointing the trustees and setting up the escrow accounts but also for exchanging trustees and transferring the trust assets to another bank. From 2015 to 2019, Citadelle Corporate Services acted as trustee, and the Oversea-Chinese-Banking Corporation in Singapore held the bank account. From the end of 2019, Mark Christopher Tolentino was appointed trustee, and BDO Unibank and the Bank of the Philippine Islands were appointed banks.

The overall picture does not meet the required characteristics of beneficial ownership within the meaning of the HGB or control according to IFRS, so the existence of an asset of Wirecard has to be denied for the trust assets in the escrow account. Wirecard could not exercise any control over the existence or availability of the account balances. However, if Wirecard had not become the beneficial owner, there could not have been a shortened payment channel. The conclusion to be drawn from this is that recognition in the balance sheet as cash or cash equivalents is out of the question. Instead, Wirecard has to recognize trade receivables and form corresponding specific or general loan loss reserves (impairments) (without having to go into more detail on the unique requirements of IAS 39 and IFRS 9 for the formation of risk provisions, as Wirecard has not shown any receivables in its financial statements).

[7] This was the testimony of the head of EY's policy department before the Investigation Committee. See Committee of Inquiry: p. 378.

4.2 Audit Procedures

Audit procedures are required to be performed once the critical audit areas have been determined before an audit. Fiduciary relationships had to be a mandatory focus. "A fiduciary relationship always entails an increased risk, as the possible purpose may be to conceal asset relationships—even beyond the audit of the financial statements."[8]

Wirecard worked in the TPA business via three subsidiaries with initially two acquirers, Al Alam and Senjo Payments, a trustee, and a bank. This is, therefore, an extreme concentration of business partners with corresponding existential risks for Wirecard. When examining the trustee relationships, it is initially a question of the (un) customary nature of establishing a trustee relationship in general, the structure of the trustee agreement, the conditions of the trustee agreement concerning the respective services, the trustworthiness of the trustees, the creditworthiness of the bank(s) managing the trustee accounts, and ultimately the existence of the trust assets. This includes an examination of whether the escrow accounts are fully documented in the books of the Wirecard companies, whether the amounts posted to the escrow accounts are traceable, whether the balance sheet item in which the amounts in the escrow accounts are reported complies with the regulations (in the present case, this relates to the designation as cash assets), and, finally, whether the disclosures required for understanding and required under IFRS have been applied.

The auditor is obliged to perform the audit procedures per IDW PS 210 para 40 based on risk assessments in such a way that misstatements based on inaccuracies or violations material to the financial statements are detected with reasonable assurance. In the event of indications of inaccuracies and violations, the auditor is forced to assess the circumstances that led to this and the possible effects on the financial reporting based on IDW PS 210 para. 58. As part of the audit, the auditor is required to perform the audit procedures so that sufficient and appropriate audit evidence is obtained to draw well-founded conclusions based on this evidence by IDW PS 300 n.F. para. 5. In this respect, the auditor is required by IDW PS 300 n.F. para. 7

[8] Schüttler: Prüfung von Treuhandkonten auf Vorhandensein; Der Betrieb (DB), 2020, pp. 1862–863, here p. 1863 with emphasis on "increased risk" and "concealment of asset relationships," who further points out that auditors are subject to increased due diligence obligations under money laundering law and must comprehensively determine who is the beneficial owner of the trust property (Section 15 GwG, Annex 2, factors for a potentially higher risk). Similarly Schüttler: Die Treuhand im HGB-Abschluss, Weder Treugeber noch Abschlussprüfer müssen über Treuhandverhältnisse berichten—das muss sich nach Wirecard ändern!; Unternehmenssteuern und Bilanzen (StuB), 2020, pp. 671–672, here p. 671.

to plan and perform the audit procedures so that sufficient and appropriate audit evidence is obtained under the circumstances of the individual case. In accordance with IDW PS 300 n.F. para. 8, the information's relevance and reliability have to be considered. Relevance means that the audit evidence is to correspond to the purpose of the audit procedures.[9] "Reliability ... is influenced by the nature and origin of the information and the circumstances in which it is obtained."[10]

In the case of information from the company, audit evidence on the accuracy and completeness of the information has to be obtained by IDW PS 300, n.F. para. 10. If the auditor has doubts about the reliability of the audit evidence, IDW PS 300 n.F. para. 12 requires the auditor to determine which adjustments or additions to the audit procedures are necessary to clarify the matter by IDW PS 300 n.F. para. A2, audit evidence includes information supporting management's assertions and information contradicting them. "In some cases, the absence of information (e.g., management's refusal to provide a requested explanation) is also relevant to the audit and therefore also constitutes audit evidence" (IDW PS 300 n.F. para. A2). Furthermore, IDW PS 300 n.F. para. A3 states that inquiries alone do generally not provide sufficient audit evidence for the absence of material misstatements at the assertion level nor the effectiveness of controls; according to IDW PS 300 n.F. para. A29, the reliability of information is influenced by its nature and origin and the circumstances under which it is obtained; according to IDW PS 300 n.F. para. A29, the reliability of copies, digitized documents, or documents otherwise converted into electronic form depends on the controls over their creation and maintenance. Regarding the sufficient scope in selecting the elements to be audited, IDW PS 300 n.F. para. A48 explicitly mentions the entire survey, the deliberate selection, and the random sample. It points out that applying one of these audit forms or their combination may be appropriate depending on the respective circumstances, such as the risks of material misstatements concerning the audited statement. In this context, a full audit per IDW PS 300 n.F. para. A49 may be appropriate if there is a significant risk and other procedures do not provide sufficient and appropriate audit evidence. In this respect, the appendix to IDW 300 n.F. points out that, irrespective of the term choice, statements have to be made on account balances at the end of the period, which may relate to the existence and attribution to the company based on existing rights to assets.

In the case of fiduciary relationships, the auditor is required to determine in particular:

---

[9] See Graumann: Wirtschaftliches Prüfungswesen, 7th revised edition, Herne 2023, p. 303.

[10] Graumann: Wirtschaftliches Prüfungswesen, 7th revised edition, Herne 2023, p. 303.

- "the trust property shown in the balance sheet exists (existence),
- the trust property is fully included in the balance sheet (completeness),
- the trust property is properly presented in the accounts (accuracy, valuation, and allocation as well as presentation and, if applicable, disclosures in the notes),
- the reporting entity has beneficial ownership of and control over the trust property (rights and obligations)."[11]

The following may be appropriate for a case-by-case review:

- "obtaining and recalculating the list in which the trust property is listed,
- inspection of the trust agreements and assessment of their authenticity, reliability, completeness, and the existence of the underlying assets,
- obtaining confirmations from the trustee as third-party confirmation,
- inspection of the trust property."[12]

The cash balances in the escrow accounts have to be investigated using a physical inventory.[13] According to IDW PS 301, stocktaking is generally carried out by taking a physical inventory (counting, measuring, and weighing). Instead of counting, measuring, and weighing, other appropriate and sufficient audit evidence may be considered. The physical inventory aims to determine target/actual deviations (stock shortages). In the case of book inventories, the control function associated with the inventory can only be performed by confirming balances. The auditor has to be allowed to be present during the inventory so that he can satisfy himself with the correctness of the inventory. For this reason, the audit assignment is also regularly issued before the end of the financial year. Sufficient audit evidence for a balance sheet item of this size, for which a physical inventory is impossible, can only be obtained through balance confirmations, whereby the individual requirements of IDW PS 301 para. 32 are to be fulfilled. This requires:

[11] Marten: Die Prüfung von Treuhandkonten im Rahmen der Abschlussprüfung; Der Betrieb (DB), 2020, pp. 1465–1469, here p. 1466.

[12] Marten: Die Prüfung von Treuhandkonten im Rahmen der Abschlussprüfung; Der Betrieb (DB), 2020, pp. 1465–1469, here p. 1467.

[13] Other view Marten: Die Prüfung von Treuhandkonten im Rahmen der Abschlussprüfung; Der Betrieb (DB), 2020, pp. 1465–1469, here p. 1469, who, however, does not address the fact that if there are significant doubts about the reliability of the trustee, this constitutes an impediment to the audit. Lenz rightly points this out very clearly. See Lenz: Die Prüfung von Treuhandkonten—das Fallbeispiel Wirecard AG, response to Marten; Der Betrieb (DB) 2020, pp. 1465–1469, pp. 2085–2089, here p. 2085.

- consideration of the integrity and independence of the custodian,
- the observation of the inventory at the custodian (by the auditor himself or by another auditor),
- confirmation of the adequacy of the custodian's inventory-related internal control system by another auditor to provide assurance that inventories are appropriately recorded, adequately stored, and safeguarded,
- inspecting documents such as warehouse receipts or obtaining third-party confirmations if the inventories have been pledged as collateral.

These principles designed for the inventory are to be applied analogously to the inventory check of cash and cash equivalents.

Obtaining third-party confirmations can contribute to obtaining relevant and reliable audit evidence. According to IDW PS 302 (n.F.) para. 6 (a), this is audit evidence that the auditor obtains directly as a written response from a third party in paper form or using an electronic or other medium. However, by IDW PS 302 n.F. para. 7, the auditor is obliged to consider whether such third-party confirmations should be obtained as audit procedures. "In such cases, the work of third parties has to be assessed to determine whether it is appropriate for the audit."[14] IDW PS 302 (revised) para. 8 requires the auditor to retain control over the confirmation process. According to IDW PS 302, the new version has no additional requirements for electronic confirmations. Given the easier modifiability of third-party confirmations in electronic form, it is essential to "carefully observe the obligation to maintain control over the confirmation process."[15]

If the legal representatives refuse to allow the auditor to send a confirmation request, the process is not over for the auditor. Instead, per IDW PS 302 n.F. para. 11 (c), the auditor is required to perform alternative audit procedures if necessary. Suppose the auditor can't obtain relevant and reliable evidence through alternative audit procedures. In that case, the auditor has to enter into discussions with the supervisory body in accordance with IDW PS 302 n.F. para. 12. In addition, the auditor is required to decide on the effects on the performance of the audit and the audit opinion—applying the principles of IDW PS 250 n.F., IDW PS 261 n.F., and IDW PS 400. Even if the auditor doubts the reliability of the response to a confirmation request, he has to obtain further audit evidence per IDW PS 302 n.F. para. 14 to eliminate these doubts. Furthermore, his (original) assessment of the associated risks of

---

[14] IDW (ed.): WP-Handbuch: 17th edition, Düsseldorf 2020, p. 1620. See also Marten: Die Prüfung von Treuhandkonten im Rahmen der Abschlussprüfung; Der Betrieb (DB), 2020, pp. 1465–1469, here p. 1468.

[15] IDW (ed.): WP-Handbuch, 17th edition, Düsseldorf 2020, p. 1626.

error, including the risk of non-compliance, has to be reconsidered by IDW PS 302 n.F. para. 15.

Special features apply to bank confirmations. In accordance with IDW PS 302, n.F. para. 26, they are to be obtained for all business relationships between a company and banks. There are no exceptions to IDW PS 302 n.F. in the present case. By IDW PS 302 n.F. para. 21, the information to be obtained via a bank confirmation includes existing accounts and their balances, existing credit lines, and collateral provided. "When bank confirmation requests are sent (e.g., in the case of foreign credit institutions or where credit institutions use external service providers to respond to confirmation requests), it is nevertheless frequently observed that the standardized information requested is not answered in full or in part. In these cases, the auditor may use his professional judgment by his risk assessment to determine the scope of the alternative audit procedures required under paragraph 16 for the information not received" (IDW PS 302, n.F. para. A28).

In the present case, the auditor is required to first question the use of escrow accounts[16] because these are not necessary to implement the business model, at least not to this extent. In this context, whether Wirecard can exercise control over the trust assets has to be examined at all.

"The security deposits in the escrow accounts were, ... as the contracts indicate, retained for a total default, i.e., a counterparty default risk."[17] The amount of the security payment was 33% of the commissions on the underlying transactions.[18] This means that for a customer transaction of 100 Euro, an assumed commission of 10% of the commission amount of 10 Euro, 33%, i.e., 3.33 Euro, was retained. To arrive at an amount of 1.9 billion Euro in this way requires an incredibly high transaction volume, which has to be checked for plausibility by the auditor.[19]

The retention of high amounts as collateral for chargeback claims and fines is not understandable, given the very low risk for Wirecard and the fact that detailed audit procedures are required. The low risk is also demonstrated by Wirecard not being utilized in the 2015 to 2019 fiscal years. "In fact, the business with third-party providers does not result in any utilization of the collateral that justifies the high collateral provided by Wirecard over time."[20]

[16] See Schüttler: Prüfung von Treuhandkonten auf Vorhandensein; Der Betrieb (DB), 2020, pp. 1862–1863, here p. 1863.

[17] According to the head of EY's policy department in the Committee of Inquiry. See Committee of Inquiry: p. 376.

[18] See Committee of Inquiry: p. 376.

[19] Cf. the example given by the head of EY's policy department in the Committee of Inquiry.

[20] Wambach Report: p. 21.

"The even more extensive provision of collateral through reclassifying receivables will continue until mid-2015, contrary to contractual regulations and business experience. The model of providing further collateral (...) means that Wirecard will hardly receive any money from this business model as business grows due to constantly increasing collateral requirements. On the other hand, Wirecard has to finance the constantly growing volume of collateral with equity and borrowed capital. Against the background of economic considerations, such action appears very unusual."[21]

Granting very high amounts as collateral for a very low risk is suspicious. The auditor is obliged to investigate this. The auditor had also noticed that the security deposits were very high—in earlier years when the escrow accounts were not yet used extensively and were actually reported as receivables. At that time, the auditor had criticized the receivables positions with the individual TPA business partners as being too high and that the solvency of these TPA did not justify the level of receivables.[22]

Wirecard did not have any direct customer data for the TPA business, but the accountants received the receipts from business partners based on which the bookings were made.[23] This is already questionable concerning proper accounting principles and constitutes a violation of Section 238 (1) HGB.[24] As Wirecard is not aware of the TPA partners' additions to the escrow accounts or the utilizations to cover risks due to the structure of the fiduciary relationships but is dependent on the business partners' documents, there is also an extremely high risk of manipulation. The immense risk of fraudulent activity can only be countered by obtaining meaningful audit evidence. Particular attention is to be paid to this.

As Wirecard and its group companies cannot provide sufficient evidence of customers or individual transactions, Wirecard cannot verify the plausibility of the additions to the escrow accounts by the TPA partners via sales.[25] However, this was the auditor's audit approach. "We have always audited the escrow accounts, as I have seen, also from the working papers, in the context of revenue recognition."[26] However, a direct audit was not possible. "The

---

[21] Wambach Report: p. 51.

[22] According to the Head of Accounting in the Committee of Inquiry. See Committee of Inquiry: p. 216.

[23] According to the Head of Accounting in the Investigation Committee. See Committee of Inquiry: p. 215.

[24] The Wambach Report: Addendum II, p. 17, also agrees with this view.

[25] See Wambach Report: p. 78 and Wambach Report: Addendum II, p. 19.

[26] This was the testimony of the head of EY's policy department in the Committee of Inquiry, see Committee of Inquiry: p. 376.

existence and amount of revenue, therefore, only appears to have been proven indirectly via balance confirmations."[27]

The contractual partners are of particular importance in a fiduciary relationship. The trustee has a unique function of trust. They are usually selected with particular care. "Lawyers, notaries or a bank are often considered as trustees."[28]

What is surprising is that Wirecard did not choose the trustee. From 2015 to 2019, the trustee was not a German or at least European company, an international auditing firm, or a renowned law firm, but a company called Citadelle Corporate Services. Due to the unique position of trust of the trustee, many jurisdictions require a particular professional background or even a license to carry out the activity. It is essential to check whether a license is required in Singapore and whether the trustee has one. In this context, some peculiarities and anomalies have to be investigated. In the present case, it is incomprehensible that the owner of Citadelle, Rajaratnam Shanmugaratnam, also ran a dance bar called Hedgehog in the Little India district of Singapore. He allegedly had scantily clad girls dancing there—and often stood behind the bar himself. According to the Trust Companies Act of Singapore, only those licensed under this law may act as trustees. In any case, the owner of Citadelle did not have a license and was, therefore, not allowed to act as a trustee in Singapore.

The auditor is obliged to assess which third party provides the more reliable audit evidence, which also depends on the reliability of the person consulted and their competence and objectivity.[29] In this respect, the auditor is forced to assess the reliability of external confirmations by IDW PS 300 n.F. para. 8 and para. A29. "Where relevant, this also includes controls over the preparation and maintenance of this information" (IDW PS 300 n.F. para. A29). With proper audit procedures, it is impossible to conceal who is behind Citadelle, especially when a large auditing firm with an international network and offices in Singapore is commissioned to audit the financial statements. Therefore, it is extremely easy to investigate locally. After all, several hundred million to over a billion Euro were managed via the trustee. "If the auditor is

[27] Wambach Report: p. 78.

[28] Marten: Die Prüfung von Treuhandkonten im Rahmen der Abschlussprüfung; Der Betrieb (DB), 2020, pp. 1465–1469, here p. 1465.

[29] Lenz emphasizes this with reference to IDW PS 302 para. A7. See Lenz: Die Verantwortung des Abschlussprüfers zur Aufdeckung von Bilanzdelikten (Täuschungen, Vermögensschädigungen), Das Fallbeispiel Wirecard AG; Zeitschrift für internationale und kapitalmarktorientierte Rechnungslegung (KoR), 2020, pp. 546–552, here p. 551. See also Schüttler: Prüfung von Treuhandkonten auf Vorhandensein; Der Betrieb (DB), 2020, pp. 1862–1863, here p. 1863, who demands that the auditor question "What reputation does he have?".

therefore considering ... basing his audit opinion on confirmations from the trustee, he has to necessarily assess the trustee's reliability or retrace the reliability check of the audited company as a trustor."[30] "Confirmations received directly from the bank (original documents) are more reliable than indirect confirmation from the trustee. Only if the auditor has good reason to assume that the audit evidence obtained via the trustee is just as reliable and convincing he can obtain the confirmations via the trustee. The latter, in turn, depends on assessing the trustee's reliability."[31]

If—in this context—the need for a license was not checked, IDW PS 230 para. 14 was violated, which requires that the auditor is required, among other things, to obtain knowledge of the company's legal environment to be audited as part of the audit, namely "legal provisions of material significance for the company."[32]

Answers will be obtained as audit evidence to the following obvious questions about the trustee:

- "What reputation does he have?
- How long has it existed? How can it be reached?
- Are there fixed business facilities, offices, etc.?
- How long has he been working for the audited company?
- Why was he chosen?
- What regulation is it subject to?
- Is he also being tested? By whom?"[33]

"Despite the close relationship with the TPA, the auditor's working papers show that no (audited) annual financial statements of the TPA were obtained in the period from 2015 to 2017 ... Analytical audit procedures, such as multi-year comparisons, post-calculations, etc. on the financial data are not

[30] Lenz: Die Prüfung von Treuhandkonten—das Fallbeispiel Wirecard AG, reply to Marten; Der Betrieb (DB) 2020, pp. 1465–1469, pp. 2085–2089, here p. 2088.

[31] Lenz: Die Prüfung von Treuhandkonten—das Fallbeispiel Wirecard AG, reply to Marten; Der Betrieb (DB) 2020, pp. 1465–1469, pp. 2085-2089, here p. 2088.

[32] See also IDW (ed.): WP-Handbuch: 17th edition, Düsseldorf 2020, p. 1475.

[33] Schüttler: Prüfung von Treuhandkonten auf Vorhandensein; Der Betrieb (DB), 2020, pp. 1862–1863, here p. 1863.

recognizable in the auditor's working papers."[34] No annual financial statements were available for Citadelle for the entire period.[35] How any statement can then be made about the trustee—regardless of whether it is reliable or unreliable—is incomprehensible.[36] The legal representatives of Citadelle were also active in other functions for the TPA partners and other business partners of Wirecard, so the independence constitutive for trustees could not be guaranteed.

Towards the end of the fourth quarter of 2019, a new trustee was (suddenly) appointed in another country—but not by Wirecard. Instead, the previous trustee sought his successor from,[37] a Filipino family law attorney, Mark Christopher Tolentino, from Makati City, Philippines. It is pretty curious and critical to question why Citadelle initiated a change of trustee in the first place and why the new trustee was selected and recommended by Citadelle. It is not apparent from the minutes of the Committee of Inquiry about the transfer of the trustee relationship that an alternative to appointing Tolentino as trustee was considered or that his reliability was examined before the decision.[38] The absurdity of the trustee relationship is taken to the extreme in that there was probably initially no trustee agreement with the new trustee. However, work continued "based on trust" on the same basis as with Citadelle.[39] In any case, a contract between Citadelle and Tolentino was only entered into the accounts in February, March, or April 2020.[40]

Despite these circumstances, the auditor only obtained audit evidence for the 2015, 2016, 2017, and 2018 financial years through confirmations from

[34] Wambach Report: p. 71. "The two audited financial statements 2016 and 2017 of the Senjo Group obtained by the auditor cannot be used in the respective audits, as they are only available to Wirecard approximately six months after the auditor's opinion." Wambach Report: Addendum II, p. 24. In connection with its investigations in 2020 into the annual financial statements of the TPA business partners, KPMG states: "As part of the investigation, Wirecard provided us with audited annual financial statements of TPA partner 1 as of December 31, 2018 and audited annual financial statements of TPA partner 3 as of December 31, 2016, December 31, 2017 and December 31, 2018. Wirecard did not provide us with any annual financial statements of TPA partner 2 until the conclusion of our investigation, although a corresponding right to information existed according to the contractual agreements from 2018." KPMG Report: p. 16. KPMG also received no evidence of a reliability assessment for the subsequent trustee during the period under review. See KPMG Report: p. 17.

[35] See KPMG Report: p. 17.

[36] Lenz: Die Prüfung von Treuhandkonten—das Fallbeispiel Wirecard AG, reply to Marten; Der Betrieb (DB) 2020, pp. 1465–1469, pp. 2085–2089, here p. 2088.

[37] See KPMG Report: p. 23.

[38] See KPMG Report: p. 17.

[39] See KPMG Report: p. 23.

[40] Cf. the testimony of Wirecard's Head of Accounting in the Investigation Committee. See Committee of Inquiry: p. 217.

the TPA partners and the trustee.[41] Wirecard itself carried out the plausibility check of sales in the same way. Balance confirmations were issued by the three TPA partners and the trustee—these were two independent bodies.[42] Furthermore, the annual financial statements included TPA revenues that were only reported by the TPA partners after the annual financial statements had been prepared.[43]

"The reliability of this audit evidence is particularly dependent on the trustworthiness of the TPA."[44] However, the auditor's working papers reveal numerous special features[45]:

- The confirmations of the trustee Citadelle were not addressed directly to the auditor in 2015 and 2016.
- The balance confirmation from the TPA business partner Al Alam, dated 28.03.2016, shows the Wirecard subsidiary with the name Wirecard Technologies GmbH as the beneficial owner. However, another subsidiary, CardSystems Middle East FZ-LLC, concluded the trust agreement with Al Alam.
- In 2016, the email addresses on the letterhead of the Citadelle trustee varied between "shan.citadelle@com.sg" and citadelle33@yahoo.sg.com, as did the names of the contact persons.
- The dates on the 2015 confirmations follow the English typology, while from the end of 2016—after the stationery was changed—they were written in German format.
- A balance confirmation dated 25.05.2016 shows a balance for the other TPA partner, Al Alam, for 31.03.2016 on an account attributable to the TPA partner Senjo (this involves as much as 41 million Euro). Wirecard UK & Ireland is named as the beneficial owner. The confirmation is made for Al Alam by another person who (strangely enough) also acts as Secretary at Senjo. In contrast, the same account is assigned to CardSystems Middle East FZ-LLC in a confirmation dated 02.12.2016. This means the escrow account changes beneficial owner within the same year (2016).
- In December 2016, Al Alam made an unusually high payment to the escrow account (amounting to 80 million Euro).

[41] According to the head of EY's policy department in the Investigation Committee. See Committee of Inquiry: p. 376 and p. 377.

[42] This was the statement of Wirecard's Head of Accounting. See Committee of Inquiry: p. 215.

[43] Cf. Committee of Inquiry: p. 215.

[44] Wambach Report: p. 78, almost identical wording also in Wambach Report: Addendum II, p. 20.

[45] See Wambach Report: p. 77 for the following special features.

- There is a confirmation for one of the escrow accounts as of 22.11.2016, but there is no confirmation for the end of the year. In the following year (2017), this account was used differently and was no longer used as an escrow account for the TPA business from the end of February 2017.

The following additional special features apply specifically to the consolidated financial statements for the 2018 financial year[46]:

- The balance confirmation was received on 11.04.2019 but is dated 12.04.2019.
- Once again, the date format is given in the German typology.
- The company names have a dot after the respective company form compared to previous years.
- Only amounts are confirmed in the balance confirmation, but no account numbers are given for the balances.
- The bank where the assets are said to have been held was not named.
- "No balance confirmation requests were sent directly to the merchant."[47]

In the auditor's working papers, these unique features were not investigated. Nevertheless, the auditor relied exclusively on this (poor) level of audit evidence. "It is not clear from the auditor's working papers whether these (balance confirmation requests to be sent directly to the merchant, author's note) or other attempts were made to obtain alternative audit evidence independent of the TPA."[48]

The auditor has not obtained a bank confirmation in recent years. The contract with Wirecard did not provide for direct contact with the bank holding the escrow account, and there was no right to information from the bank.[49] "The trust agreement does not stipulate any rights to information, such as the monthly dispatch of account statements, bank balance confirmations, proof of the establishment of the escrow accounts or similar for Wirecard."[50] In addition, test transactions were carried out.

Given the extraordinary importance of the TPA business for Wirecard's earnings situation, the account-holding bank has a central function. Apart from the fact that it would be entirely unusual for other companies to process such a significant business activity via a single bank and to take an extreme

[46] See Wambach Report: Addendum II, p. 18.
[47] Wambach Report: Addendum II, p. 20.
[48] Wambach Report: p. 78.
[49] Cf. Committee of Inquiry: p. 378.
[50] Wambach Report: p. 77.

credit risk, it is surprising that it was not an internationally renowned bank with an outstanding credit rating. Instead, the Overseas-Chinese Banking Corporation in Singapore managed the escrow account from 2015 to 2019. The economic environment in which the business activities took place was the Asian region. Nevertheless, the account was in Euro. This should have given the auditor food for thought.

The same applies to the two banks appointed to manage the account after the trustee change was made: BDO Unibank and the Bank of The Philippine Islands.

Apart from the fact that maintaining an account in Euro is unusual for an activity in Asia, the question of account management conditions arises. At least in Europe, it was common practice in the low-interest rate environment to charge negative interest on balances of a specific size. Companies, therefore, usually endeavor to maintain credit balances only to a necessary minimum amount. With this in mind, checking whether the account management conditions align with the market is necessary. Additional audit evidence should be obtained to allow a reliable audit opinion. After all, without charging negative interest on balances of several million to over one billion Euro, banks would forgo very high earnings.

It is, therefore, insufficient to obtain confirmations from third parties, i.e., only from the trustee.[51] "In connection with the audit of credit balances with credit institutions, the auditor is obliged to also obtain an overview of the company's other business relationships with the credit institution. For this purpose, bank confirmations are to be obtained for all types of business relationships of the company to be audited with credit and financial services institutions and for all business relationships with financial companies within the meaning of Section 1 (3) KWG."[52] "In this respect, obtaining bank confirmations is a necessary and generally appropriate measure to assess whether the company's business relationships with credit institutions are fully covered."[53]

If bank confirmations are dispensed with, there can be no sufficient and appropriate audit evidence within the meaning of IDW PS 300 n.F. para. 7. Due to the dubious trustworthiness of the trustee Citadelle alone, it is imperative to obtain bank confirmations directly from the account-holding bank.[54]

---

[51] In agreement with Schüttler: Prüfung von Treuhandkonten auf Vorhandensein; Der Betrieb (DB), 2020, pp. 1862–1863, here p. 1863.

[52] IDW (ed.): WP-Handbuch, 17th edition, Düsseldorf 2020, pp. 1586, 1789.

[53] IDW (ed.): WP-Handbuch, 17th edition, Düsseldorf 2020, p. 1789.

[54] Lenz: Die Verantwortung des Abschlussprüfers zur Aufdeckung von Bilanzdelikten (Täuschungen, Vermögensschädigungen), Das Fallbeispiel Wirecard AG; Zeitschrift für internationale und kapitalmarktorientierte Rechnungslegung (KoR), 2020, pp. 546–552, here p. 552.

It is, therefore, essential to release the bank from its duty of confidentiality in this respect. Finally, the auditor can request all information and evidence necessary for a thorough audit by Section 320 (2) HGB. "If the trustor cannot even force the trustee to provide simple direct bank information by instruction, it is more than questionable whether there is a genuine trust relationship at all, which entitles the trustor to recognize the trust property as beneficial ownership."[55]

Given the central importance of the business activity for Wirecard, it can only be assumed in highly exceptional cases that the auditor may be satisfied with corresponding confirmations, even without the unique features of the trustee and the account-holding bank. This would mean that a sales and earnings volume of existential importance for the business success of the entire group, which could jeopardize the going concern assumption, would be audited without its audit procedures. "The third-party acquirer business is growing very strongly and is becoming the main source of success for the Group as a whole."[56] After all, it accounts for more than 50% of sales, more than 95% of EBTA, virtually all cash and cash equivalents, and 25% of total assets.[57] This would clearly violate IDW PS 300 (n.F.) para. 5, according to which audit procedures are required to be carried out to obtain sufficient and appropriate audit evidence to draw substantiated conclusions for forming an audit opinion. The statutory obligation under Section 317 (1) of HGB is to conduct the audit in such a way that it is possible to identify whether there are any misstatements or violations that would be disregarded.

A careful and in-depth examination of the escrow accounts is also essential to assess the business activities of the Wirecard subsidiaries completely independently of checking the existence of the credit balances. After all, Wirecard shows sales that the company has not managed independently at all, but from which income flows on the one hand, which trigger commission payments on the other and are ultimately responsible for cash collateral to be provided.

"In most relations to merchants, we could not identify any communication throughout the company that could be linked to these merchants. We found no price or commission lists and no corresponding sales reporting. We found no dedicated onboarding, i.e., no dedicated merchant audit. We found no

---

[55] See Lenz: Die Prüfung von Treuhandkonten—das Fallbeispiel Wirecard AG, response to Marten; Der Betrieb (DB) 2020, pp. 1465–1469, pp. 2085–2089, here p. 2087.

[56] Wambach Report: p. 21.

[57] According to the Chairman of the Supervisory Board of Wirecard; see Committee of Inquiry: p. 294.

risk analysis that dealt with economic risks, i.e., partner failure, merchant failure, or the business model itself."[58] The auditor has to notice this.

"If the auditor had insisted on the audit of real cash transactions (payments to the trustee, stating the invoices paid) by its internal guidelines, then further indications of the existence or non-existence of the associated transactions could possibly have emerged."[59]

Even if control over the trust property, i.e., the credit balances in the escrow accounts, is to be denied, this is assumed below as a working hypothesis. The question then arises whether the assets are cash, cash equivalents, or receivables. This is to be checked first in the balance sheet.

[58] This was the testimony of Wirecard's Head of Compliance in the Committee of Inquiry; see Committee of Inquiry: p. 235.

[59] Wambach Report: Addendum II, p. 18.

5

Trade Receivables versus Cash and Cash Equivalents

Wirecard reported the credit balances in the escrow accounts as cash. Here, the development of cash and cash equivalent has been 185 million Euro in 2010, 213 million Euro in 2011, 358 million Euro in 2012, 479 million Euro in 2013, 695 million Euro in 2014, 1,063 million Euro in 2015, 1,333 million Euro in 2016, 1,901 million Euro in 2017, and 2,720 million Euro in 2018.[1] That line item is not obvious (assumed that Wirecard is the beneficial owner which, in fact, is not the case as has been shown in the previous chapter). In principle, it should be considered to report those assets as trade receivables. The different nature of the assets entails differences in subsequent measurements, such as the recognition of value adjustments (loan loss reserves and impairments). Receivables arise when a payment claim has arisen per the accounting rules but has not yet been fulfilled.

"The first doubts on the way Wirecard accounted for its TPA partners were raised in a series of blog articles in the FT Alphaville House of Wirecard series in 2015. Such allegations were also brought to FREP's attention by a whistleblower, who in 2016 expressed concerns with Wirecard's accounting with respect to the receivables and payables related to Wirecard's acquiring business. These allegations regarded the way in which the acquiring receivables and the acquiring payables were accounted for at subsidiary level, since they appeared to be approximately equal at group levels. This seemed particularly

[1] Cf. ESMA: p. 37. See also Wirecard's financial statements of the respective years.

© The Author(s), under exclusive license to Springer Nature Switzerland AG 2024
E. Löw and R. Heyd, *The Audit Failures of the Wirecard Scandal*,
https://doi.org/10.1007/978-3-031-59854-8_5

problematic with regard to subsidiaries based in jurisdictions where Wirecard did not have a licence and used acquiring parties (e.g. Dubai, Ireland). Allegedly, inconsistencies arose from the fact that no such balance seemed to exist at subsidiary level and therefore the corresponding liabilities were missing."[2]

Wirecard's business activities lead to different cash inflows, namely from its activities as a PSP, as an acquirer with the involvement of Wirecard Bank, and as a guarantor.

As a PSP, Wirecard provides the service of making its platform available for processing transactions. This platform is used by all other parties involved: the customer who orders the goods, the bank that issued the credit card, the credit card company through which the payment is made, the acquirer bank that forwards the payment to the merchant, and the merchant itself, which is the payment recipient. Depending on with whom Wirecard has concluded the contract for the provision of the service from PSP activity, there is a claim to a fee from this contractual partner. If this fee is not paid immediately, a claim for payment arises. It is, therefore, conceivable that a receivable should be reported here.

In countries where Wirecard Bank had a banking license, Wirecard could assume the function of the acquirer bank itself. The name is derived from the relationship with the credit card institution for which the customers are effectively recruited. The acquirer, therefore, receives a fee for acquiring customers. Once the acquisition has taken place, the acquirer is entitled to payment. If payment is not made immediately, a claim is made against the credit card company.

Finally, Wirecard is responsible for defaulting on receivables from a (partial) reversal of the original (goods) transaction by issuing a guarantee. It can be assumed that this guarantee was exclusively committed to payments by Wirecard as guarantor in the event of a proven default by both the merchant and the acquirer to the credit card company as the guarantee holder and payments for other reasons, such as due to rating downgrades or changes in indices, are more likely to be ruled out, the facts of the case are probably not a credit default swap, but a financial guarantee. While a credit default swap under IAS 39 (since 2018 under IFRS 9) would have to be recognized as a derivative at fair value through profit or loss, different rules apply to financial guarantees. Irrespective of this, a receivable may arise if the credit card company does not meet its payment obligations to Wirecard on time.

---

[2] ESMA: p. 43.

As these business activities are in payment services and funds to settle the various activities are retained directly from the customer's payment flow to the business, it is unlikely that receivables will build up to any great extent.

Something different could apply if the cash collateral retained as part of the guarantee exceeds an amount higher than the contractual obligations. Depending on the contractual structure, an agreement is necessary to be made regarding whether the trustee will transfer the excess credit balance to an account, which will be determined by Wirecard, presumably at Wirecard Bank. Alternatively, the credit balance can remain in the escrow account, but Wirecard's disposal is not subject to any restrictions. It is nevertheless to be expected that a repayment has to be made to Wirecard if a certain amount is exceeded or Wirecard will call up the amount in question.

The auditor is obliged to inspect and interpret the contractual terms and conditions. The audit procedures have to focus on the appropriateness of the amount of the cash collateral, the compensation rules, and their implementation. Cash collateral is only considered appropriate if it is in an economically reasonable proportion to the default risk assumed. Firstly, it is necessary to take into account that Wirecard only has to step in if the merchant fails to meet its (return) payment obligations and the cash collateral retained by the acquirer bank is insufficient—or the acquirer bank defaults. In this respect, Wirecard only bears a very small piece of the risk. Apart from why Wirecard is needed as a guarantor, a very high level of cash collateral can hardly be explained in terms of turnover.

Apart from the amount that exceeds the collateral to be deposited, the issue is ultimately the cash collateral itself. Assuming the working hypothesis that Wirecard would be allocated control in accordance with IFRS, recognition as a receivable cannot be considered for the cash collateral itself—only for the excess collateral, and only if it was agreed that this was to be transferred to an account specified by Wirecard but was not transferred.

Otherwise, cash collateral is a cash reserve. In practice, the term cash reserve is often used as a generic term for cash and cash equivalents defined in IAS 7. In the literature, particularly before adopting IAS 7, the term cash and cash equivalents is generally used, and its definition is discussed. In the (longer) past, broad definitions have been proposed, including net current assets and net monetary assets.[3] Net current assets are the balance of all current assets and liability items. In contrast, net monetary assets include,

[3] See Wysocki von: Grundlagen, nationale und internationale Stellungnahmen zur Kapitalflussrechnung, in: Wysocki (ed.): Kapitalflussrechnung, Stuttgart 1998, pp. 1–33, here p. 10. See also fundamentally IDW: Stellungnahme des Hauptfachausschuß des Instituts der Wirtschaftsprüfer in Deutschland e.V.: Die Kapitalflußrechnung als Ergänzung des Jahres- und Konzernabschlusses, (SG/HFA 1/1995); Die Wirtschaftsprüfung (WPg), 1995, pp. 210–213.

in addition to cash and cash equivalents, all monetary receivables less monetary liabilities with a remaining term until the next balance sheet date. Such deferrals were justified in practice by the possibility of a simple derivation of cash flow statements. The legislator disagreed with such arguments when formulating IAS 7. Instead, cash and cash equivalents under IAS 7 have been deliberately defined very narrowly.

According to IAS 7.6, cash and cash equivalents include cash and demand deposits. Cash equivalents are short-term, highly liquid financial investments that can be converted into fixed amounts of cash at any time and are only subject to insignificant fluctuations in value. They are used to meet short-term payment obligations and, by IAS 7.7, are not usually held for investment or other purposes and generally have a remaining term of no more than approximately three months from the date of acquisition. The key reason for the narrow definition is that a financial investment may only be classified as a cash equivalent "if it is readily convertible to a known amount of cash and is subject to an insignificant risk of changes in value" (IAS 7.7).

Prima facie, in the case of the escrow accounts, it could be questioned whether the funds can be converted directly into a fixed amount of cash because Wirecard's ability to dispose of them is restricted. According to such a consideration, disposable means that the funds may not be disposed of in any other way but have to be at the free disposal of the Wirecard companies. The amounts in the escrow accounts are intended to cover any financial losses that the TPA partners may incur from transactions with the credit card customers referred. They are left to the trustee for appropriate disposal and thus withdrawn from the beneficial owner, the Wirecard companies. However, this only applies in the event of a claim. In this respect, such an interpretation is subject to a misunderstanding.

It could also be argued that short term means a total period of no more than around three months from acquisition. The chargeback risk, the settlement of which was guaranteed by the Wirecard companies, and this guarantee was secured by the cash balances in the escrow accounts, can extend over a longer period, for example, for 180 or even up to 560 days (e.g., for subscription contracts and longer-term travel or flight bookings) in the case of corresponding transactions with high-risk customers. This case is also not covered by IAS 7.7.

The expansion of cash and cash equivalents is based on a different consideration. The original version of IAS 7 was published back in 1977. Unlike in phases of low or even negative interest rates on cash investments, at other times, a company's treasury does not leave funds in a bank account without interest as part of liquidity management but instead invests them in short-term money market securities, fixed-term deposits or time deposits, while at the same time including them in the cash management of asset/liability management. Against this background, equating cash equivalents with actual cash and cash equivalents is appropriate. However, the prerequisite is that they are incredibly close to money. In terms of their character, cash equivalents are, therefore, an (active) cash investment by the treasury of a very short-term nature, usually to generate additional income for a minimal period but in conjunction with liquidity management. This explains that such short-term uses of funds may only be included in cash and cash equivalents if there is no capital investment, and they are not subject to significant fluctuations in value. In this respect, speculation in derivatives with short maturities, for example, is excluded from inclusion in cash equivalents.

This is not the case for Wirecard. The cash collateral in the escrow accounts does not represent a short-term, highly liquid financial investment. It is not invested for the reason to generate interest income. Furthermore, the question of conversion into cash does not arise in the present case, as account balances already constitute cash by definition in accordance with IAS 7.6 without the need for conversion.

IAS 7 also does not state that availability without penalty is necessary to qualify as a means of payment. The deposit of cash as collateral does not change its classification as cash—provided that control generally remains with the collateral provider.

This is also supported by the provisions of IAS 39 on accounting for financial instruments, which was applicable up to and including 2017, and IFRS 9, which replaced it in 2018, on the derecognition of assets. According to IAS 39.20 and IFRS 9.3.2.6, financial assets, which incidentally also include cash on hand, are only to be derecognized if the risks and rewards have been transferred from the transferor of a security to the transferee. This is not the case for genuine securities repurchases or securities lending transactions, for example, so the transferor of the collateral retains the accounting treatment despite granting collateral (for a limited period). The same applies to banks depositing a minimum reserve with central banks. The corresponding financial resources are held in an account of the bank at the relevant central bank.

This means that the cash collateral transferred by Wirecard (via a shortened payment channel) qualifies as cash—always assuming that Wirecard would be the beneficial owner. The requirements of IAS 7.6 are met. The matter is regulated otherwise, and Wirecard violated this in its financial statements from 2015 to 2018.

IAS 7.48 requires an entity to disclose, in conjunction with a management commentary, the amount of significant cash and cash equivalents held by the entity that are not available for use by the group. According to IAS 7.49, this also applies if the parent company or other subsidiaries restrict the availability of the holdings.

In addition, IFRS 7.14 (a) requires an entity to disclose for financial instruments "the carrying amount of financial assets that it has pledged as collateral for liabilities or contingent liabilities … ."

Compliance with the disclosure requirements is not a marginal matter. The disclosure of the amounts posted to escrow accounts as cash and cash equivalents is particularly important for investors and analysts because this item has a specific informative value for an insolvency forecast as part of the analysis of the annual financial statements. To assess insolvency or the threat of insolvency as a reason for insolvency, the focus has to be on the amount of and changes in cash and cash equivalents. Therefore, IAS 7.48 and IFRS 7.14 (a) disclosure requirements are essential information. This applies to Wirecard, as granting guarantees has been an important business activity.

Given the volume of funds held in escrow accounts ranging from several hundred million Euro to over one billion Euro, it is incomprehensible that the auditors did not complain about the missing information. This gives the shareholder a wholly inadequate and distorted picture.

6

Sales Revenue and Commissions

6.1 Presentation in the Income Statement

Wirecard worked in various areas of business models for which the company received different types of consideration. Until the 2017 fiscal year, revenue recognition was governed by IAS 18. IFRS 15 was to be applied for the 2018 fiscal year. IAS 18.7 defines revenue as the gross inflow of economic benefits arising from the ordinary activities of an entity during a period. According to IAS 18.8, revenue only covers gross inflows a company has received (or can claim) for its account. In contrast, IAS 18.8 clarifies that amounts collected in the interest of third parties do not generate economic benefits. "The same applies to amounts included in the gross inflows of economic benefits collected on behalf of the principal that do not increase the equity of the arranging entity. Amounts the company collects for the client's account do not constitute sales revenue. Revenue, on the other hand, is the commission" (IAS 18.8). By IAS 18.9, revenue is measured at the fair value of the consideration received or receivable, which, according to IAS 18.10, usually consists of cash or cash equivalents.

IFRS 15, which Wirecard had to apply for the 2018 fiscal year, is also based on the civil law structure. IFRS 15.10 assumes a contract establishing enforceable rights and obligations for the parties concerned. By IFRS 15.22, the promised services has to be examined, and the performance obligation has to be identified when the contract is concluded. According to IFRS 15.22, a performance obligation is (a) a separately identifiable service, which via IFRS 15.26 (f) also includes the provision of a service to a third party that results in the transfer of services to a customer and (i) the granting of

© The Author(s), under exclusive license to Springer Nature Switzerland AG 2024
E. Löw and R. Heyd, *The Audit Failures of the Wirecard Scandal*, https://doi.org/10.1007/978-3-031-59854-8_6

licenses. Revenue is recognized in accordance with IFRS 15.31 when it satisfies a performance obligation by transferring a promised service. According to IFRS 15.46, the revenue is the transaction price, which is required to be determined in accordance with IFRS 15.47, taking into account the terms of the contract and commercial practice. If a transaction price were paid for the provision of several distinct services, the price would have to be allocated to the service components by IFRS 15.73. According to IFRS 15.97 (b), the costs of fulfilling the contract include material costs (such as for inventories used to provide the service) and (e) other costs that are incurred only because the entity has entered into the contract. Payments to subcontractors are explicitly mentioned. In addition, disclosure requirements are formulated, the aim of which, according to IFRS 15.110, is for companies to provide sufficient information to enable users of financial statements to obtain an understanding of the nature, amount, timing, and (un-) certainty of revenue and cash flows arising from the contracts. To this end, IFRS 15.114 requires a breakdown by category. IFRS 15.115 also refers to the cross-reference to breakdowns in segment reporting.[1]

In the actual PSP business, Wirecard provides a platform that brings together the merchant and customer, acquirer bank, card organization, and issuer bank. This platform provides various detailed services, such as verifications, plausibility checks, and other services—virtually simultaneously and in real time. Depending on with whom Wirecard has concluded the contract for the provision of the service from PSP activity, a claim for payment arises against this contractual partner. If Wirecard acts as a PSP, payment is made for this service. In terms of billing, the merchant is withheld a percentage of each Euro of its turnover. In this respect, the amount of the purchase price represents the basis for calculating the fee—but nothing more. Wirecard generates sales from deliveries and services, which are to be reported as such in the income statement.

However, Wirecard did not work on its platform until 2019. Wirecard's external presence cannot be definitively decided without insight into the relevant contracts. Two possibilities are conceivable in principle. Either Wirecard acted contractually as a PSP and used a subcontractor, so to speak, who was the actual PSP and invoiced Wirecard directly for its services. In this case, the third party's service is effectively a preliminary product and is required to be reported under the cost of sales. This would result in a kind of gross presentation. Alternatively, Wirecard has merely arranged the order for this

[1] See Karami: Das kollektive Kontrollversagen—ein Fall für die Lehrbücher; Karami (ed.): Skandalfall Wirecard: Eine wissenschaftlich-fundierte interdisziplinäre Analyse, Wiesbaden 2022, pp. 1–85, here p. 14.

PSP. In this case, Wirecard would not have to report its sales revenue, only a commission.

As the TPA business presents itself, the three subsidiaries, Wirecard UK and Dublin, Wirecard Technologies, and Wirecard Middle East, referred customers to third-party acquirers. Al Alam and Senjo operated as independent companies until the end of 2017, and Wirecard took over on 1 January 2018. Both have just been operating on the Wirecard platform since 2019. A third acquirer was only added in 2018, namely PayEasy. All three companies worked as BIN sponsors for Wirecard. As the processing fees were charged to the credit card customers by the TPA partners, it can be assumed that they acted independently in the external relationship. Wirecard was responsible for the customer relationship with the respective merchant. The customers were referred to Al Alam Solution Provider by Wirecard. The (gross) commission was collected from the TPA partners during processing. However, specific amounts from the portion due to the Wirecard companies were paid into escrow accounts to secure Wirecard's guarantee commitment for the assumption of risk for chargebacks and fines, and another portion was transferred to accounts that were freely accessible to Wirecard.

Al Alam Solution Provider was responsible for the technical connection of the merchants and had contacts and technical interfaces to acquire banks. Furthermore, Al Alam Solution Provider was responsible for payment processing (settlement), chargeback management, and merchant control. In addition, Wirecard provided Al Alam Solution Provider with the liquidity required for the so-called Merchant Cash Advance business. Before accepting Wirecard customers, Al Alam Solution Provider conducted a due diligence review of these customers. Al Alam Solution Provider decided which acquiring banks would be used to process the customers—the customers then concluded contracts with Al Alam Solution Provider and the acquiring banks. Al Alam Solution Provider concluded a contract with each merchant for the technical processing of credit card transactions. The contracts concluded between Al Alam Solution Provider and merchants were negotiated by Al Alam Solution Provider, whereby the conditions negotiated by Al Alam Solution Provider were always within a framework specified by Wirecard. The activity with Senjo Payments Asia has been similar. Since 2018, it has also been with PayEasy Solutions.

For Wirecard, this would mean that commission income, rather than sales revenue, would have to be reported for customer referrals. From the acquirer's perspective, the costs charged by the acquirer for the service are sales revenues. However, they were to be paid by the corresponding customers. Wirecard did not incur any expenses in this constellation.

The opposite would be the case if Wirecard had acted towards the customer and used the acquirers, who were, in fact, not acquirers at all but PSP, like a subcontractor. Wirecard would then have provided a service to the outside world that would have been charged to the customer. The TPA partners would have had to pay a processing fee. In this respect, the service would have had to be reported as sales revenue and the processing fee would have been presented as an expense to generate sales revenue. However, even Wirecard does not appear to have argued accordingly. Instead, Wirecard relies on the fact that the company can dispose of transactions and fulfill the performance obligation towards the respective merchant. The latter would be regarded as a customer despite the lack of a direct contractual relationship between Wirecard and the respective merchant.[2] However, this means that the control criteria are not met per IAS 18 or IFRS 15.[3]

By the contracts between the three Wirecard subsidiaries and the TPA partners, it was agreed that the TPA partners would process the corresponding credit card transactions for customers referred by Wirecard. "The sales revenues paid by the respective customers were collected or reported. The TPA partners, in turn, received commissions for the processing services they provided, which were reported as "cost of materials" by the Wirecard companies. For the Wirecard companies concerned, the quarterly statements thus resulted in receivables from the TPA partners that corresponded to the amount of the (gross) sales revenues reduced by the "cost of materials" (or commission claims of the TPA partners)."[4]

However, the fact that Wirecard itself did not have contracts with the acquiring banks and merchants and had no direct contractual influence and control over the operational provision of services speaks against gross accounting.[5] This applies to the PSP business and acquiring.[6] "The TPA provides accounting-relevant documents in the form of quarterly sales reports and evaluations to Wirecard, which are based on the payment transaction data of the supported merchants (or website operators). The TPA thus provides the data on which Wirecard's revenue and cost of materials accounting is based."[7] "On the basis of the evidence and information received and our investigations carried out on this basis, we were unable to fully understand the appropriateness of the "gross accounting" chosen by Wirecard for

[2] See KPMG report: p. 33.
[3] See also ESMA: page 35.
[4] KPMG report: p. 14.
[5] See Wambach Report: p. 60.
[6] See Wambach Report: p. 60.
[7] See Wambach Report: p. 64.

the sales revenues generated with the TPA partners due to a lack of sufficient evidence of the respective contractual relationships, among other things."[8] The auditor was aware of the contradiction between the contracts with the TPA partners and the procedure practiced based on the audit evidence provided. This has to be investigated, and the accounting has to reflect the actual circumstances. The auditor is required to insist on this.[9]

In any case, it is not sufficient to be satisfied with Wirecard's explanation that the deviations between the contractual agreements and the actual settlements were since the contracts merely had the character of framework agreements, some of which were deviated from for operational reasons. "According to the information provided, there was no written documentation on deviations and adjustments; rather, the contractual partners' commercial agreement was established in all cases by implied action. About the traceability of the respective valid conditions by third parties, this procedure does not meet the requirements for proper documentation, in particular of the respective relevant contractual agreements."[10] "The completeness of the accounting-relevant documents and their correct representation in the external accounting system is not ensured without an appropriate contract archive or contract management."[11] Against this background, compliance with generally accepted accounting principles, independently under which accounting regime, seems challenging.

Another astonishing discrepancy between the contracts and reality is the timing of the invoices. The contract provides monthly billing, but quarterly billing was implemented—to Wirecard's disadvantage.[12]

Whether the payment flow speaks against a gross presentation is questionable if it were actually a shortened payment method.[13] In the present overall context, however, the payment flow is an additional indication against a gross presentation, as the TPA retains all fees from the payment flow and only forwards Wirecard's share.[14] The payment flow takes place on a net basis. The TPA handles the technical payment processing via its systems as an outsourced service provider.[15]

---

[8] KPMG report: p. 32.

[9] See as well, SMSG: p. 17.

[10] KPMG report: p. 21.

[11] KPMG report: p. 21.

[12] See KPMG report: p. 21.

[13] Different view Wambach Report: p. 60.

[14] See Wambach Report: p. 60.

[15] See Wambach Report: p. 63.

In 2018, there were probably contractual changes (in connection with the first-time application of IFRS 15), which should lead to Wirecard having control over the revenues according to the contracts. It is, therefore, conceivable that gross accounting can be justified based on the contract design—provided that the reality practiced corresponded to the contracts.[16]

Regardless of how the contract is structured and how the transaction is carried out, under no circumstances can gross proceeds in the amount of the merchant's turnover be reported. The purchase price that the customer has to pay to the merchant is merely the mathematical basis for calculating the fees of the other contracting parties involved in the transaction. Each party ultimately receives a particular percentage share of the sales revenue. Suppose Wirecard presents the remuneration received on a gross basis. In that case, it can, therefore, be that percentage of the actual sales of the delivery transaction to which Wirecard and other parties involved are entitled.[17] This is either a commission income not offset by any expenses (third parties) or a sales revenue corresponding to a usage fee within the meaning of IAS 18.5 (b) if the fee to be paid to the actual PSP is paid for the use of its platform. IFRS 15 does not contain any special features in this respect.

In certain countries, Wirecard has acted independently as an acquirer due to the license held by Wirecard Bank. The acquirer acts as a customer intermediary for the benefit of the credit card company. For this, the card organization has to pay a commission to Wirecard Bank, which is to be reported as such in the income statement.

Finally, Wirecard developed the business activity of a guarantee for defaults on reversals and penalty payments. Assuming that the contract is structured accordingly, this is not a credit default swap but a financial guarantee within the meaning of IAS 39/IFRS 9. For the assumption of a default guarantee, Wirecard receives a guarantee commission payment to be accounted for with a clear identification of the activity that allows the addressee of the Financial Statements of Wirecard to recognize the nature of the service. Direct inclusion in the income statement is not possible. Instead, the commission payment is to be distributed throughout the guarantee service.

Provisions have to be made for the threat of utilization. IAS 39 applied until 2017. IFRS 9 has been relevant since 2018. According to IAS 39.9, a financial guarantee contract is defined as a contract that requires the issuer to make specified payments to reimburse the holder for a loss it incurs as a result of a default. Per IAS 18, the premium received is to be distributed over the

---

[16] See Wambach Report: Addendum II, pp. 7–9.

[17] According to the KPMG Report, all transaction fees borne by the merchant were recognized as revenue.

guarantee period using the effective interest method. In most transactions, (partial) refunds are made within a very short period. An interest component can be excluded for these cases. However, some transactions take a long time, such as purchasing airline tickets. In this case, the term of the contract underlying the guarantee may be longer than one year, so distributing commissions for guarantees may be necessary. Guarantees are measured by IAS 37. Based on IAS 37.23, a provision is required to be recognized if the utilization probability is over 50%. In this case, this is a specific provision. If the criteria for a specific provision are not met, general provisions have to be recognized by IAS 37.24, whereby experience about default rates can be used as a basis.

IFRS 9.5.5.1 transferred the measurement of a guarantee to the application area of the impairment requirements for financial instruments. This means that general loan loss provisions for guarantee commitments have to be allocated to stage 1 of the impairment hierarchy, and an impairment loss is required to be recognized in the amount of the 12-month expected credit loss. In the event of a significant deterioration in creditworthiness, the loan is obliged to be allocated to stage 2 in accordance with the classification for the remaining term. If objective default indications exist, the guarantee has to be allocated to stage 3, and the gross amount reported in the income statement is to be changed to the net amount. Most of the guarantee terms are less than one year, so the term consideration is of secondary importance.

6.2 Audit Procedures

"The assessed risks of error are to be linked to the further audit procedures to be performed, and the audit procedures to be performed are to be linked to the relevant statements in the financial reporting to be able to issue the audit opinion with reasonable assurance (common thread of the audit). It is necessary to consider "whether there is a risk for which statement-related audit procedures alone do not provide sufficient appropriate audit evidence (e.g., risks from mass transactions)."[18] "An audit of whether all transactions have been included in the financial statements cannot be performed using substantive audit procedures alone. Ultimately, the question is whether, for example, a transaction that has taken place (an incoming invoice) has not been recorded. Only recorded transactions can be audited using a sample."[19]

[18] IDW (ed.): WP-Handbuch, 17th edition, Düsseldorf 2020, p. 1607 with reference to IDW PS 261 n.F. para. 10 and para. 68.

[19] IDW (ed.): WP-Handbuch, 17th edition, Düsseldorf 2020, pp. 1583–1585.

Particular risks may exist in connection with revenue recognition. "When assessing the risks of non-compliance, the auditor, therefore, is required to assume that such risks exist in connection with revenue recognition (e.g., accounting manipulations such as early revenue recognition, the recognition of fictitious revenue or the inadmissible deferral of revenue to a later reporting period)."[20]

When developing the audit strategy and audit program, the risks of error are taken into account,

- in which areas of the audit it is necessary or appropriate to rely on internal controls relevant to the audit,
- in which audit procedures are to be performed to obtain additional information relevant to the judgment in the individual audit areas,
- in which areas special and more extensive audit procedures are required due to an increased risk assessment (especially significant risks) or where an audit appears possible to a lesser extent due to a lower risk."[21]

The type of audit field concerned depends on the statement in the financial reporting.[22]

Statement in financial reporting	Type of audit field concerned
Existence	Account balances
Entry	Business transactions, disclosure
Attribution	Account balances, disclosure
Completeness of the information	Business transactions, account balances
Measurement and allocation	Account balances, disclosure
Accuracy	Business transactions, disclosure
Accrual	Business transactions
Disclosure and comprehensibility	Business transactions, disclosure

All of these areas are relevant here. TPA transactions require particular attention. They are characterized by a strong lack of transparency, leading to

[20] IDW (ed.): WP-Handbuch, 17th edition, Düsseldorf 2020, p. 1645 with reference to IDW PS 210 para. 39. Similar reference in Lenz: Die Verantwortung des Abschlussprüfers zur Aufdeckung von Bilanzdelikten (Täuschungen, Vermögensschädigungen), Das Fallbeispiel Wirecard AG; Zeitschrift für internationale und kapitalmarktorientierte Rechnungslegung (KoR), 2020, pp. 546–552, here p. 550. See also Farr: Wirecard und seine Folgen für die Abschlussprüfung, Aufdeckung doloser Handlungen nach ISA (DE) 240; Die Wirtschaftsprüfung (WPg) 2021 pp. 66–74, here p. 70.

[21] IDW (ed.): Prüfungspraxis, Leitfaden für Prüfungsmitarbeiter, 2nd updated edition, Düsseldorf 2020, p. 72. See also 3rd updated edition, Düsseldorf 2023, pp. 58–60.

[22] See IDW (ed.): Prüfungspraxis, Leitfaden für Prüfungsmitarbeiter, 2nd updated edition, Düsseldorf 2020, p. 77–78. See as well 3rd updated edition, Düsseldorf 2023, p. 62 and IDW (ed.): WP-Handbuch, 17th edition, Düsseldorf 2020, p. 1610 and p. 1613 et seq.

a particular risk of inaccuracies and violations per IDW PS 210. If reference is made solely to unusual business activities, which—among other issues—is explicitly listed in IDW PS 210 para. 35, some of the indicators mentioned are fulfilled, for example, transactions with a material impact on profits, complicated transactions or unusual accounting of transactions, or about the service received, excessive expenses for brokerage commissions. Furthermore, there may have been massive difficulties obtaining audit evidence, which is another area covered by IDW PS 210 para. 35. The risk of errors in the financial statement documents by IDW PS 261 (n.F.) is to be taken into account.

The mere interposition of escrow accounts, to which very substantial amounts were booked, leads to a strong lack of transparency. Given the risk involved, limiting the audit procedures to inquiries of management was by no means sufficient in this case.[23]

The lack of transparency is particularly evident in the fact that

- the sales revenues with end customers are not proven to Wirecard on an item-specific basis but rather according to merchants, groups of merchants, or another payment solution provider,
- the statements did not contain any information on transaction numbers and volumes or commissions due,
- the payment transactions could not be precisely allocated to the individual sales transactions,
- the payments were allegedly made partly to bank accounts available to Wirecard and partly to escrow accounts,
- this allocation was based on neither contractual agreements nor structured risk assessments,
- the reconciliation of the figures was presented using Excel tables and screenshots at different levels of aggregation, and this information was also the basis for the Wirecard companies to post the corresponding revenue and cost of materials,
- reconciliations were carried out on a quarterly basis, and deviations of up to 5% were considered tolerable,
- the comparison of the receivables of the Wirecard companies and the liabilities of Senjo Payment Asia, as well as the associated sales revenues and cost of materials, showed implausibilities.

[23] Lenz notes that Wirecard's business model leads to a very high number of transactions and that it is therefore difficult to obtain sufficient audit assurance based on the audit of selected individual transactions. See Lenz: Die Verantwortung des Abschlussprüfers zur Aufdeckung von Bilanzdelikten (Täuschungen, Vermögensschädigungen), Das Fallbeispiel Wirecard AG; Zeitschrift für internationale und kapitalmarktorientierte Rechnungslegung (KoR), 2020, pp. 546–552, here p. 550.

Some peculiarities are noted in the auditor's working papers, but they do not trigger further audit procedures.[24] "Payments are documented that are not made by the TPA partner itself, but by unknown companies ... Al Alam makes the majority of payments by check (39.9 million Euro) from 2015 to 2017 and thus without an intended use. ... The checks are printed in German."[25]

"According to the working papers, the TPA were billed without an invoice number. Payments for the TPA are made without reference to individual invoices. It is not possible to itemize outstanding invoices. In some cases, payments are made by third parties and can therefore only be attributed indirectly."[26] "These significant deficits in the accounting of the TPA business are also fraud indicators and could have been recognized as such by an auditor."[27]

Parts of the invoicing process have been outsourced in the TPA business. "The TPA takes over the technical payment processing via its systems as an outsourced service provider."[28] The extent to which this complies with generally accepted accounting principles (independently of the underlying accounting regime) is questionable, but it depends, in particular, on how the business partner's control system is structured. "An audit of the internal control system outsourced by Wirecard (by IDW PS 331 (2010)) at the individual TPA could well have led to further indications in connection with the accounting fraud."[29] As the service provider's activities are material for Wirecard, the auditor is obliged to obtain sufficient information to understand its internal control system.[30] The omission constitutes a breach of IDW PS 331 para. 14.

In 2018, Senjo and Al Alam were acquired by Wirecard with retroactive effect from 1 January 2018. At this point, the auditor could audit the systems and internal control system of the (new) subsidiaries now belonging to the group.[31]

If sales represent a significant risk of error (IDW PS 210 n.F. para. 39, IDW PS 261 para. 67) and there are numerous indications of a lack of transparency that make it difficult to obtain an audit opinion and, in addition, there are substantiated indications of irregularities in the reporting of

24 See Wambach Report: p. 74.
25 Wambach Report: p. 75.
26 Wambach Report: p. 54, see also p. 74.
27 Wambach Report: p. 54.
28 Wambach Report: p. 63.
29 Wambach Report: p. 64.
30 See also Wambach Report: S. 63.
31 See Wambach Report: Addendum II, p. 13.

sales through public reporting. The audit is required to be performed with particular intensity.[32] Assurance-related audit procedures include case-by-case reviews and assurance-related analytical audit procedures on individual types of transactions and account balances. However, this is not sufficient in these cases.[33] If necessary, the audit should switch from a pure sampling procedure to a procedure with deliberate selection. This is based on the consideration that the risk of misstatements is more significant in the samples selected by the auditor than in the other areas.[34] "Further audit procedures would include, for example, requesting additional documentation at the level of individual transactions, i.e., examining individual settlements between third-party partners and their customers on a sample basis, verifying the existence of customers, or tracing payments into the escrow account."[35]

Furthermore, certain sales can be confirmed, whereby criteria for a deliberate selection can be, for example, the amount of an inevitable turnover or the volume of business transactions with a customer.[36] If there is a risk of fictitious sales being reported, the posted values should be compared with the underlying contract documents, and information on significant customers should also be obtained.[37]

Nevertheless, inadequate audit procedures appear to have been carried out—and not only in 2018. "Based on the documentation situation at Wirecard regarding the business transactions between the TPA and Wirecard in 2018 (no consecutive numbering and signature on the statements, no clear reference of the payments to specific invoices), it was not possible to directly allocate and trace individual statements to payment as part of the revenue audit. Therefore, the existence and amount of revenue only appear to have been proven indirectly via balance confirmations from the TPA and the trustee. Due to the outsourcing of the legal and operational processing of customer relationships to the TPA, numerous audit evidence (settlements, risk management analysis, interviews with the TPA as part of site visits,

---

[32] See also Lenz: Die Verantwortung des Abschlussprüfers zur Aufdeckung von Bilanzdelikten (Täuschungen, Vermögensschädigungen), Das Fallbeispiel Wirecard AG; Zeitschrift für internationale und kapitalmarktorientierte Rechnungslegung (KoR), 2020, pp. 546–552, here p. 550.

[33] See Lenz: Die Verantwortung des Abschlussprüfers zur Aufdeckung von Bilanzdelikten (Täuschungen, Vermögensschädigungen), Das Fallbeispiel Wirecard AG; Zeitschrift für internationale und kapitalmarktorientierte Rechnungslegung (KoR), 2020, pp. 546–552, here p. 550.

[34] See IDW (ed.): WP-Handbuch, 17th edition, Düsseldorf 2020, p. 1501.

[35] Lenz: Die Verantwortung des Abschlussprüfers zur Aufdeckung von Bilanzdelikten (Täuschungen, Vermögensschädigungen), Das Fallbeispiel Wirecard AG; Zeitschrift für internationale und kapitalmarktorientierte Rechnungslegung (KoR), 2020, p. 546–552, here p. 551.

[36] Based on Graumann: Wirtschaftliches Prüfungswesen, 7th revised edition, Herne 2023, p. 554 on the audit of receivables.

[37] The examples are provided by Marten/Quick/Ruhnke: Wirtschaftsprüfung, 6th, revised edition, Stuttgart 2020, p. 593.

balance confirmations) is primarily based on the TPA's own information, as Wirecard is still not involved in the payment flow with the merchants."[38] The basis for an audit opinion on the revenue in the TPA business was, therefore, in particular, balance confirmations from the TPA partners to the auditor, contracts with the TPA partners and corresponding pricing schedules, screenshots of transaction volumes, etc., from the TPA partners' systems and minutes of quarterly meetings with the TPA partners, which document the reconciliation of relevant billing parameters.[39] Statements of business activities were sent electronically by email quarterly.[40] For the TPA business partners, the statements included information on the number and volume of credit card transactions processed and the commissions due.[41] An Excel file was also provided for two TPA partners, which formed the basis for corresponding postings of sales revenue and cost of materials for two of the Wirecard subsidiaries.[42] At the other TPA partner, the postings were made directly based on the statements. In some cases, account names were specified for transactions in the statements.[43] These were alias names under which sales were recorded, but not the names of the merchants.[44] Wirecard was unable to assign specific customers to fictitious collective names. Due to the alias names, sales could not be traced.[45]

The general problem with the evidence provided is that it only shows the relationship between Wirecard and the TPA partners. In contrast, the entire transaction chain from the merchant to the customer via all parties involved is not traced. "A substantive analysis and review of the transaction data on which the settlement is based, including at individual transaction level, is not evident from the documents submitted."[46]

"In this respect, there is no evidence that, for example, the acquiring banks and card networks have accepted the transactions. Therefore, the reliability of the audit evidence obtained depends largely on the trustworthiness of the TPA. Further audit evidence that is not dependent on the TPA is not included in the documentation. An audit of the entire transaction chain by the TPAs

38 Wambach Report: p. 19.

39 Cf. KPMG Report: p. 13 and p.18; see also Committee of Inquiry: p. 336.

40 See KPMG Report: p. 18.

41 See KPMG Report: p. 18.

42 See KPMG Report: p. 18.

43 See KPMG Report: p. 18 and p. 28.

44 See KPMG Report: p. 28.

45 Cf. KPMG Report: p. 28. In 2019, the Financial Times speculated that no customers were recorded behind 34 such account names in 2017. Cf. for example KPMG Report: p. 28.

46 KPMG Report: p. 20.

did not take place. No balance confirmation requests were sent directly to the merchant."[47]

The account statements also did not provide any proof of turnover. For example, some account statements have no recognizable references to Wirecard or Wirecard subsidiaries.[48] Based on the account statements, no links could be established between the bank accounts and the sales revenues (not even indirectly).[49] In this respect, it is impossible to make reliable audit statements on the origin of the amounts in the accounts or verify the sales revenues.[50]

Concerning the required audit procedures, it should be recalled that the revenues generated with the TPA business partners accounted for the vast majority of the total revenues and EBIT of the entire Group for Wirecard's three subsidiaries.[51] "For the TPA business we examined, i.e., third-party partner business in Asia, which accounted for more than half of the revenues and the majority of the profit of the entire Wirecard Group, there is no appropriate and sufficient evidence, neither for the existence of the revenues nor for the alleged customer relationships."[52]

There are serious deficiencies because sufficient and appropriate audit evidence has not been obtained to permit an audit opinion. It was imperative to take further audit measures,[53] which may well include a full audit for a specific sub-area in accordance with IDW PS 200 para. 19 if necessary. If this does not sufficiently cover the information requirements, there is an audit impediment,[54] which would lead to the refusal of the audit opinion

---

[47] Wambach Report: p. 19-20.

[48] See KPMG Report: p. 24.

[49] See KPMG Report: p. 24.

[50] See KPMG Report: p. 24.

[51] See KPMG Report: p. 15.

[52] Testimony to the Investigation Committee by a partner involved in the KPMG special investigation. See Committee of Inquiry: p. 333. "Three articles published in the FT newspaper (...) denounced that half of the worldwide revenues and almost all of the reported profits of Wirecard came from three opaque partner companies, which in 2016 contributed to 95 % of the EBITDA and over half of revenues of the Wirecard group." ESMA: p. 43.

[53] See IDW (ed.): WP-Handbuch, 17th edition, Düsseldorf 2020, p. 1495.

[54] This is also the case with Lenz, who, however, "only" demands a qualification of the audit opinion due to an audit impediment, but already refers to the deficiencies in the internal control system. Lenz: Die Verantwortung des Abschlussprüfers zur Aufdeckung von Bilanzdelikten (Täuschungen, Vermögensschädigungen), Das Fallbeispiel Wirecard AG; Zeitschrift für internationale und kapitalmarktorientierte Rechnungslegung (KoR), 2020, pp. 546–552, here p. 550. If necessary, the audit opinion should "even be refused", cf. p. 546.

by IDW PS 400.[55] The points listed by KPMG very clearly demonstrate an audit impediment.

[55] See Lenz: Die Prüfung von Treuhandkonten—das Fallbeispiel Wirecard AG, Erwiderung auf Marten; Der Betrieb (DB) 2020, pp. 1465–1469, pp. 2085–2089, here p. 2088, who also points out that if no reliable audit evidence of the existence of very material means of payment is obtained, the audit opinion "must be qualified at least due to an audit impediment." This applies without restriction to the sales revenues that were posted to the corresponding escrow accounts to the extent that cash colateral was to be provided by Wirecard.

7

Segment Reporting

7.1 Requirements for Segment Reporting

The legal basis for mandatory disclosure of segment reporting by capital market-oriented parent companies is set out in IFRS 8. According to IFRS 8.BS 4-BC 17, one of the main objectives when the standard was adopted in November 2006 was implementing the so-called management approach. An insight is to be provided into the internal organizational structure, which forms the basis for the internal assessment of segment success and the allocation of resources to the segments, as the standard setter believes that segment information that is used for internal decision-making tends to be more useful than information compiled solely for external reporting purposes. In this respect, IFRS 8.1 establishes the fundamental principle that an entity should disclose information that enables users of financial statements to evaluate the nature and financial effects of its activities and the economic environment in which it operates.

According to IFRS 8.5, operating segments are components of an entity that can generate internal or external income and expenses and are subject to internal financial reporting. According to IFRS 8.6, not all company areas are necessarily part of an operating segment if revenue generation is only incidental to the company's management (e.g., internal administration).

In accordance with IFRS 8.12, several segments may only be combined into one segment if they have similar economic characteristics and all of the following aspects:

© The Author(s), under exclusive license to Springer Nature Switzerland AG 2024
E. Löw and R. Heyd, *The Audit Failures of the Wirecard Scandal*,
https://doi.org/10.1007/978-3-031-59854-8_7

- type of products and services,
- type of production process,
- customer structure,
- forms of distribution,
- regulatory environment, if applicable.

There is a separate reporting obligation for a segment combined in this sense by IFRS 8.11 and IFRS 8.13. IFRS 8.13 if (alternatively) (firstly) the revenue, consisting of external and internal revenue, amounts to at least 10% of the corresponding total amount of revenue of all operating segments, (secondly) the total comprehensive income represents at least 10% of the higher amount of either the total reported profits of all operating segments that do not report a loss or the total reported losses of all operating segments that report a loss, or (thirdly) the assets comprise at least 10% of the assets of all operating segments.

Operating segments that do not meet the quantitative thresholds are required, nevertheless, to be presented separately if, by IFRS 8.13 and IFRS 8.17, the Executive Board considers information on an operating segment to be useful for decision-making or, by IFRS 8.15, the external income of all reportable operating segments represents less than 75% of the company's income.

By IFRS 8.16, non-reportable operating segments and other business activities have to be presented in a collective item and with a description of their sources of income.

The segment result has to be disclosed in accordance with IFRS 8.21. If included either in the segment result or in internal reporting, the following income statement items are required to also be disclosed separately (IFRS 8.23):

- external revenues,
- internal revenues,
- interest income,
- interest expense,
- depreciation and amortization,
- material expenses and income to be recognized by IAS 1.86,
- result from valuation using the equity method,
- tax result,
- material non-cash items (except depreciation and amortization).

Segment assets are to be disclosed in accordance with IFRS 8.24. If they are included in segment assets or internal reporting, they also are to be disclosed separately (IFRS 8.24):

- investments in affiliated companies and joint ventures accounted for using the equity method and
- additions to non-current assets (except for financial instruments, deferred tax assets, plan assets from pension obligations, and rights from insurance contracts).

According to IFRS 8.28, the following reconciliations are required to be disclosed:

- total income of the reportable segments on the company's income,
- overall result of the reportable segments on the company's earnings before taxes and discontinued operations,
- sum of the assets of the reportable segments to the assets of the company,
- total amount of each material item of the reportable segments to the corresponding amount of the company,
- significant reconciliation amounts have to be described separately.

IFRS 8.25 to IFRS 8.27 contain an obligation to use internal accounting policies as well as the following minimum disclosures on the measurement of segment items:

- principles of accounting for internal transactions,
- disclosures on measurement differences between segment items and corresponding items in the financial statements, if not evident from the reconciliation, for example
  - o accounting and valuation methods,
  - o allocation policy for centrally incurred costs or shared assets,
- changes in the valuation methods used to determine the segment result,
- reason for asymmetrical item allocation to segments (e.g., depreciation allocation without the corresponding asset allocation).

By IFRS 8.21 and IFRS 8.22, the following has to be disclosed about geographical markets:

- the determinants of reportable segments (including organizational structure and aggregation of operating segments into an overall segment),

- a description of the products and services per (geographical) segment.

In addition to the regions it has to be disclosed by IFRS 8. 33:

- external income and
- non-current assets (except for financial instruments, deferred tax assets, plan assets from pension obligations, and rights from insurance contracts), in each case for
    - o amounts attributable to the company's country of domicile,
    - o amounts attributable to foreign countries as a total amount (if the amounts are material in a specific country, they must be stated individually),
- indication of how external income is allocated to the segments (e.g., customer location),
- creation of additional subtotals for groups of regions permitted,
- amounts are based on the information on the financial statement.

Finally, IFRS 8.34 requires the following information on significant customers to be disclosed:

- income from transactions with a single customer, provided the amount represents at least 10% of the company's income,
- identification of the segment or segments to which this income is allocated.

Individual companies in a group of companies, as well as a government and the companies it controls, are considered individual customers.

7.2 Contents of Segment Reporting in Wirecard's Consolidated Financial Statements over time

The Segment Reports of Wirecard AG for the years 2015–2018 can be found on pages 238–241 for the 2015 Consolidated Financial Statements, on pages 248–251 for the 2016 Consolidated Financial Statements, on pages 265–268 for the 2017 Consolidated Financial Statements, and pages 192–194 for the 2018 Consolidated Financial Statements.

The Segment Reports differ only marginally and can, therefore, be summarized. There are no discernible changes in the operating segments. The

Segment Reports comprise just over three pages and begin with a brief description of how the reportable segments are determined according to internal reporting. The internal performance indicator is EBITDA, defined by Wirecard as operating earnings before interest, taxes, depreciation, and amortization. Internal cost allocation is carried out based on third-party comparisons. In internal reporting, balance sheet values, interest, and taxes are not reported at the segment level.

Sales are segmented into three areas: Payment Processing and Risk Management, Acquisition and Issuing, and Call Center and Communication Services.

The Payment Processing and Risk Management segment, reported as the largest segment, includes all products and services for electronic payment processing and risk management. Wirecard AG (as the Group holding company) was also allocated to this segment. No other subsidiaries are mentioned by name.

In the Acquiring and Issuing segment, merchants are offered the settlement of credit card transactions for online and terminal payments. In addition, it is described that merchants process their transaction-oriented payments via accounts with Wirecard Bank AG. Furthermore, prepaid cards are issued to private and business customers, and private customers are offered current accounts in combination with cards. The segment is described as completing and expanding the value chain. Wirecard Bank AG and Wirecard Card Solutions Ltd. are mentioned by name.

The Call Center and Communication Services segment is the segment in which the entire value chain of call center activities is mapped, including other products such as after-sales support for customers or mailing activities.

There are no further explanations of the operating segments. The following breakdowns are provided for these operating segments in two different tables:

- Sales (without consolidation as well as separately consolidation and a total) and
- EBITDA (without consolidation as well as in a total consolidation and a total).

Information on geographical segments is also provided. Numerous subsidiaries listed by name are allocated to production locations. Wirecard Payment Solutions Holdings Ltd, Dublin, is allocated to Europe, but Wirecard UK and Dublin Ltd, Dublin, is not mentioned by name. The company CardSystems Middle East FZ-LLC, Dubai, belongs to the Other International segment, and Wirecard Technologies GmbH, Aschheim, is not mentioned by name, which is why it probably belongs to the segment named Germany, in which all companies not listed individually by name are included. Apart from the allocation of legally independent companies and the information that the allocation is based on production locations (which does not necessarily mean legal entities), no further explanatory information is provided.

The following breakdowns are provided for the geographical segments (Germany, Europe, and Other Countries) in three different tables:

- Sales (without consolidation as well as separately consolidation and a total),
- EBITDA (without consolidation as well as in a total consolidation and a total),
- Segment assets (without consolidation as well as in a total consolidation and a total).

From the 2017 financial year, the previous geographical segments are broken down into Europe (including Germany), Asia together with the Pacific, the Americas together with Africa (including North and South America). The previous year's figures have been adjusted.

The relevant table shows that intangible assets, property, plant, and equipment are regarded as assets.

The segment reporting does not explain further the figures or incorporates reconciliation statements.

7.3 Violations of the Segment Reporting Requirements

The segment reports do not mention the TPA business at all. It is neither presented nor allocated to one or more segments, neither recognizable in the segmentation according to operating areas nor according to geographical characteristics. The requirement of IFRS 8.1 is violated, as the addressee of the financial statements cannot assess the nature and financial impact of Wirecard's business activities, which account for around half of revenue, as well as the economic environment in which the Wirecard Group operates.

Segment reporting breaches IFRS 8.5, which requires operating segments to be determined based on internal or external expenses or income and internal financial reporting. The fact that business activities with (only) three business partners, which contribute half of the entire Group's turnover, are not reported individually to the Management Board is ruled out. This means that segment reporting does not comply with the management approach and internal reporting requirements.

In accordance with IFRS 8.12, several segments may only be combined into one segment if they are similar in terms of their economic characteristics and all of the following aspects: type of products and services, namely type of production process, customer structure, forms of distribution, regulatory environment if applicable.

Wirecard was active as a payment service provider (PSP), sometimes without its platform. The activities, therefore, differ according to the type of production process. Wirecard was partly active as a PSP and acquirer at the same time. The activity as a PSP without simultaneous acquirer activity and as a combination of payment service provider and acquirer represents different business models (products) with different risks and is aimed at different customers. They also differ in distribution channels and are offered in different regulatory environments. The provision of financial guarantees is entirely different from the other activities. It differs fundamentally in the type of product, how the service is presented using escrow accounts, the customers that were involved or on which Wirecard was dependent, the type of distribution and the regulatory environment, including the legal framework for escrow activities, legal access to the deposited cash assets, and other legal framework conditions. Not a single characteristic is consistent with the other group activities. The segmentation of the operating segments fundamentally violates IFRS 8.12 in many respects.

The disclosure of a separate segment is required to be made after certain thresholds of IFRS 8.13 are exceeded, which alternatively relate to revenue, total comprehensive income, or assets. If even one of the thresholds is exceeded, this segment is obliged to be disclosed separately. Disclosure is mandatory if the TPA business (Third Party Acquiring) accounts for more than 10% of revenue or profit. If the granting of guarantees accounts for more than 10% of revenue or profit, this segment also has to be shown separately. By not reporting the TPA business and also (separately) the guarantee business, although the 10% thresholds were far exceeded, IFRS 8.13 was breached.

It is also noticeable that assets are reported geographically. This is only permissible if this is reported to the management. Otherwise, the separate disclosure violates IFRS 8.5, namely the (top) management approach. However, if segment assets are reported to the (top) management on a geographical basis, it is ruled out that they are not also reported to the (top) management on an operating basis. As operating segment reporting is the primary parameter for the corporate management at Wirecard, assets are also a mandatory management parameter. For Wirecard, segment assets are intangible assets plus property, plant, and equipment. IFRS 8.13 was violated because the required individual disclosures on segments to be separated were not made.

It cannot be ruled out that the Management Board had other segments reported on individually that were not disclosed, contrary to the requirements of IFRS 8.13. This could only be clarified by comparing the documents passed on to the (top) management.

Wirecard reports revenue and EBITDA for the operating segments. If included in the segment result or internal reporting, further individual items have to be shown for each segment. Wirecard states that interest and taxes are not passed on to the chief operating decision-makers in internal reporting. Material expenses and income that are required to be reported by IAS 1.86 are, therefore, particularly relevant here. This refers to expenses and income that have to be reported separately in the income statement. The following items are shown there before EBITDA, which consequently also had to be shown separately in segment reporting in accordance with IFRS 8.23:

– capitalized own contributions,
– cost of materials,
– personnel expenses,
– other operating expenses,
– other operating income.

All of these disclosures are missing. This constitutes a breach of IFRS 8.23.

As the assets are reported geographically, it can be assumed that they are also reported to the (top) management as part of primary management. This is all the more true as it comprises intangible assets and property, plant, and equipment, whereby intangible assets include, for example, the value of the customer-relationship to be disclosed in the event of acquisitions as well as goodwill. It is almost inconceivable that the Management Board does not receive any information about this at the segment's operating level. However, the segment assets are obliged to also be broken down operationally. Once again, this has not been done and constitutes a breach of IFRS 8.24.

Furthermore, by IFRS 8.24, additions to non-current assets are required to even be shown in a separate item. This was also violated.

IFRS 8.28 contains various requirements for reconciliations, some of which have also been breached.

Finally, a key requirement for Wirecard was breached, namely IFRS 8.34. This formulates disclosure requirements if income is derived from transactions with a single customer, provided that the amount represents at least 10% of the company's income. This applies to each of the three business partners in the TPA business. After all, Wirecard does not know the (allegedly) underlying merchants and customers, has no control over the business activity, and has no contractual relationship with the merchants. The one segment or the segments to which this income is allocated are to be identified. This is vital information for the financial statements user. On this basis, Wirecard's dependence in the TPA business on only two or three business partners and the associated risk could have been recognized by the addressee of the financial statement (so-called cluster risk). In this respect, this is a fundamental breach of IFRS 8.34—by intention.

The segment reporting of Wirecard, therefore, contradicts the requirements of IFRS 8 concerning numerous individual disclosure requirements. It does not even begin to give an impression of the actual business activities. Instead, significant business activities are concealed, and a completely misleading picture of the individual areas controlled by the company management is presented. Segment reporting fundamentally contradicts the requirements of IFRS 8.1.

Per Section 317 (1) HGB, the auditor is obliged to satisfy that the accounting requirements have been complied with. Segment reporting in accordance with IFRS 8 is one of the fundamental reporting elements of consolidated financial statements by IFRS, which provides insight into the aggregated results reported at the Group level and their sources. It is imperative that the auditor compares the internal reporting with the segment reporting and insists on compliance with the management approach. It cannot be allowed to happen that a company so immensely violates numerous individual regulations on segment reporting without the auditor reporting on this in the auditor's report. This constitutes a fundamental breach of Section 317 (1) HGB and of fundamental duties of care in the exercise of the profession, which means a breach of the principle of diligence in accordance with Section 43 (1) WPO.

8

Risk Reporting in the Notes to the Consolidated Financial Statements and Group Management Reports

8.1 Requirements for Financial Risk Reporting in Accordance with IFRS and Violations

The obligation to report on opportunities and risks as part of (Group) management reporting arises from Section 289 (1) sentence 4, (2) no. 1 HGB and Section 315 (1) sentence 4, (2) no. 1 HGB. The regulations on risk reporting structure can be found in GAS 20 and IFRS 7. The obligation to audit the company or group-wide risk management system for listed companies arises from Section 317 (4) HGB.

Capital market-oriented parent companies are subject to a twofold risk reporting obligation. The first obligation arises from applying IFRS accounting rules, which are standardized in IFRS 7. The other results from the fact that per Section 315e (1) HGB, parent companies that have to present consolidated financial statements by IFRS are also obliged to provide risk reporting as part of the group management report in accordance with Section 315 (1) HGB. The requirements under the HGB are specified in GAS 20, which has the status of a Generally Accepted Accounting Principle following publication in the Federal Gazette by the Federal Ministry of Justice and Consumer Protection. The requirements for risk reporting by Section 315 HGB go beyond IFRS 7 in two respects. Firstly, not only risks but also opportunities have to be reported. Secondly, IFRS 7 relates exclusively to financial risks, whereas the (group) management report in accordance with the German Commercial Code (HGB) has to also address business, operational, and legal risks, for example.

© The Author(s), under exclusive license to Springer Nature Switzerland AG 2024

E. Löw and R. Heyd, *The Audit Failures of the Wirecard Scandal*,
https://doi.org/10.1007/978-3-031-59854-8_8

As the IASB was aware at the time of publication of IFRS 7 that companies had to report on risks due to national requirements and that these rules continue to apply after IFRS 7 comes into force, IFRS 7.21B contains the option of integrating the risk report by IFRS 7 into another report and referring to the relevant section in the (consolidated) notes to the financial statements. This cross-reference means that the corresponding disclosure requirements have the same binding and, therefore, an auditing effect as a presentation in the (consolidated) notes.

Wirecard has not made use of this option. Risk Reports can, therefore, be found in two places in the annual reports: once in the Notes to the Consolidated Financial Statements and once in the Group Management Report. Both reports refer to the other. There is no allocation to the legal requirements under IFRS or HGB.

In their unqualified audit opinions for the years 2015 to 2018, the auditors of the Wirecard's Consolidated Financial Statements for these years certified that the Management Report of the Wirecard Group "as a whole provides a suitable view of the Group's position" and "suitably presents the opportunities and risks of future development."[1]

The following explanations in this chapter relate to IFRS 7. The standard formulates disclosure requirements and goes beyond the obligation of (narrow) risk reporting in that disclosures on financial instruments per se also have to be made. IFRS 7.1 has two objectives: to provide information so that readers of financial statements can independently assess the significance of financial instruments for net assets, financial position, and operations results (see also IFRS 7.7). In addition, the mandatory disclosures under IFRS 7 serve to inform readers of the financial statements about the nature and extent of the risks arising from financial instruments to which the company is exposed during the reporting period and as at the reporting date and how the company manages these risks (see also IFRS 7.31).

Some disclosures are required for classes of financial instruments. Classes are formed by the company in accordance with IFRS 7.6 in such a way that they do justice to the characteristics of these financial instruments. In applying IFRS 7.B2, it is necessary to distinguish between cash and cash equivalents, irrevocable loan commitments, and financial guarantees as further individual classes in addition to the categories for measuring financial instruments. In the present case, cash and cash equivalents, receivables, and financial guarantees are significant. The inclusion of financial guarantees,

[1] See Wirecard: Annual Report 2015, p. 261, ibid. 2016, p. 273, ibid. 2017, p. 289 and thes. 2018, S. 218.

although in principle not recognized in the balance sheet, results from IFRS 7.4.

Concerning collateral provided, the carrying amount of the financial assets transferred as collateral for liabilities or contingent liabilities and the contractual terms and conditions of the collateral are to be disclosed per IFRS 7.14.

Per IFRS 7.32, risks have to be differentiated (at a minimum) into default, liquidity, and market risks. Disclosure requirements of a qualitative and quantitative nature have to be fulfilled for each risk type separately.

IFRS 7.33 requires the following qualitative disclosures for each risk type:

- scope and cause of the risks,
- objectives, methods, processes for managing these risks, and the methods used to assess them, and
- changes in the past period.

By IFRS 7.34, quantifications are to be made for each risk type as follows:

- summarized quantitative data relating to each risk, with the level of aggregation resulting from the information provided to decision-makers,
- certain information from later text paragraphs (which are discussed separately below), and
- risk concentrations.

IFRS 7.B8 clarifies the quantitative disclosures on risk concentrations that risk concentrations arise when financial instruments with similar characteristics react similarly to economic or other changes. The disclosures by this regulation have to include:

- a description of how management determines the concentration,
- a description of the common feature that characterizes each risk bundle (with examples of counterparties, geographical area, currency, or market), and
- the total number of risk positions of all financial instruments that have this common characteristic.

If the quantitative data do not represent the period under review, it is not allowed to be omitted but supplemented with additional representative data per IFRS 7.35.

IFRS 7 contains further disclosure requirements relating specifically to default risk. In turn, many of these relate to financial instruments subject to the impairment rules of IFRS 9, such as financial guarantees. Some of these relate to the impairment model, which has changed from an incurred loss model to an expected credit loss model since the 2018 financial year. Of these disclosures, particular reference is made to the need to provide an impairment table for each class of financial instrument in accordance with IFRS 7.35H with the individual disclosure requirements listed there. In addition, for financial instruments within the scope of the impairment rules of IFRS 9, the amount of the maximum default risk has to be disclosed for each class in accordance with IFRS 7.35K (a). IFRS 7.35M requires an entity to disclose the gross carrying amount of financial assets and the default risk for loan commitments and financial guarantees for each default risk rating class because users of financial statements can assess an entity's exposure to default risk and understand significant concentrations of these default risks.

For the 2015–2017 financial years, a similar disclosure requirement was applied to default risk, namely disclosure of the maximum default risk for each class of financial instrument by IFRS 7.36, including the financial guarantees issued. IFRS 7.B10 (c) specifies that for granting guarantees, the maximum default risk corresponds to the maximum amount a company could have to pay if the guarantee is called upon. The regulation explicitly states that this amount can be much more significant than what has been recognized as a liability.

Regarding liquidity risk, IFRS 7.39 is limited to very few disclosure requirements related to the liability side. It can be broken down into the requirement to provide a maturity analysis for financial liabilities that are not derivatives and the requirement to provide a maturity analysis for derivatives. The management of liquidity risk has to be described as well. IFRS 7.B11E states: "For financial assets held to manage liquidity risk (such as assets that are available for immediate sale or that are expected to generate cash inflows that offset the cash outflows from financial liabilities), an entity shall present a maturity analysis if it is necessary for users of financial statements to assess the nature and extent of liquidity risk."

In the disclosures required by IFRS 7.39, the entity could consider, among other things, in accordance with the examples given in IFRS 7.B11F, whether it

- can access committed credit facilities or credit lines to cover its liquidity requirements,
- has deposits with central banks,

- has significant liquidity risk concentrations in its assets or financing sources, and
- has instruments that could require the deposit of collateral.

Sensitivity analyses are to be presented for market risks by IFRS 7.40, whereby specific methods may be used if they are used for management purposes, such as a value-at-risk analysis. If such analyses are not representative, the company is obliged to justify this accordingly. Concerning currency risks, IFRS 7.B24 indicates that a sensitivity analysis is mandatory to be disclosed for each currency to which an entity is particularly exposed.

Wirecard publishes statements on debtors and financial risks in the Consolidated Financial Statements' Notes because they directly impact individual items of the balance sheet or income statement. In addition to the section in the Notes to the Consolidated Financial Statements explicitly entitled "Risk Reporting," Wirecard provides specific breakdowns of financial assets and liabilities in a subsequent section. Finally, the Notes to the Consolidated Financial Statements also contain a small section on other obligations and contingent liabilities.

The structure and main content have been retained for the 2015–2018 financial years. However, the Notes to the Consolidated Financial Statements for the 2018 financial year take into account the first-time application of the standard on the recognition and measurement of financial instruments, namely IFRS 9, insofar as the resulting adjustments were integrated into IFRS 7 for the disclosure of risk provisioning in particular by the new impairment model and other adjustments were made on this occasion (such as a change in the order of presentation).

The following explanations, therefore, apply equally to all Risk Reports and further explanations on financial instruments in the Notes to the Consolidated Financial Statements for the 2015–2018 financial years unless an exception is explicitly stated.

Seven risk areas are differentiated in a table, and examples are provided. However, not all of these risks are addressed separately in the Notes to the Consolidated Financial Statements. Firstly, it is emphasized that all risks can lead to intangible assets being written down and the earnings situation developing negatively.

In principle, such risks should be limited by entering into hedging transactions. This is surprising, as it is subsequently stated that interest rate derivatives are probably not used to manage either interest rate or liquidity risks. In this respect, derivatives are probably only used in the currency area.

However, there were no currency options at the end of the year (apparently, only currency options are used, as other derivatives are not listed by name).

Investment and derivative transactions would only be concluded with banks that meet the creditworthiness requirements from the group's risk assessment and—if external ratings are available—are classified by renowned rating agencies as minimal risk in terms of their creditworthiness. No specific information is provided on the company's creditworthiness requirements or on how many banks do not have an external rating (which is unusual in any case but occurs at Wirecard) and what is described as a minimum risk rating—a rating of AAA is rather unlikely. Furthermore, whether the rating agencies are Moody's, Standard & Poor's, or Fitch is not stated.

The first sentence of the section on interest rate risks states that the group has considerable cash and cash equivalents, which are invested as demand deposits, term deposits, and/or overnight money at reputable banks. Liquid funds as a cash reserve in an escrow account are not mentioned.

An uninformative sensitivity analysis follows this about the total investment portfolio, which is stated at over 1 billion Euro (2015), according to which an interest rate increase (decrease) of half a percentage point would have a relatively small negative (positive) effect. This is presumably intended to comply with IFRS 7.40 in a very formal manner.

Furthermore, reference is made to an interest rate risk for long-term, variable-interest liabilities. This is surprising because the investment of cash and cash equivalents is short term. Therefore, there is either no interest rate risk or a very small interest rate risk in the overall interest rate management. The addressee is not informed of this. Instead, it is stated about the interest rate risk of the liabilities that although it exists in principle, it can be responded to quickly due to repayment options. The fact that the deposit of a cash reserve in escrow accounts effectively prevents this is not mentioned. It, therefore, remains unclear how repayment can counteract an interest rate risk.

The Payment Processing and Risk Management and Acquiring and Issuing segments are increasingly affected by currency risks. Around 60% (2015, 65% in 2016, 69% in 2017, and 71% in 2018) of revenue in both segments is generated in foreign currencies, with the USD being the most important foreign currency. Again, an elementary sensitivity analysis is presented, which is based on a reduction (increase) in exchange rates by one percent (presumably meaning percentage points, with this error continuing from year to year), which would lead to a certain unrealized income (expense). Again, these disclosures serve to comply with IFRS 7.40 formally.

Liquidity risks are treated separately (from interest rate risks). Wirecard strives to maintain a comfortable level of liquidity. Liquidity management is limited to holding cash and cash equivalents, credit lines, monitoring forecasts, and actual cash flows. A liquidity risk would exist in the event of mismatches between the defined investment period and the time of the liquidity requirement. However, the Management Board assumes a low risk as only a base amount of liquidity less a security reserve would be invested for the longer term.

To illustrate the remaining terms of the liabilities, a table is shown, and a residual term structure is presented, broken down into three maturity bands, and differentiated by type of liability. This complies with IFRS 7.39 in formal terms. Corresponding residual terms of financial assets, as is usual in the banking sector, are not shown.

Finally, Wirecard deals with debtor risks. For Wirecard, these are the default risks of business partners' contractual payment flows. For this reason, business partners are comprehensively assessed according to relevant criteria before a business relationship is concluded. Creditworthiness, liquidity, market positioning, and management experience are examples. This also applies to business relationships with commercial banks, acquiring partners, and merchants.

According to the company, the default risks from the acquiring business resulting from potential chargebacks following a merchant's insolvency or inability to deliver are very low. This is justified by the current volume covering outstanding receivables from customers, individual security retentions (reserve), or a delayed payment to the merchant. Furthermore, this would be adjusted continuously due to close monitoring of the dealer business. The 2018 Annual Report also states that anomalies and possible fraud patterns are monitored. As a rule, the security retention is sufficient.

Most receivables result from the acquiring business and the underlying payment cycles. This is processed either via the Wirecard Bank or acquiring partners. In both cases, Wirecard bears the main risks and rewards from the processing (i.e., the technical risks). The default risks for receivables from the acquiring business are defined identically to the default risks from the business itself, whereby the receivables used for hedging would have a revolving character.

The carrying amount is designated as the maximum default risk of the financial instruments, but the amount is not specified. IFRS 7.36 (for the 2015–2017 financial years—IFRS 7.35K (a) for 2018) is only complied with in formal terms. In terms of content, this is too vague as long as the reader of the financial statements cannot recognize the maximum default risk as a figure. This is followed by a short schedule of impairments for the (small) receivables portfolio—without a breakdown into specific and general loan loss reserves (impairments). The default risk of financial guarantees issued has not been reported.

Some classifications in accordance with IFRS 7 are to be made by class. Certain statements can be found in connection with the classification of carrying amounts. The classification at Wirecard is based on the balance sheet items, some of which are summarized or divided into further subclasses. For this purpose, a balance sheet carrying amounts table is shown, broken down according to IAS 39 measurement categories. The financial assets and liabilities are broken down according to a more commercial and legal distinction, namely cash and cash equivalents (which surprisingly do not form a separate class in this respect), interest-bearing securities and time deposits, receivables, and financial and other assets/interest-bearing securities for the assets side and liabilities from acquiring and trade payables as one item and other liabilities as a separate liability item. In formal terms, this complies with IFRS 7.6.

In the section on other obligations and contingent liabilities, the contingent liabilities refer exclusively to an appeal process and other lawsuits against Wirecard without further specification. The maximum risk is described as theoretical and stated as an amount in the single-digit million range. Financial guarantees are not reported.

The main objective of IFRS 7.1 remained unfulfilled. This applies both to assessing the significance of financial instruments for the net assets, financial position, and results of operations, and to assessing the nature and extent of risks assumed. Both are significantly influenced by the business activity of issuing financial guarantees and providing cash collateral.

The granting of financial guarantees and the provision of cash collateral affect all three risks that are mandatory to be reported by IFRS 7. Both form part of Wirecard's Management Board's risk strategy. The reader of the Financial Statements has to be informed of this in accordance with IFRS 7.1, IFRS 7.7, and IFRS 7.31. By remaining silent about both activities, the addressee cannot obtain a picture of the significance of these financial instruments for the net assets, financial position, and results of operations. The disclosures are also not designed to assess the nature and extent of the risks associated with these financial instruments, as there are no disclosures at all. Wirecard is thus in breach of IFRS 7.1, IFRS 7.7, and IFRS 7.31.

Furthermore, the requirement of IFRS 7.14 is violated, according to which the carrying amounts of financial assets transferred as collateral for liabilities or contingent liabilities and the contractual terms of the collateral are obliged to be disclosed. Neither the carrying amount nor any contractual terms and conditions are disclosed. As this is a very significant activity, the breach of this provision is all the more serious.

Classes of financial instruments are to be formed for certain disclosures. In principle, the company is free to form classes. However, IFRS 7.6 requires that the classes be appropriate to the characteristics of the financial instruments. IFRS 7.B2 points out that further classes have to be formed in addition to the IAS 39 measurement categories. For example, irrevocable loan commitments and financial guarantees are explicitly distinguished. The need to include financial guarantees, although in principle not affecting the balance sheet, arises from IFRS 7.4. For Wirecard, the cash reserve, financial guarantees, and possibly even irrevocable loan commitments would have had to be formed as additional classes due to their significance. Although the cash reserve does not appear as a separate class at Wirecard (only in the 2018 Annual Report, p. 198, p. 205), the corresponding information can nevertheless be found in the table disclosed by Wirecard. What is missing, however, are financial guarantees and, depending on the contract design and significance, irrevocable loan commitments. Accordingly, there is a violation of the class formation by IFRS 7.6 in conjunction with IFRS 7.4. IFRS 7.4 necessarily affects all class disclosures.

For each type of risk, IFRS 7.33 requires qualitative disclosure of the scope and cause of the risks, the objectives, methods, and processes for managing these risks, and the methods used to measure them (as well as any changes in the past period). These are disclosure requirements regarding interest rate, currency, liquidity, and debtor risks (i.e., default risks) at Wirecard.

The leading cause of interest rate risks is the risk of interest rate changes for long-term, variable-interest liabilities. Viewed in isolation, interest rate increases can occur on the liabilities side if the general market interest rate rises. However, the reason for this is not explained, and it is not explained why this results in an interest rate risk at the overall company level. According to the company's statements, cash and cash equivalents are invested short term and are not subject to long-term interest rate risks. Something similar may be meant to be expressed by the comment that interest costs (interest expenses are meant in financial accounting terms) would increase if interest rates rise. However, rising interest income would compensate for this additional expense. However, no reference is made to the risk of maturity-mismatched refinancing. With a normal yield curve, interest rates are lower at the short end and higher at the long end. This means there is a risk that interest rates on the liabilities side will increase more than they can be passed on the assets side. A (reverse) maturity transformation should be indicated if this results in a noticeable interest rate risk.

In addition, it is stated about the interest rate risk of the liabilities that, although it exists in principle, it is possible to react quickly due to repayment options. This is unclear in several respects. If the liabilities are subject to a variable interest rate, early termination and new borrowing would not result in any interest rate advantage—assuming the same terms. Therefore, the alleged interest rate risk cannot be reduced by early liability repayment in the event of an existing refinancing requirement. If, on the other hand, the repayment of long-term liabilities (should) be made using liquid funds, this presupposes that these are available. However, this requirement is not met if a cash reserve is deposited in escrow accounts, which is not mentioned.

Apart from the fact that no interest rate derivatives are used—which is very unusual in the interest rate management of a treasury—the user of the financial statements is not informed about the interest rate management methods.

The disclosures on interest rate risks cannot provide users with the necessary information that IFRS 7.33 requires. There is a substantive violation of IFRS 7.33.

The management of currency risks at Wirecard appears to consist almost exclusively of contractual arrangements that the treasury influences in this respect. No risks can arise by ensuring that receivables and liabilities are (as far as possible) in the same currency and amount when drawing up contracts with merchants and banks. Open (low) risks are mitigated with derivatives. Speculation is not permitted.

Although more than 60% of sales are generated in foreign currencies, the other information is limited to a rudimentary sensitivity analysis of the overall position of all currencies without differentiation. This is too little, given the importance of foreign currencies. Apart from the USD, no other currency is explicitly mentioned. The emphasis on the USD, in particular, is surprising as business activities in the US did not account for any significant share of total revenue even in 2018, when the Americas appeared as a separate segment in the segment reporting for the first time. It is, therefore, essential to clarify in which countries with which currencies what proportion of the business exists and what country- and currency-specific risks exist, whether the currencies are freely convertible, and to what extent there are transfer restrictions.

Currency risks and financial guarantees granted are not reported. However, there could be a high foreign currency risk here if the guarantee event occurs but is not hedged against currency fluctuations. If financial guarantees are backed by cash collateral, the question of foreign currency risk and its hedging also arises. Depending on the geographical business activity, it is not to be expected that a buyer in Asia, for example, will invoice a dealer in Euro.

As the scope of activities was highly significant to Wirecard's earnings situation, larger open currency risks are to be expected. Given the requirements of IFRS 7.33, the statements on currency risks are generally not convincing. Concerning the complete lack of statements on potential currency risks from cash collateral deposited in foreign currencies, IFRS 7.33 is violated.

The presentation of liquidity risks and their management suggests that the management has adequate holdings of cash and cash equivalents and credit lines with banks and that the monitoring of cash flows fully covers such risks. In addition, the Management Board states that it sees only a low risk. Active short-term liquidity management is only possible with highly liquid holdings, which include the cash reserve. A high amount of cash and cash equivalents suggests availability at all times. This is why the disclosure of cash collateral is extremely valuable for the addressee. These funds are blocked for short-term disposal and are, therefore, wholly withdrawn from liquidity management. There is not a single word about this in connection with liquidity risks. Liquidity management is therefore—deliberately—completely misrepresented because reference is made to high cash and cash equivalents that are not available.

Instead, a complete sideshow is being played out, writing about premature bond repurchases which, firstly, were not planned at all because, secondly, the refinancing was urgently required and would have been completed by an alternative refinancing at similar conditions if the bonds had been repurchased prematurely and, thirdly, the cash assets reported would not have been available in the short term. Wirecard, therefore, needed to refinance via bonds.

Furthermore, the table on the residual terms of liabilities does not show any long-term bonds as issues. The maximum residual term of liabilities is 5 years. Only two items fall below this: interest-bearing loans, credits (taken out), and other liabilities. They account for around one-third of the total liabilities (2015). Despite this, no word of explanation is provided.

Reporting on liquidity should have included a detailed explanation as to why, given the extremely high level of cash and cash equivalents reported and the alleged investment of surplus liquidity, it was only necessary to raise a substantial amount of debt capital (without further explanation) less a substantial security reserve. The presentation of the liquidity situation is wholly inadequate and suggests a false picture to the addressee by deliberately avoiding side issues and intentionally omitting important information. The statements on liquidity, therefore, seriously violate IFRS 7.33.

A maturity analysis table is provided for liabilities, but no table is provided for financial assets. However, this would have been necessary for Wirecard, as

IFRS 7.B11E states that an entity is required to present a maturity analysis for financial assets held to manage liquidity risk if this is necessary for users of financial statements to assess the nature and extent of the liquidity risk. This is the case here.

It is highly unusual to narrowly describe non-payment risk as debtor risk instead of default or credit risk. In terms of definition, this only considers a section of all default risks. From the very definition, it should not be expected to be informed about impending claims from financial guarantees. A risk that Wirecard's contractual partners consider to be so severe that they require a cash reserve to be deposited is not included in Wirecard's reporting on default risks due to the narrowing of the statements to pure debtor risks.

A second, extremely dangerous default risk is also not mentioned—the default of the only bank where the cash reserve is deposited, the Oversea-Chinese-Banking Corporation in Singapore. If this bank, where around a quarter of the total assets and almost all of the cash assets are deposited, defaults, Wirecard's very existence would be threatened, raising the question of the company's ability to continue as a going concern.

Instead, reference is made to default risks in the acquiring business and risks relating to receivables in the acquiring business. These are presented as low and justified with references to current volumes, individual security retentions, and delayed merchant payouts.

It is extraordinary that when dealing with Wirecard's default risks, it is pointed out that Wirecard bears the opportunities and risks from the settlement. This is, at most, an operational risk, namely if Wirecard or the business partners it commissions do not provide the PSP services. This means the topic is entirely wrong and has nothing in common with the default risks to which Wirecard is exposed.

The reporting on default risks, therefore, shows a very low risk. In reality, however, Wirecard was subject to highly significant default risks by entering into financial guarantees, which were not reported on, and by depositing the cash reserve with only one bank, which also cannot be described as internationally first-class in terms of creditworthiness, which was also not mentioned. The reporting on default risks is therefore not only misleading by suggesting a low risk to the addressee, it is also utterly false by concealing potentially existence-threatening risks. It violates IFRS 7.33.

Even though the 2018 Annual Report reports on default risks in more detail, the overall picture is the same. The newly added disclosures do not relate to IFRS 7.33 but meet particular requirements for the disclosure of impairment losses by the newly introduced expected loss method. The extent to which this model is part of internal management remains open. As the impairments are not discussed in detail here, certain statement inconsistencies are not followed up.

In addition to qualitative information, IFRS 7.34 requires separately quantified data for each type of risk. IFRS 7.B7 states that quantitative data on the risks to which a company is exposed are obliged to be based on internal management and specifies that, in the case of management using various methods, the information that provides the most relevant and reliable information for users of the financial statements is to be disclosed.

Concerning interest rate risks, figures are published in connection with sensitivities. This may fulfill the reporting obligation of IFRS 7.40 on sensitivity analysis, albeit in a less meaningful way, but not IFRS 7.34. No further quantitative disclosures on interest rate risks are made. This constitutes a violation of IFRS 7.34 for interest rate risks.

The situation is similar for currency risks. Sensitivities are given at the highest aggregation level, which at least goes towards fulfilling IFRS 7.40 on sensitivity analysis. Nevertheless, IFRS 7.B 24 requires sensitivity analyses to be disclosed for each currency with a particular currency risk to comply with IFRS 7.40. This has not been done, not even for the USD, and constitutes a breach of IFRS 7.40. No further quantitative disclosures are made. This constitutes a violation of IFRS 7.34 for currency risks.

The liquidity risks include a table of undiscounted cash flows by contractual payment dates for the liabilities (plus a comparison with the previous year). Therefore, it can be stated that IFRS 7.39 is fulfilled for the liabilities side regarding this breakdown. No further quantitative disclosures are made. This represents a breach of IFRS 7.34 for liquidity risks.

There is no single figure on debtor risks in the reporting apart from information on value adjustments. It is only stated that the maximum default risk is the carrying amount of the financial instruments. It can, therefore, be assumed for the financial instruments recognized (not for the financial guarantees) that the maximum default risk was stated by IFRS 7.36. No further quantitative information is provided. No further quantitative disclosures are made. This constitutes a breach of IFRS 7.34 for default risks.

IFRS 7.34 also requires disclosures on concentrations of risk. IFRS 7.B8 provides more specific details. In addition to the requirement for a description of the method used to determine concentrations, a description of common characteristics for each risk bundle (IFRS 7.B8 lists examples including contractual partners, geographical areas, currencies, and the market), the total amount of the risk positions of all financial instruments that have this common characteristic is required to be specified.

Wirecard had numerous concentrations in the TPA business. The company worked with (only) two (three) central business partners, which was not reported. Wirecard was exposed to concentration risk in the assumption of guarantees vis-à-vis three business partners. Wirecard deposited almost all its cash assets with just one bank, representing an extreme concentration risk. There were, therefore, several concentrations, each of which had to be reported separately, along with the amount disclosed. This was not done, which could have had existential consequences given the threat posed by these dependencies and therefore constitutes a blatant violation of IFRS 7.34.

IFRS 7.36 requires disclosure of the maximum default risk for each class of financial instruments. Wirecard has only complied with this concerning the financial assets reported in the balance sheet. According to IFRS 7.4, a separate class had to be formed for financial guarantees given. Wirecard has not complied with this requirement. Consequently, the maximum default risk according to IFRS 7.36 is not disclosed. Instead, it is merely specified that for granting guarantees, the maximum default risk corresponds to the maximum amount that a company could have to pay if the guarantee is called upon. It is fully acknowledged that this amount may be considerably higher than the amount recognized as a liability. Such a disclosure is missing in Wirecard's reporting. This represents a breach of IFRS 7.36.

Accordingly, there is also no impairment table for the class of financial guarantees, although impairments are not considered in detail here.

The 2018 Annual Report contains a disclosure on financial guarantees allegedly recognized at fair value through profit or loss under liabilities. This is technically astonishing, as using a fair value option is subject to access restrictions. However, the amount is negligible, and reference is also made to an allocation to the balance sheet item called other provisions—without any meaningful explanation (including the supposed contradiction (p. 206)). The further explanations elsewhere are also not particularly enlightening (p. 209).

However, an important statement is made in the 2018 Annual Report (p. 209). "Due to the contractual regulations for the processing of transactions with credit card organizations, providers of other payment methods and also within interbank transfers in payment transactions, Wirecard generally considers the total transaction volume of 124.9 billion Euro (previous year: 91.0 billion Euro) to be a financial guarantee, as a fundamental liability cannot be completely excluded" (p. 209). This is followed by statements on the expected credit loss calculation and the note: "The maximum, but highly improbable, guarantee amount calculated here is 3.1 billion Euro as of 31 December 2018 (1 January 2018: 2.0 billion Euro)." Although this business activity was not previously explained in the Risk Report, the maximum default risk can still be found in the 2018 Annual Report, meaning that IFRS 7.35K (a) (equivalent to the previous requirement of IFRS 7.36) is met there.

Reporting on financial assets and liabilities and the resulting risks does not meet the general requirements of IFRS 7.1 due to the numerous violations of individual requirements of IFRS 7 for important financial instruments. In some cases, the addressee is even deliberately presented with a very low risk, although there were serious risks, including risks that could potentially jeopardize the company's existence. By omitting very significant risks, a completely false picture is conveyed.

By Section 317 (1) HGB, the auditor is obliged to ensure that the accounting regulations are complied with. The auditor is (actually) aware of the actual business transactions due to its auditing activities in accordance with the relevant auditing standards.

It is imperative that the auditor compares the reporting by IFRS 7 with reality and vehemently insists on compliance with the accounting rules in accordance with their meaning and purpose. It cannot be allowed to happen that a company so blatantly violates numerous individual regulations on risk reporting without the auditor providing information about this in the auditor's report. This constitutes a fundamental breach of Section 317 (1) HGB and of fundamental duties of care in the exercise of the profession, which means a breach of the principle of diligence in accordance with Section 43 (1) WPO.

8.2 Requirements for Risk Reporting in Accordance with National Rules, Audit Procedures, and Violations

The consolidated financial statements and the group management report are subject to the audit of the (consolidated) financial statements per Section 316 (2) HGB. A vital component of the group management report, which has to be prepared by national regulations, is the forecast, opportunity, and risk report in accordance with Section 315 (1) sentence 4 HGB, which is specified in more detail in a German Accounting Standards (GAS), namely GAS 20.135–187. By Section 315 (1) HGB, the management report contains both retrospective and prospective elements due to its descriptive statements on the course of business since the last reporting date (retrospective view), the presentation of the group's position as a description of the actual situation on the current balance sheet date and the explanation and analysis of the expected development with its significant opportunities and risks, and thus represents a part of the annual report that is particularly relevant to the future investment behavior of the addressees of the capital market.

In accordance with Section 315 (1) sentence 4 HGB, the group management report is required to assess and explain the expected development, including the main opportunities and risks. The underlying assumptions have to be stated. In addition, by Section 315 (2) No. 1 a) and b) HGB, the group's risk management objectives and methods, including its methods for hedging all major types of transactions recognized in hedge accounting, as well as the price, default and liquidity risks and the risks from cash flow fluctuations to which the group is exposed. This refers to the use of financial instruments within the group, to the extend that it is relevant for assessing the group's situation or expected developments.

GAS 20.36–37 requires the presentation of the group's fundamental principles and explaining the business model. The statements on opportunities and risks are derived from this presentation. The requirements for the risk report are described in GAS 20.135–187. According to GAS 20.135, risk reporting has to include information on the risk management system, individual risks, and a summarized presentation of the risk situation.

A risk management system is the controlled handling of risks within the company as part of an institutionalized risk management process. It comprises the following individual aspects:

- risk analysis as risk identification,
- risk assessment in terms of probability of occurrence, impact, and operational urgency,
- risk management through transfer, reduction, avoidance, or assumption, and
- risk monitoring by continuously recording target/actual deviations and designing appropriate adjustment measures.

In accordance with GAS 20.P137, the description of the risk management system in the management report is required to include information on the characteristics, in particular the objectives and strategies, as well as the structures and processes of risk management. Following GAS 20.P138, the risk management system should be presented in the risk report so that a knowledgeable reader can assess handling risks in the group. A generally accepted framework concept is to be disclosed if such a concept is used as the basis for risk management (GAS 20.P139). Finally, GAS 20.P140 requires disclosures as to whether and, if so, which risks are generally not recognized or avoided. When describing the risk management system, GAS 20.P144 requires the identification, assessment, management, and control of risks and the internal monitoring of these processes to be explained—mainly whether an internal audit department carries out this monitoring.

According to GAS 20.147, risk factors are to be described as internal group factors associated with the specific circumstances of the Group and its business activities, as well as external circumstances and events relating to the corporate environment.

In accordance with the explicit emphasis in GAS 20.148, risks that could jeopardize the company's continued existence are of particular importance in risk reporting.

Material risks have to be presented individually and analyzed about their significance and consequences (GAS 20.148–150). If risk quantifications are used for internal management, they are mandatory to also be included in risk reporting by GAS 20.152–159. The effects of risks have to be presented and assessed in accordance with GAS 20.157, taking into account the measures taken to limit risks. By the requirements of GAS 20.160, risk reporting is required to be summarized to provide an overall picture of the group's risk situation.

Reporting on significant opportunities is to be carried out analogously (GAS 20.165–167), whereby opportunity reporting is not discussed below in this chapter.

In accordance with GAS 20.P168–P178, particular attention should be paid to reporting on the internal control system and the risk management system about the consolidated financial reporting process. According to GAS 20.P168, this should present its critical features to enable users to better assess the risks associated with the group accounting process. GAS 20.P170 specifies the reporting requirements for the structures and processes of the internal control and risk management system. In particular, the principles and procedures that are in place are to be pointed out to ensure that the consolidated financial statements and the group management report comply with standards. This expressly includes the internal audit system geared toward the control objective (GAS 20.P170).

Exemplary demand GAS 20.P175–P176 statements on:

- accounting policies,
- structure and process organization of accounting and the preparation of financial statements,
- separation of functions between departments and assignment of tasks as part of the financial statement preparation process,
- involvement of external service providers,

- access regulations to the IT systems,
- internal audit functions in connection with group accounting, and
- related control processes.

By GAS 20.P177, it is mandatory to report on:

- measures to identify and assess risks that prevent group financial reporting from conforming to standards,
- measures to limit recognized risks, and
- measures to review identified risks concerning their impact on the consolidated financial statements and risk reporting.

If there is no internal control or risk management system regarding the group accounting process, this is mandatory to be disclosed in the group management report per GAS 20.P178.

Risk reporting is subject to a separate audit, for which there is a specific auditing standard, IDW PS 350 n.F., on the audit of the management report. Reference is made at various IDW PS 350 n.F. points to a business model analysis, including the associated inherent risks. This applies, for example, to quantitative and qualitative disclosures, past, present (as at the balance sheet date) and forecast disclosures, the interlinking of accounting and performance data, the inclusion of strategic planning and planning determinants (framework conditions, business model parameters, objectives and methods, management quality, professional and personal suitability of the persons involved), as well as management instruments and controlling methods.

Following IDW PS 350 (revised) No. 12, the objectives of the audit of the management report (which includes the audit of the risk report) are to obtain reasonable assurance about whether the management report is consistent in all material respects with the financial statements and the knowledge obtained in the audit and whether the management report as a whole provides an appropriate view of the group's position. In particular, it is to be examined whether the risks of future development are appropriately presented in all material respects. Findings from the audit of the financial statements are to be taken into account per IDW PS 350 n.F. para. 12. The audit strategy and audit planning, therefore, do not differ significantly between an audit of the management report (the audit of the risk report) and an audit of the financial statements, which is why numerous auditing standards designed for the audit of the financial statements are to be applied analogously. In this sense, there are no differences in obtaining audit evidence for the general audit of the risk report. In this respect, the principles of conducting audits of financial statements (IDW PS 200), detection of irregularities during the audit of financial statements (risk-oriented audit approach, IDW PS 210), knowledge of the business activities and the economic and legal environment of the company to be audited during the audit of financial statements (IDW PS 230), principles of planning audits of financial statements (IDW PS 240), materiality during the audit of financial statements (IDW PS 250 n.F.), identification and assessment of risks of error and the auditor's response to the assessed risks of error (IDW PS 261 n.F.), and audit evidence in the context of the audit (IDW PS 300 n.F.) also apply to the audit of (group) management reports.

However, an assessment of the appropriateness and effectiveness of precautions and measures (systems) for recording and evaluating the material risks of future development have to be carried out in accordance with IDW PS 350 n.F. no. 20. Furthermore, IDW PS 350 n.F. refers to specific features, for example:

- there is a need for a risk assessment concerning material misstatements in quantitative and qualitative terms (IDW PS 350 n.F. para. 32),
- if risks of material misstatement in the financial statements and the management report arise simultaneously, the auditor has to take into account the results of the risk assessment of the financial statements in the audit of the management report (IDW PS 350 n.F. para. 33),
- the auditor is obliged to gain an understanding of the company and its environment (IDW PS 350 n.F. para. 37–38), and
- furthermore, an understanding of the relevant precautions and measures (systems) for preparing the management report and determining forecast disclosures has to be obtained (IDW PS 350 n.F. para. 39–42, and para. A45 and A46).

The last point, in particular, is very similar to assessing the internal control system in accounting.

A review of the Risk Reports in Wirecard's Consolidated Financial Statements shows that the requirements of GAS 20 are largely formally fulfilled.[2] The existence of a risk management system is confirmed, and its functions are

[2] See Wirecard: Annual Report 2015, consolidated financial statements 2015, pp. 123–128, Wirecard Annual Report 2016, consolidated financial statements 2016, pp. 128–132, Wirecard Annual Report 2017, consolidated financial statements 2017, pp. 144-148, Wirecard Report 2018, consolidated financial statements 2018, pp. 92–98.

described.[3] Reference is made to identifying, assessing, and perceiving opportunities, and a link is established between opportunity and risk management. The group-wide instruments of the risk management system are integrated into all business processes, operating business units, and group companies. Reference is made to the orientation of the risk management system to ISO 31000:2009. The individual risk management functions—identification of risks and risk relationships, analysis and assessment using risk metrics and threshold values, risk reporting for the Management Board as part of a formalized reporting system, and, finally, responsibility for risk management decisions in the respective group units, including central risk controlling—are presented and described. The allocation of responsibilities and the delineation of functions between risk management, internal audit, and project risk management are described, and references are made to the ongoing development and adaptation of the risk management system to changing circumstances.[4]

The risk assessment is categorized according to the probability of occurrence and the presumed impact, presented in a risk matrix. However, there is no reference here to the group-specific circumstances or risk aggregation, for example, in the form of a Monte Carlo simulation.[5]

The explanations in the section on the internal control and risk management system concerning the (Wirecard Group) accounting process show that this has suitable structures and processes and that their implementation in the organization ensures that all business processes and transactions are recorded promptly, uniformly, and correctly in the accounts. Compliance with legal standards, accounting regulations, and the group's internal accounting guidelines is ensured. Therefore, changes to the law are taken into account in the same way as changes to the internal guidelines and systems used. Defined control mechanisms, system-based and manual reconciliation processes, separation of functions and compliance with guidelines and work instructions characterize the internal control system.

The processes described for preparing the consolidated financial statements, responsibilities, IT access rules, and applying the dual control principle are just as exemplary as establishing a policy department for special technical issues and complex matters. Measures to ensure the reliability of the accounting system are described, as are quality assurance measures to avoid

[3] See Chapter 2.1 of the opportunity and risk reports within the Wirecard consolidated financial statements 2015–2018 (Wirecard: Annual Reports 2015–2018).

[4] See Chapter 2.2 of the opportunity and risk reports within the Wirecard consolidated financial statements 2015–2018 (Wirecard: Annual Reports 2015–2018).

[5] See section 2.3 of the opportunity and risk reports within the Wirecard consolidated financial statements 2015–2018 (Wirecard: Annual Reports 2015–2018).

possible misreporting in the consolidated financial statements. Reference is made to the monitoring functions of the Executive Board and Supervisory Board.[6]

The individual risk areas relevant to Wirecard are presented below, whereby the order in which they are presented gives no indication of their significance for Wirecard. The presentations follow the uniform structure of a verbal description, a presentation of how the respective risks are dealt with, the factors influencing the development of the risk, and an explanation of the potential impact and the extent of the risk, as estimated by the Management Board. They are divided into:

- business risks, subdivided into business strategy risks, market risks, risks from existing customer business, and risks from the development of products,
- operational risks, subdivided into personnel risks, project risks, risks from the use of third-party services and technologies, and risks from acquisitions,
- information and IT risks, subdivided into risks from the unauthorized publication and modification of data, risks from the design and operation of information systems,
- financial risks, subdivided into exchange rate risk, interest rate risk, and liquidity risk,
- debtor risks are divided into debtor risks, legal and regulatory risks, risks from breaches of contract, and risks from legal disputes, and
- other risks.[7]

The Risk Report concludes with a summarized presentation of the overall risk, in which the effects of identifiable developments for Wirecard AG are presented in condensed form. On the one hand, the categorization of the risk content (very low, low, medium, high, very high) is discussed, and on the other hand, the effects of the measures with the instruments of the group's risk management system are shown and evaluated.[8]

---

[6] See section 2.4 of the opportunity and risk reports within the Wirecard consolidated financial statements 2015–2018 (Wirecard: Annual Reports 2015–2018).

[7] See sections 2.5–2.12 of the opportunity and risk reports within the Wirecard consolidated financial statements 2015–2017 (Wirecard: Annual Reports 2015–2017). Sections 2.6–2.13 of the opportunity and risk report within the Wirecard consolidated financial statements 2018 (Wirecard: Annual Report 2018).

[8] See section 2.13 of the opportunity and risk reports within the Wirecard consolidated financial statements 2015–2017 (Wirecard: Annual Reports 215-2017). Section 2.14 of the opportunity and risk report within the Wirecard consolidated financial statements 2018 (Wirecard: Annual Report 2018).

By GAS 20.12–35, the disclosures in the risk reporting in the 2015 to 2018 consolidated financial statements of Wirecard AG that meet the formal requirements for risk reporting according to GAS 20.146–187 are required to be complete, accurate, reliable, and balanced.

"One of the most crucial aspects for a robust system of corporate governance is an efficient organization of internal controls. The internal controls, which are composed of compliance (permanent controls) and internal audit (periodic controls), did not work efficiently in the Wirecard case."[9]

The description in Wirecard's Risk Reports did not correspond to reality, which the auditor has to be aware of when dealing with the business model on the one hand and the risk management system, including the entire internal control system, on the other. In reality, there were obvious weaknesses in the control and risk management system of the accounting process.

The Risk Reports in Wirecard's 2015 to 2018 Consolidated Financial Statements claim that the risk management system is efficiently organized.[10] The internal control and risk management system ensures that business processes and transactions are recorded promptly, uniformly, and correctly in the accounts. It ensures compliance with legal standards, accounting regulations, and the group's internal accounting guidelines.[11]

According to the generally accepted view and following GAS 20, a functional risk management system includes standard-compliant processes and their monitoring by the operating units involved in the processes and by a process-independent body (internal audit). Another part of a functional risk management system is the quality-assured recording, processing, monitoring, and archiving of accounting data. This involves compliance with the Generally Accepted Accounting Principles (independently from the underlying accounting regime) and its compliance requirements:

- principle of the systematic structure of accounting (the system of double-entry bookkeeping),
- principle of individual recording of all business transactions by Sects. 239 (2), 246 (1) HGB and their orderly posting immediately after they occur (in a timely manner) and in their chronological order, and.

[9] SMSG: p. 24/25.

[10] See Wirecard Consolidated Financial Statements 2015 (Wirecard: Annual Report 2015) pp. 123–124, see Wirecard Consolidated Financial Statements 2016 (Wirecard: Annual Report 2016) p. 128, see Wirecard Consolidated Financial Statements 2017(Wirecard: Annual Report 217) p. 144, see Wirecard Consolidated Financial Statements 2018 (Wirecard: Annual Report 2018) pp. 92–94.

[11] See section 2.4 of the opportunity and risk reports within the Wirecard consolidated financial statements 2015–2018 (Wirecard: Annual Reports 2015–2018).

- documentation principle as a fundamental requirement for the formal and factual accuracy of accounting. The posting document forms the basis of every posting (no posting without a document). The relationship between the entry and the document always has to be verifiable and traceable using mutual references.

"A properly functioning accounting organization has to ensure certain quality standards in accounting:

- all transactions are recorded (completeness);
- transactions exist and have occurred (existence);
- transactions are recorded at the appropriate amounts (valuation);
- rights and obligations are appropriately recorded and classified;
- disclosure and presentation of corporate reporting are appropriate;
- unauthorized acquisition, use or disposition of assets is prevented or detected in a timely manner (safegurading)."[12]

The accounting of Wirecard AG was based on checks carried out by the companies CardSystems Middle East, Wirecard UK & Ireland, and Wirecard Technologies on the figures contained in the statements of the main acquiring partners. Wirecard only posted what was provided by the TPA partners. Normally, however, the party providing the service prepares the statement. If, on the other hand, the sales are prepared based on the customers' statements, this indicates a relationship of dependence on the customer.

The control activities performed by Wirecard AG itself were limited to mere plausibility assessments. Any differences were discussed in quarterly meetings, whereby deviations of up to 5% were accepted without objection. The results of the meetings were only documented using screenshots in the minutes, although there were probably no minutes at all until 2018.[13] In addition, only comparisons of figures in TPA partner statements with sales forecasts of the Wirecard sales units responsible for the respective customers were carried out.[14] In contrast to controlling, however, reconciliations in financial accounting are not carried out between target and actual figures but between document data for individual business transactions and posted

12 Beerbaum: The future of audit after the Wirecard Accounting scandal—Consideration of the "Wambach Report", Working Paper Aalto University School of Business, Department of Accounting, Helsinki, Finland, June 2022, p. 7 and Beerbaum: The future of audit after the Wirecard Accounting scandal—Proposal for a change in the payment model, working paper Aalto University School of Business, Department of Accounting, Helsinki, Finland, https://ssrn.com/abstract=3934773, p. 7.

13 See KPMG Report: p. 19.

14 See KPMG Report: p. 19.

account entries. Data reconciliation via screenshots at quarterly meetings without an agenda and minutes does not ensure timely, uniform, and correct accounting recording of business processes or transactions in compliance with legal standards (e.g., no posting without a receipt) and accounting regulations.

Even when accepting new merchants, Wirecard had no internal control system. Wirecard did not check the existence of new customers, but it completely depended on the TPA partners. Wirecard did not even track their compliance checks or monitor them. Obtaining proof of the existence of customers was entirely the responsibility of the TPA partners[15]—with corresponding risks for Wirecard, about which nothing can be found in their Risk Reports.

Instead, there were a large number of—far-reaching—control deficits that indicated serious deficiencies in the internal control system, which could not have remained hidden from the auditor and therefore firstly had to be included in the Risk Report and secondly had to trigger correspondingly more in-depth audit procedures by the auditor. It is difficult to understand how the auditor would have tested the rudimentary control mechanisms in place.

Wirecard did not have any organizational guidelines or work instructions regarding the control activities to be carried out.[16]

Wirecard never checked the contractual conformity of the statements received, particularly the commission rate amount per "account name."[17]

Foreign currency conversions and postings in the inventory management systems were not carried out in a form secured by a documented dual control principle.[18]

The content of the transaction data on which the settlements are based, including at the individual transaction level, was not analyzed or verified.[19]

According to the Risk Reports in the Wirecard Group Management Reports from 2015 to 2018, the foundations of the internal control system, apart from defined control mechanisms, are, for example, systemic and manual reconciliation processes, the separation of functions, and compliance with guidelines and work instructions.[20]

---

[15] See KPMG Report: p. 30.

[16] See KPMG Report: p. 19.

[17] See KPMG Report: p. 20.

[18] See KPMG Report: p. 20.

[19] See KPMG Report: p. 20.

[20] See section 2.4 of the opportunity and risk reports within the Wirecard consolidated financial statements 2015–2018 (Wirecard: Annual Reports 2015–2018).

This represents a deliberate misleading of the addressee of the Financial Statements by Wirecard, which was to be prevented by the auditor.

Defined control mechanisms, system-based reconciliation processes, and segregation of duties, as required by IDW PS 261 n.F. para. 52, could not be identified for large parts of the accounting process. "It is obvious that there were grave failures at the company, and that its internal corporate governance structures were inadequate."[21] Compliance with guidelines and work instructions was impossible because there was no formal documentation before 2018. Instead, the figures were merely checked on the screen with the partners. Wirecard did not have any organizational guidelines, work instructions concerning the control activities to be carried out, or formal documentation of the quarterly meetings essential for control purposes. The control activities performed by Wirecard itself were limited to mere plausibility assessments.

As a result, neither the auditors nor the internal auditors were able to test the procedures and control mechanisms for updating the receivables portfolio and evaluating receivables that were contractually agreed with the acquiring partners and defined internally. Neither the initial selection, the contractual agreements and compliance with them, nor the ongoing activities of the acquiring partners could be monitored and controlled as part of the risk management process. The structuring and monitoring of this existentially important part of the business model for the Wirecard Group was removed from the reach of internal group monitoring bodies and was transferred to the direct control sovereignty of the Group Management Board as "group strategic matters."

Suppose the inadequate precautions of the accounting-related internal control system at Wirecard are considered. In that case, the description of the internal control system in the Risk Report as fully functional and in line with legal requirements cannot be affirmed. Serious deficiencies were found, for example, in the:

- audit of the accounting material from the TPA business as well as accounting and control modalities in the Wirecard Group,
- review of the assessment of the recoverability of receivables, in particular on escrow accounts,
- examination of counterparty, concentration, and currency risk,
- examination of the risks for the Wirecard Group from chargebacks and penalties,
- review of documentation and archiving of contracts with TPA partners,

[21] Möllers: The Wirecard accounting scandal in Germany, and how the financial industry failed to spot it; The International Lawyer, vol. 54, no. 3, 2021, pp. 325–360 here p. 331.

- verification of actual incoming and outgoing payments to Wirecard accounts,
- verification of the existence and authenticity of account statements and balance confirmations for the fiduciary accounts recognized in the IFRS Financial Statements of Wirecard AG, and
- review of third-party confirmations and the selection of audit evidence IDW PS 302 n.F. and IDW PS 300.

In this sense, it remains unclear how the auditors could have concluded that there was sufficient and appropriate audit evidence to confirm an appropriate risk management process given the list of deficiencies. On the contrary, the auditor noted during the 2018 financial audit that there were extensive control and process weaknesses.[22] Nevertheless, the resulting risks were not mentioned in the Risk Report.

Concerning reporting on individual risks, GAS 20.146–164 initially stipulates in general terms that such risks are to be reported that could influence the decisions of a reasonable addressee. Risks that could jeopardize the company as a going concern are required to be identified as such (GAS 20.148) and deserve special attention. Internal Group factors associated with the specific circumstances of the Group and its business activities, as well as external circumstances and events relating to the corporate environment, are to be described as risk factors (GAS 20.147).

Significant risks are obliged to be presented individually following GAS 20.148–150 and analyzed about their significance and consequences. If risk quantifications are used in internal management, these have to be included in risk reporting as well by GAS 20.152–159. The effects of risks are to be presented and assessed in accordance with GAS 20.157, taking into account the measures taken to limit risks. GAS 20.160 requires a summary of risk reporting to provide an overall picture of the group's risk situation.

According to GAS 20.146–152, risk reporting has to begin with the risk inventory, i.e., the identification, recording, and quantifying assessment of the risks to which the group and its segments are exposed. The consequences to be expected if they occur have to be analyzed. Per the requirements of GAS 20.147, the risk inventory depends on the specific circumstances of the Group and its companies regarding the risks associated with their business activities and their market and industry-specific environment.

By the end of 2017, Wirecard had only provided two services that should have enabled Wirecard to generate profits with the TPA business. Firstly,

[22] See KPMG Report: p. 45.

Wirecard referred customers to the TPA partners, and secondly, Wirecard assumed default risks. Wirecard played no role in the TPA business as a PSP until the end of 2017 and only partially after that. Wirecard never assumed the function of an acquirer. The fact that Wirecard's platform was not used in the TPA business contrasts with the statements in the business model in the management report. Without its platform, the statements on the allegedly flourishing TPA business were in no way plausible. On the contrary, there were blatant business risks. As the auditor dealt intensively with the business model, he was aware of this. Nevertheless, the misleading and, in part, deliberately false Risk Reporting to the detriment of the readers of the financial statements was not criticized.

For years, Wirecard did not publish detailed information on risks relating to the TPA business in its annual reports—particularly not on the business with the three underlying business partners Al Alam, Senjo, and PayEasy. This meant that the concentration risk of the three TPA partners, which were responsible for half of the Group's turnover was completely concealed. Only the risk that a "significant number of existing customers decide not to continue the business relationship with Wirecard (...)" and that this could harm the course of business in the form of a loss of sales is reported. This is not only misleading, as it is about three direct business partners. It implicitly suggests the false impression that there is such a significant number of existing customers, which was entirely wrong for the TPA business. In particular, it should not be disregarded that, according to Wirecard's account, it was largely unaware of the "real"merchants behind the master merchants. There were no contracts between Wirecard and these merchants. In case of doubt, Wirecard would have had no chance of retaining the merchants for the TPA business if a TPA partner had ceased to exist.

Apart from the concentration risk, the three TPA business partners, the trustees, and the banks involved were exposed to considerable counterparty risks, which were also not reported.

The serious errors in presentation run like a red thread through every annual report.[23] They are, therefore, blatant and deliberate violations of accurate and complete reporting. This concealment of the actual risks had to be objected to by the auditor, who had dealt intensively with Wirecard's business model and was, therefore, fully aware of the actual risks.

Concerning the summarized presentation of the group's risk position, Wirecard's Consolidated Financial Statements describe the overall risk structure as stable, refer to the ongoing optimization of risk management, which

---

[23] See Wirecard: Annual Report 2015, p. 130, ibid. 2016, p. 135, ders. 2017, p. 152 and thes. 2018, p. 100.

adapts to the development of the volume and complexity of the business, refers to recognized industry standards, and implements a large number of risk-minimizing measures. The risk assessment identifies 63% of all risks as low or very low, 37% as medium, and no as high or very high. Express reference is made to the structured processes for early risk identification, which provide the Management Board with tools to counter the aforementioned risks at any time.[24]

The overall assessment of the group's risk situation completely dispenses with risk quantification and aggregation. While GAS 20.152 requires risks to be quantified in the event that this is also carried out for internal management purposes, risk aggregation is methodically considered a recognized form of assessing the overall scope of risk, taking into account the interactions of several individual risks about a group's risk-bearing capacity. It makes it possible to assess whether individual risks, which are of secondary importance when viewed in isolation, could aggregate in their interaction or through accumulation over time to form an overall risk that could jeopardize the company's continued existence. Given the significance of the TPA business for Wirecard, it can be assumed that quantifications were available to management—even if they may have been based on incorrect figures. Missing quantifications in the Risk Report, therefore, fundamentally violate GAS 20.152.

If the risks from the TPA business, the lack of transparency regarding the escrow accounts, the counterparty risks from the business relationships with the TPA partners, and the banks managing the escrow accounts, including the concentration risk from the limited number of TPA partners and banks and the inadequate monitoring options due to the underdeveloped control and risk management system—particularly about the accounting process—had been aggregated as part of a Monte Carlo simulation, either a going concern risk would have been identified immediately (with corresponding disclosure requirements in the risk reporting by GAS 20.148) or at least a very high probability of a going concern risk would have been indicated. However, no statement was made in the annual reports about the overall risk situation and significant risks that could jeopardize Wirecard's continued existence. In this respect, it was not only the specific risks from the TPA business that were not mentioned. The overall risk was also presented in a wholly false and concealing manner. In the unqualified audit opinions for the years 2015 to 2018, the auditors of the Wirecard's Consolidated Financial Statements certified that the Management Reports of the Wirecard Group for these years

[24] Cf. Wirecard: Annual Report 2015, p. 147, ibid. 2016, p. 153, thes.2017, p. 169, thes. 2018, p. 114.

each convey "an accurate overall picture of the Group's position" and that the "opportunities and risks of future development are accurately presented."[25] However, this was factually incorrect in each year. The auditor would, therefore, have had to object to such Risk Reporting. If Wirecard had not complied with Risk Reporting that reflected the actual circumstances of the net assets, financial position, and results of operations and fully disclosed all risks, this would at least have had to be reported in the auditor's report.

[25] See Wirecard: Annual Report 2015, p. 261, ibid. 2016, p. 273, thes. 2017, p. 289 and thes. 2018, p. 218.

9

Audit Opinion and Auditor's Report

At the end of an audit, the auditor forms an audit opinion. The opinion is visible in the auditor's report for the external addressee of the company's financial reporting. IDW PS 400 applied until 2017 and was replaced by IDW PS 400 n.F. from the end of November 2017. At the same time, modifications to the audit opinion were newly regulated in IDW PS 405.

Important documents of the auditor remain hidden from the addressees of the consolidated financial statements themselves, his working papers as the most important documentation on the audit planning, audit procedures, and obtaining the necessary audit assurance to reach an audit opinion, as well as the audit report, in which the auditor has to inform the client in writing and with the necessary clarity about the nature and scope as well as the result of the audit based on IDW PS 450 para. 8 and IDW PS 450 n.F. para. 1. Under Sect. 321 a (1) sentence 1 HGB, a creditor or shareholder may only inspect the auditor's reports on the audit of the last three financial years in the event of insolvency. Before this, the audit opinion is of the greatest importance for the addressee of the financial statements.

According to IDW PS 400 para. 8, the auditor's report has to contain a concluding assessment of whether the accounting records and the annual financial statements (if applicable, the consolidated financial statements), as well as the management report (if applicable, the group management report), comply with the statutory provisions including Generally Accepted Accounting Principles or IFRS and other national regulations (in this case, e.g., the group management report). By IDW PS 400 para. 14, the auditor's report may only be issued after the audit required for the assessment in accordance with the auditor's professional judgment has been materially

© The Author(s), under exclusive license to Springer Nature Switzerland AG 2024

E. Löw and R. Heyd, *The Audit Failures of the Wirecard Scandal*,
https://doi.org/10.1007/978-3-031-59854-8_9

completed. By IDW PS 400 para. 41, the audit result may take the form of an unqualified or qualified audit opinion or a disclaimer of opinion due to objections or serious audit impediments. IDW PS 400 para. 68a states that the prerequisite for a refusal due to audit impediments is that the auditor, after exhausting all reasonable possibilities to clarify the matter, is not in a position to arrive at a—possibly qualified—audit opinion with a positive overall statement on the financial statements. Due to the significance of the audit opinion, it has to be provided with a professional seal in accordance with IDW PS 400 para. 86.

"If, exceptionally, the auditor can't obtain an overall opinion as part of the audit (e.g. due to impediments to the performance of audit procedures), it has to be clarified whether this is due to a circumstance that constitutes good cause for cancellation of the audit engagement within the meaning of Section 318 (6) HGB. If an audit engagement is terminated, neither an audit opinion nor a certificate is to be issued. Still, a report on the results of the audit to date is to be issued by Section 318 (6) sentence 4 HGB (see IDW PS 450, para. 150 et seq.)." (IDW PS 400 para. 10).

Due to its importance, IDW PS 400 (n.F.) devotes several sections with numerous paragraphs to the formation of an audit opinion. Firstly, IDW PS 400 (n.F.) para. 13 stipulates that the auditor has to form an audit opinion. According to IDW PS 400 n.F. para. 14, the auditor has to conclude "whether reasonable assurance has been obtained as to whether the financial statements as a whole are free from material misstatement, whether due to fraud or error." According to the explicit reference in this paragraph, the conclusion drawn by the auditor in accordance with IDW PS 261 n.F. as to whether sufficient appropriate audit evidence has been obtained has to be taken into account. The same applies to the management report by IDW PS 400 (n.F.) para. 19. For certain companies, including Wirecard, the auditor's report has to report on particularly important audit matters in accordance with IDW PS 400 n.F. para. 50 (to which IDW PS 401 applies). According to IDW PS 405 para. 4, there are three types of modified audit opinions: the qualified audit opinion, the disclaimer of opinion, and the declaration of non-issuance of an audit opinion. In accordance with Section 322 (4) sentence 2 HGB, a report containing a disclaimer of opinion or a declaration of non-issuance may not be labeled as an auditor's report, but as a disclaimer of opinion. By IDW PS 405 para. 9, an audit opinion has to be modified in the auditor's report if it impedes the audit. By IDW PS 405 para. 13, a declaration of non-issuance of an audit opinion has to be made if the auditor comes to the conclusion that the possible effects of audit impediments could be not only material but also comprehensive.

A large number of auditing standards were breached during the audits of Wirecard's financial statements and insufficient audit evidence was obtained for numerous matters. Against this backdrop, it is incomprehensible that the auditor issued unqualified audit opinions for the 2015 to 2018 financial years.[1] Numerous indicators suggest that the required audit had not yet been materially completed when an unqualified audit opinion was issued. This would be a massive violation of IDW PS 400 para. 14. There were serious audit impediments in the TPA business in all years. By IDW PS 400 para. 68a, the audit opinion had to be refused in these years.

The accounting and auditing regulations in place at the time of the audits would have required a more careful and in-depth audit of Wirecard's financial statements if the audit had been properly subsumed. There were serious breaches of disclosure requirements—for example in the segment reportings and in the risk reports—which the auditors were obliged to criticize. This was particularly because the disclosure practiced massively (consciously and intentionally) misled the recipients of Wirecard's financial statements about the group's actual business activities and risk situation. It is inconceivable that the auditor would not have noticed the fraudulent actions if the principles of proper auditing had been observed.

Obvious deficiencies in the audit of Wirecard's financial statements were already evident in the application of the risk-oriented audit approach by IDW PS 261 as amended. It should be noted here that the main risk for the auditor is that it overlooks a material error in the annual or consolidated financial statements. Significant weaknesses can be seen in the risk assessment before and during the audit, particularly if there are sufficient indications of inaccuracies and violations (suspicion of fraud, IDW PS 210).

The starting point for every audit is the risk-oriented audit approach, which makes the audit strategy and audit procedures dependent on an initial risk assessment that is updated throughout the audit. In general, and particularly in the case of suspicion of fraud, which in the present case was present at Wirecard due to numerous press releases in advance[2] and the risk indicators to be dutifully collected by the auditor in accordance with IDW PS

---

[1] See Orlandi: The Wirecard case: Challenges for German and European supervision; working paper Luiss University Rome, Department of Economics and Finance, Chair of Market Law and Regulation, Coordinator Prof. Paola Lucantoni, Advisor Prof. Mirella Pellegrini, Academic Year 2020/2021, pp. 65–66, see also Zeranski/Sancak: Does the 'Wirecard AG'Case Address FinTech Crises?; working paper, ZWIRN Zentrum für wissenschaftliches, interdisziplinäres Risikomanagement und Nachhaltigkeit, working paper ZWP/2020/2, 17 October 2020, p. 11.

[2] See Orlandi: The Wirecard case: Challenges for German and European supervision; working paper Luiss University Rome, Department of Economics and Finance, Chair of Market Law and Regulation, Coordinator Prof. Paola Lucantoni, Advisor Prof. Mirella Pellegrini, Academic Year 2020/2021, pp. 65–66.

210 para. 22–57, the auditor's critical mind toward the audited company, its legal representatives, employees, and supervisory bodies is of particular importance. Clearly, IDW PS 210 para. 22–57 was violated. At least fifteen indicators from the catalogue of possible indications of fraud in IDW PS 210 para. 35 have been identified. In this context, IDW PS 210 para. 72 requires the auditor to qualify or refuse the audit opinion (with an obligation to give reasons) if the company prevents the auditor from carrying out investigations to uncover possible fraud. Either the auditor has not sufficiently investigated the fraud indicators, which is a massive violation of the risk-oriented audit approach, or the auditor has withheld key documents. In the present case, there is a great deal of evidence to suggest that both offenses were fulfilled and that the audit opinion should be refused accordingly.

According to IDW PS 210 para. 58, the existence of significant inherent and control risks given recognizable serious indications of misstatements and violations, to take just one of the fifteen fraud indicators as an example, required the auditor to carry out further investigations into the circumstances that led to the indications of misstatements and violations and the possible effects on the financial reporting. The auditor had to draw conclusions for the audit and reporting and align the audit strategy and audit procedures accordingly or adjust them in this direction during the audit if the indications of inaccuracies and violations were identified according to IDW PS 210 para. 18.

There was no doubt that Wirecard had an inadequate internal control system, of which the auditor was aware. Depending on the appropriateness and effectiveness of the internal control system, which is to be determined using a structural and functional audit, the audit strategy and the audit procedures are to be determined in accordance with IDW PS 261 (n.F.) para. 19–85, which have to influence the type, scope, and intensity of the audit procedures. Indications of inaccuracies and violations trigger extended auditing, documentation, and reporting obligations for the auditor based on IDW PS 210 para. 58–72. This was to be taken into account to a greater extent in the massive deficiencies and inadequacies identified in the (group) accounting-related control and risk management system at Wirecard, but was clearly not sufficiently recognized by the auditor. In this case, it is not only about the inadequate internal control system at Wirecard itself. Rather, Wirecard did not scrutinize the controls allegedly carried out by the business partners, for example about merchants, which was accepted uncritically by the auditor.

IDW PS 300 n.F. para. 10 requires the auditor to obtain audit evidence regarding the accuracy and completeness of information originating from the company to be audited. This was violated on several occasions. Such audit evidence is not available.

When assessing the relevance and reliability of the audit evidence used in accordance with IDW PS 300 n.F. para. 8, the auditor at Wirecard had considerable doubts when, for example (and by no means conclusively),

- screenshots from sources of TPA partners at non-recorded meetings showing the booking documents for sales and cash flow transactions,
- primarily statement-related audit procedures are used as the basis for assessing key audit matters (a clear violation of IDW PS 300 n.F. para. A3) and
- account statements and account balances of the (fiduciary) account-holding banks of the fiduciary accounts material to the overall statement of the Wirecard consolidated financial statements are not inspected (violation of IDW PS 302 n.F. para. 7).

According to IDW PS 302 (revised) No. 5, the auditor has to plan and perform the obtaining of third-party confirmations in such a way that relevant and reliable audit evidence is obtained based on which the auditor can form an opinion with reasonable assurance. The reliability of information in accordance with IDW PS 300 n.F. para. A29 is influenced by the type and origin as well as the circumstances under which it is obtained. In the case of Wirecard, it is particularly striking in this context about IDW PS 302 n.F. para 11–13 that the legal representatives did not enable the auditor to request confirmation from the (fiduciary) account-holding banks. The auditor should not have been satisfied with waiving the right to inspect the account statements and balance confirmations of the (fiduciary) account-holding banks. Rather, in the application of IDW PS 302 para. 11, the effects on the assessment of the associated risks of error, including the risk of non-compliance and the nature, timing, and extent of other audit procedures, as well as alternative audit procedures aimed at obtaining relevant and reliable audit evidence had to be assessed. Furthermore, to fulfill IDW PS 302 n.F. para. 11 c) as well as para. 12 and para. 13, it was imperative that the auditor assesses the effects of this audit impediment on the audit opinion and, in particular, on the audit findings.

Since the auditor used the statements of the trustees on the development and amount of the balances in the escrow accounts as a substitute for inspecting the account statements and balance confirmations of the (escrow) account-holding banks, special requirements would have had to be placed on the competence, skills and objectivity of the expert, in this case, the trustees, based on IDW PS 300 n.F. para. 9. IDW PS 300 n.F. para. A3 states that interviews alone do not normally provide sufficient audit evidence. According to IDW PS 300 n.F. para. 14, if the auditor has doubts about the reliability of the confirmation request, he has to obtain further audit evidence to eliminate these doubts. In the present case, it was obvious to raise such doubts. It is not apparent that the auditor has reconsidered his assessment of the related risks of error, including the risk of non-compliance, as well as the nature, timing and extent of the corresponding audit procedures, which is contrary to IDW PS 302 n.F. para. 15. Again, there is insufficient and appropriate audit evidence (IDW PS 300 n.F. para. 7 and 8). It is unacceptable that the existence of—alleged—assets on escrow accounts of up to EUR 1.9 billion remains effectively unaudited.

Wirecard did not even comply with the fundamental principles of proper accounting. For example, the financial reporting in the years 2015 to 2018 revealed numerous violations of Generally Accepted Accounting Principles, such as the principle that no entry may be made without a supporting document, which calls into question both the correctness and the accuracy and reliability of the accounting system as a whole and not just in parts. Wirecard itself thus violated Section 238 (1) HGB and the auditor had to reject the inadequate accounting.

"External auditors and their audit opinions certifying the financial statements play a critical role in the oversight system, not least because of their privileged access to corporate information."[3] The fundamental violations of numerous relevant auditing standards that were identified led to the auditor issuing unqualified audit opinions in the years 2015 to 2018, although it became apparent that the auditor could not have had sufficient audit evidence. Instead, the audit opinion should have been refused. The fraud could have been detected by the auditor at an early stage if the audit had been carried out properly in accordance with the rules applicable at the time.

[3] Langenbucher/Leuz/Krahnen/Jan/Pelizzon (2020): What are the wider supervisory implications of the Wirecard case?; SAFE White Paper, No. 74, ISBN 978-92-846-7442-8, Leibniz Institute for Financial Research SAFE, Frankfurt a. M., p.13, https://doi.org/10.2861/936827; this Version is available at: http://hdl.handle.net/10419/226215.

10

Concluding Remarks

The Wirecard fraud is considered the biggest economic scandal in Europe since the Second World War. A scandal of this magnitude needs to be analyzed with the aim of drawing conclusions and making improvements. This process was initiated immediately and will continue for many years to come. This applies in particular to the ongoing court proceedings. In particular, the following are involved in the investigation:

- the capital market supervision,
- the insolvency proceedings,
- the jurisdiction,
- the parliament,
- the legislator.

Capital market supervision has a variety of tasks in order to protect the groups involved in the capital market in different ways. This includes monitoring compliance with regulations by companies utilizing the capital market, for example in the area of corporate management and control, and the acceptance of accounting regulations by the company in question or compliance with generally accepted auditing principles in relation to the auditor.

In 2005, a two-stage enforcement procedure was introduced in Germany for auditing compliance with International Financial Reporting Standards (IFRS) by capital market-oriented companies. In the first stage, enforcement was mainly carried out by the German Financial Reporting Enforcement Panel (FREP) as an organization under private law. Only in the second stage

© The Author(s), under exclusive license to Springer Nature Switzerland AG 2024
E. Löw and R. Heyd, *The Audit Failures of the Wirecard Scandal*,
https://doi.org/10.1007/978-3-031-59854-8_10

did the Federal Financial Supervisory Authority (BaFin) take on a sovereign role.

The introduction of effective enforcement in Germany was also to be seen in the context of developments towards the creation of an integrated European capital market. In February 2001, the Lamfalussy Group set up by the EU Commission submitted proposals for an integrated European capital market. In addition to the demand for high-quality auditing, the main proposals concerned the mandatory preparation of the consolidated financial statements of European capital market-oriented companies in accordance with IFRS and the simultaneous introduction of effective enforcement in order to achieve a standardized and consistent application of IFRS.

In accordance with Sections 342b to 342e HGB, the FREP's task was therefore to examine whether the most recently adopted annual financial statements and the associated management report or the most recently approved consolidated financial statements and the associated group management report of a company comply with accounting standards. This essentially involves determining whether a chosen accounting method is in line with the relevant accounting regulations—primarily IFRS and supplementary national and European regulations on disclosure. The aim of the enforcement procedure is to improve the quality of accounting as a preventative measure, to uncover irregularities in the application of accounting regulations and thereby strengthen confidence in the capital market. At the FREP, the examination itself primarily focused on matters where experience has shown that accounting is prone to error due to complex issues, difficult-to-apply presentation rules that require interpretation or unwelcome disclosure requirements. The complete financial statements are neither re-examined a second time after the audit by the auditors nor is the objective of a fraud examination. The FREP was not equipped for either in terms of the number of people or the relevant expertise. The companies co-operated with the FREP on a quasi-voluntary basis. In the event of a refusal to cooperate, the procedure was transferred to the BaFin, which, as the sovereign authority, had coercive measures at its disposal, meaning that the company in question was effectively unable to avoid an examination.

In 2020, the FREP had 15 employees and managed an annual budget of around EUR 6 million. If the FREP identified an error at a company that was not disclosed and corrected by the company upon request by the FREP, the BaFin, as the sovereign authority, was tasked with further proceedings. During its fifteen years of existence, the FREP has uncovered more than 300 accounting errors. In the second stage, the BaFin enforced the publication of violations by sovereign means. The combination of enforcement under private law and by the state was intended to give companies the opportunity to resolve disagreements about accounting issues under private law with a panel of highly qualified—and appropriately remunerated—experts. This system should therefore combine the advantages of both a private enforcement solution, as used to exist in the UK, and a public law solution, as is traditional in France and the USA, for example.

At Wirecard, the enforcement proceedings led to a lack of clarity with regard to competences and responsibilities when responding to accounting fraud. It would have been perfectly possible to retain the two-stage procedure. However, it would have required strict clarification of the responsibilities and accountability of the individual organizations. However, in view of BaFin's actions as a securities supervisory authority against journalists and short sellers in the specific case of Wirecard, it is questionable what the reaction of BaFin as the sole enforcement body would have been in a one-stage system. The effectiveness of the two-stage enforcement system has been examined in several studies. Incidentally, the studies were viewed quite positively.[1] It is not known whether a one-stage enforcement (like in the USA) works more effectively than a two-stage enforcement.[2]

The German legislator has decided otherwise and, in the wake of the Wirecard scandal, has organized enforcement into a single-stage system. The single-stage system is based on the assumption that a single competent authority with the necessary powers and accountability can react more appropriately and quickly to suspected cases of fraud. The corresponding Financial Market Integrity Strengthening Act (FISG) implements a more centralized procedure in which BaFin can intervene directly and immediately in cases of concrete suspicion of fraud. Almost all of the FREP's employees were taken on by the BaFin, which is an indication of its professional quality. In addition, the BaFin's staff has been significantly increased.

While there was an enforcement procedure with the FREP and BaFin for capital market-oriented companies with balance sheets, which has since been converted into a single-stage procedure, there is a body that has reviewed and continues to review the activities of auditors. Auditors who audit capital market-oriented companies, such as Wirecard, have been subject to the Auditor Oversight Authority (APAS) in Germany since 2016. The APAS functions autonomously and independently of the auditing profession. In organizational terms, it is integrated into the Federal Office of Economics

---

[1] See Sellhorn: Wirecard—der Weckruf, Skandal zeigt dringenden Bedarf nach mehr Transparenz und evidenzbasierter Regulierung auf; Der Betrieb (DB) 2020 M4-M5, p. M5.

[2] See Sellhorn: Wirecard—der Weckruf, Skandal zeigt dringenden Bedarf nach mehr Transparenz und evidenzbasierter Regulierung auf; Der Betrieb (DB) 2020 M4-M5, p. M5.

and Export Control (BAFA), which in turn is a federal authority that is part of the Federal Ministry of Economic Affairs.

Beginning in October 2019, APAS examined in the case of Wirecard whether the auditors

- has refrained from carrying out its own research and, if necessary, audit procedures at key points,
- has not reacted appropriately in the event of delays or refusal to hand over documents,
- has interpreted contradictions in the statements of the Executive Board and Supervisory Board in favor of the company,
- the assumption that a long auditor–client relationship goes hand in hand with the risk of personal familiarity is correct,
- the auditor may have relied on the integrity of the client instead of examining matters himself or planning and conducting the audit with a critical attitude.

APAS finalized its report in December 2023. It covers the financial statements for the years 2016 to 2018,[3] but the APAS report has not been made publicly available. The report is said to comprise a total of 2,000 pages.[4] At the same time, sanctions were imposed on the auditor. Part of the penalty includes a two-year ban on accepting new audit mandates at public interest entities. The auditor has lodged an appeal against the decision of the APAS and the sanctions imposed therein—presumably initially with the aim of having sufficient time to comprehensively review the next steps. However, a long delay in the proceedings is not in the interests of the auditor, as the corresponding sanctions only take effect once the decision becomes legally binding, meaning that the two-year ban on accepting new audit mandates for public interest entities only begins to run at that point. Although it is to be expected that the very comprehensive APAS report will contain highly interesting details on the work of the auditor—which, incidentally, are also likely to be of interest in some of the court cases, namely when it comes to the misconduct of the auditor—the report will probably be able to contribute little to clarification for the time being due to the secrecy. However, the sanctions imposed prove that the work of the auditors was seriously flawed.

---

[3] See Großeastroth/Koch: The Wirecard scandal – Does the loss of auditor reputation cross borders?; working paper Johannes Gutenberg University Mainz (Germany) Draft Date: December 2023, p.1.

[4] See Bender/Fröndhoff/Votsmeier: Wirecard-Skandal—Aufseher gehen mit EY hart ins Gericht, Handelsblatt 21.12.2023, retrieved on March 06, 2024 from https://www.handelsblatt.com/unternehmen/dienstleister/wirecard-skandal-aufseher-gehen-mit-ey-hart-ins-gericht/100002306.html.

The Wirecard Management Board filed for insolvency on 25 June 2020 due to imminent insolvency and over-indebtedness. Insolvency proceedings were opened at Munich Local Court on 25 August 2020. By the same resolution, the insolvency creditors were requested to file insolvency claims with the insolvency administrator in writing by 26 October 2020. In a judgment dated 23 November 2022, the Regional Court of Munich I ruled that Wirecard shareholders with any claims for damages under capital market law cannot participate as insolvency creditors in the insolvency of the issuer.

During the insolvency proceedings, the insolvency administrator was able to successfully realize sales processes for the core business of the insolvent Wirecard AG, the acquiring and issuing business, as well as for Group companies that operated their own business areas.[5] The core business and the valuable foreign subsidiaries were sold by mid-2021, generating total proceeds in the triple-digit millions for the various insolvency estates. Other areas of activity of the insolvency administration continue to be the pursuit of liability and other claims against the parties involved in numerous jurisdictions worldwide and the clarification of legal issues relating to liabilities and equity providers. The insolvency proceedings are ongoing. It is hoped that the proceedings will bring to light far-reaching information on the Wirecard scandal, including the role of the auditor.

During the years when the press published suspicions of balance sheet manipulation and fraud against Wirecard, the courts had supposedly adopted Wirecard's position by prosecuting journalists and short selling. In the meantime, there are a number of pending court proceedings in connection with the Wirecard scandal, which are also expected to shed further light on the activities of the auditors, such as[6]

- the capital investor test case against the former Wirecard Management Board,
- around 1,200 individual lawsuits filed by aggrieved investors against the auditor,
- the capital investor test case against the auditor,
- lawsuits filed by aggrieved business partners against Wirecard,
- the criminal proceedings against the former Wirecard Management Board and individual executives,

[5] See Jaffe Rechtsanwälte: Referenzverfahren Wirecard AG, retrieved on March 06, 2024 from https://www.jaffe-rae.de/referenzverfahren/detail/wirecard-ag/.

[6] See also Großeastroth/ Koch: The Wirecard scandal—Does the loss of auditor reputation cross borders?; working paper Johannes Gutenberg University Mainz (Germany) Draft Date: December 2023, p. 8.

- the civil proceedings against the former (four) Wirecard Management Board members,
- a civil action brought by the insolvency administrator against the former Chairman of the Management Board,
- the insolvency proceedings against Wirecard AG and individual Group companies.

In order to clarify the Wirecard scandal, above all politically, a parliamentary committee of enquiry of the Bundestag was launched on 8 October 2020. The committee of enquiry has 18 full members, including 6 from the CDU/CSU parliamentary group, 4 from the SPD parliamentary group and 2 representatives each from the AfD, FDP, Die Linke and Bündnis 90/ Die Grünen parliamentary groups. There is also a corresponding number of deputy members. The main issue to be discussed was who bears the political responsibility for the fact that the supervisory authorities waited far too long and were too cautious in scrutinizing the payment service provider Wirecard, even though there were numerous concrete indications. Why did BaFin report journalists from the FT who had reported on the suspicions instead of investigating the allegations at Wirecard? Why did BaFin employees not trade in any share as often as in Wirecard shares? Why didn't the auditors uncover the fraud?[7]

The investigation period extends from 1 January 2014 to the establishment of the committee of enquiry. The remit of the committee of enquiry mainly included scrutinizing the following points:

- behavior of the German government and its agencies with regard to the investigations,
- uncovering possible connections between government agencies and Wirecard,
- clarification of whether BaFin recognized or could have recognized criminal acts,
- clarification of the possible submission of evidence of balance sheet falsification, money laundering or any illegal activities,
- investigating whether the auditors violated applicable law or deviated from auditing standards during audits for Wirecard and clarifying any conflicts of interest,
- conclusions for a possible revision of control structures.

---

[7] Löw/Kunzweiler: Der Fall Wirecard, Bilanzierungsgerüchte und Reaktionen von BaFin, Wirtschaftsprüfern und Wirecard in den Konzernabschlüssen, Berlin 2021, p. 84.

The committee of inquiry should also make recommendations and draw conclusions on the following reform points:

- reform of financial supervision,
- reform of auditing and balance sheet control,
- reform of money laundering supervision, including further development of the money laundering guidelines and criminal prosecution of accounting fraud and disclosure of the exchange between the federal government and its stakeholders.

The report of the committee of enquiry is available to the public. The evaluation of the auditor's documents was assigned to four auditors under the direction of special investigator Martin Wambach (Rödl & Partner). The relevant findings relating to the committee of enquiry and the special investigator have been included in the previous chapters of this book.

On 26 October 2020, the Ministry of Finance and Consumer Protection and the Ministry of Justice published a draft bill for a law to strengthen financial market integrity. This was followed by the government draft, which was published on 16 December 2020. This initiative is part of an action plan by the Federal Ministries of Finance and Consumer Protection as well as Justice from 6 October 2020 in response to the Wirecard scandal.

Ultimately, the legislator responded to the events surrounding Wirecard with two laws that are now in force, the Financial Market Integrity Strengthening Act (FISG) and the Corporate Stabilization and Restructuring Act (StaRUG).

Of particular importance in this context is the Financial Market Integrity Strengthening Act (FISG) of 3 June 2021 (Federal Law Gazette I 1534 et seq. of 10 June 2021). It came into force on 1 July 2021 (partly with transitional provisions as of 1 January 2022).

It comprises three regulatory areas

- strengthening corporate governance,
- tightening up the audit of financial statements,
- improving supervision.

The FISG established the obligation to set up an Internal Control System (ICS) and Risk Management System (RMS) for listed companies in the legal form of a stock corporation (Section 91 (3) AktG as amended). In addition to the provisions on an Early Risk Detection System (Section 91 (2) AktG), Section 91 (3) AktG requires an appropriate and effective Internal Control

System and Risk Management System. It is no longer sufficient to merely recognize risks at an early stage. They have to also be managed systematically. There were undoubtedly deficiencies in the control system at Wirecard, although it was not apparent that the auditor had drawn any consequences from this for the risk-oriented audit approach. Given the apparent ignorance of numerous fraud indicators by the auditor when planning and carrying out his audit procedures, it is to be feared that a more efficient control system at Wirecard would not have been able to directly influence the auditor's behavior. The quality of the audit was far too poor and the auditor's errors were too numerous and too profound. These regulations would only have had an indirect effect on the work of Wirecard's auditor. Even if the new rules in this sense would probably not have led to this auditor uncovering the Wirecard scandal at an early stage, they are still very welcome overall.

The Supervisory Board of Public Interest Entities (PIEs, Section 316a HGB new version) are obliged to have at least one member with expertise in accounting and at least one other member with expertise in auditing (Section 100 (5) AktG new version). There is an obligation to establish an Audit Committee as a subgroup of the Supervisory Board (Section 107 (4) sentence 3 AktG, new version). An additional mandatory task of the Audit Committee is to monitor the quality of the audit (Section 107 para. 3 sentence 2 AktG, new version). In the future, the members of the Audit Committee (Section 107 para. 4 sentence 4 AktG (new version)) will also have a right to information from the heads of the central departments, for example, the Heads of Internal Audit, Accounting or Risk Management. The aim here is to ensure that the Supervisory Board obtains an independent picture of the risk situation and the quality of the Risk Management System, which is also influenced as little as possible by the Management Board. In this area of governance, Wirecard also lagged significantly behind all other companies listed in the Prime Index of Deutsche Börse—in deviation from the German Corporate Governance Codex. In this respect, it is at least conceivable that a different composition of the Supervisory Board, which would have acted much more confidently toward the Management Board, would have at least made the fraud case more difficult, perhaps even uncovered it. Advantages will also arise from strengthening the Supervisory Board in its collaboration with the auditor. If the Supervisory Board makes use of these legal changes, it becomes a more competent contact for the auditor and, conversely, can challenge him more clearly. The Supervisory Board not only has the task, but also an interest, in recognizing a negligent financial statement audit at an early stage and taking action against it. It is therefore to be expected that the quality of the professional exchange will increase, which could have a positive interaction with the audit procedures.

To tighten up the audit of the financial statements, both an external and an internal rotation obligation will be introduced in the audit of the financial statements. Empirical studies show an inconsistent evidence.[8] The external rotation relates to the obligation to regularly replace the audit firm appointed. The maximum term for the audit mandate is 10 years. Internal rotation refers to the obligation to regularly replace the responsible audit partner as head of the audit team every five years (instead of every seven years previously) (Section 43 (6) WPO new version). The prohibition of incompatible auditing and consulting services has been revised. The regulations on the critical mindset were also revised and tightened in the Auditors' Code (Section 43 (3) WPO new version), as was the criminal liability for accounting offences, e.g., Section 331a HGB new version. Furthermore, the auditor's liability under civil law was tightened depending on the degree of fault. In the case of Wirecard, it is not recognizable that the new regulation would have led to the auditor behaving differently in the audits. Inadequate internal or external rotations were not responsible for the fact that an audit opinion was issued without sufficient audit procedures.

The two-stage enforcement procedure was abolished. At the same time, BaFin's powers have been extended. In future, it will be possible to summon and question members of the executive bodies and the auditor, as well as having the right to search and seize (business and residential premises) (Section 107 (5) WpHG as amended). In the case of investigations of public interest, transparency may not be restricted by confidentiality obligations, for example, on the part of the auditor (Section 107 (5) WpHG as amended).

The German Corporate Stabilization and Restructuring Act (StaRUG) specifies and expands the risk management requirements for German companies with the legal form of a stock corporation. Whereas previously the Management Board was only required to take suitable measures, in particular to set up a monitoring system, to ensure that developments jeopardizing the continued existence of the company are recognized at an early stage (risk early warning system Section 91 (2) AktG), risk management and risk control are now required. In addition, the management of companies with limited liability is obliged to implement suitable measures to safeguard the company's continued existence if necessary. Furthermore, the executive board and its subordinate bodies are obliged to inform the supervisory board.

[8] See Quick: Kritische Würdigung der geplanten wesentlichen Änderungen bei handelsrechtlichen Jahresabschlussprüfungen nach dem RegE eines Gesetzes zur Stärkung der Finanzmarktintegrität; Der Betrieb (DB), 2021, pp. 125-129, here p. 126.

This information should include an assessment of the risk situation as well as a description of the planned suitable countermeasures and an assessment of their effectiveness as entrepreneurial decisions within the meaning of Section 93 AktG. These stricter legal requirements are to be welcomed, as they emphasize the already very high priority that internal control and internal risk systems should have and are legally binding.[9]

Nevertheless, as with the discussion of the legal changes to the internal control system, it can be assumed that there would have been no impact on the auditor's behavior in the Wirecard scandal. This is all the more true as the Risk Reports that were published in Wirecard's Consolidated Financial Statements and were supposed to show the real risks of Wirecard's business activities gave a completely incorrect and misleading picture of the risk situation. Despite knowledge of the real business risks, this was tolerated by the auditor for years and never objected to. In fact, the auditor participated in deceiving the addresses of the financial reporting through inaction.

Ultimately, however, it should be noted that further findings are more likely to come from the course and conclusion of the insolvency proceedings and the court proceedings, while the legal changes would have made the fraud more difficult because a functioning internal control and risk system would have had to be introduced. In contrast, the fraud could have been uncovered by the auditors if the existing auditing standards had been applied conscientiously, either by carrying out further audit procedures to obtain sufficient audit evidence or by determining that sufficient audit evidence could not have been obtained and therefore no audit opinion should have been issued. Instead, the auditor committed numerous and very serious breaches of existing auditing standards. There is no need to tighten the law in this area.

---

[9] „Based on Wirecard´s CG report and CG statement issued on March 29, 2018, the management and Supervisory Board declared that the Company had complied with the recommendations of the Government Commission German Corporate Governance Code (Code) with the following exceptions: 1. Supervisory Board committees (the Audit Committee, the Remuneration, Personnel and Nomination Committee, and the Risk and Compliance Committee) were not formed until the first quarter of 2019. 2. Wulf Matthias is both the Chairman of the Supervisory Board and the Chairman of the Audit committee due to the special expertise and experience possessed by Mr. Matthias beginning in 2019." See Jo/Hsu/Llanos-Popolizio/Vergara-Vega: Corporate Governance and Financial Fraud of Wirecard; European Journal of Business and Management Research www.ejbmr.org DOI: http://dx.doi.org/10.24018/ejbmr.2021.6.2.708 Vol 6 | Issue 2 | March 2021, p. 101.

"Wirecard also failed to apply numerous provisions of the German Corporate Governance Code. But this did not alarm the markets, as the Code is overwhelmingly regarded as non-binding soft law." See Möllers: The Wirecard accounting scandal in Germany, and how the financial industry failed to spot it; The International Lawyer, vol. 54, no.3, 2021, pp. 325-360, p. 335. See also Orlandi: The Wirecard case: Challenges for German and European supervision; working paper Luiss University Rome, Department of Economics and Finance, Chair of Market Law and Regulation, Coordinator Prof. Paola Lucantoni, Advisor Prof. Mirella Pellegrini, Academic Year 2020/2021, p. 61.

In contrast, simple compliance with the existing rules and regulations and a careful audit by Ernst & Young, as is to be expected of a conscientious auditor, could have uncovered Wirecard's fraud, which had been going on for years, at an early stage. An optimistic and positive conclusion can be drawn for both young students and experienced auditors. Anyone who carries out their work seriously in the interests of the public and behaves professionally, carefully, straightforwardly, and uprightly towards the audited company does not need to worry about a damage of the own reputation or even liability regulations.

Bibliography

Aktionär, D. (16. Oktober 2019): Wirecard: So äußert sich das Unternehmen (D. Aktionär, ed.); retrieved on February 27, 2024 from https://www.deraktionaer.de/artikel/aktien/wirecard-so-aeussert-sich-das-unternehmen-20192275.html.

Almeling/Flick/Scharr: Abschlussprüfung klipp und klar, Wiesbaden 2020.

Bayram/Meier: Marktmanipulation durch Leerverkaufsattacken; Zeitschrift für Bank- und Kapitalmarktrecht (BKR) 2018, S. 55–63.

Beck'scher Bilanzkommentar: 13. edition Munich 2022, 14. edition Munich 2024.

Beerbaum: The future of audit after the Wirecard Accounting scandal—Consideration of the „Wambach Report"; working paper Aalto University School of Business, Department of Accounting, Helsinki, Finland, June 2022.

Beerbaum/Jani: Satyam versus Wirecard—A case study research on two accounting corporate scandals; Journal of Applied Research in the Digital Economy, February 2021.

Beerbaum: The future of audit after the Wirecard Accounting scandal—Proposal for a change in the payment model; working paper Aalto University School of Business, Department of Accounting, Helsinki, Finland, https://ssrn.com/abstract=3934773.

Bender/Fröndhoff/Votsmeier: Wirecard-Skandal Aufseher gehen mit EY hart ins Gericht; Handelsblatt December 21, 2021; retrieved on March 6, 2024 from https://www.handelsblatt.com/unternehmen/dienstleister/wirecard-skandal-aufseher-gehen-mit-ey-hart-ins-gericht/100002306.html.

Bergermann/Haseborg: Die Wirecard Story; 4. edition Munich 2021.

Betz/Kim: Economic regulation and corporate governance: The case of Wirecard Institute for policy models; Seattle, WA, USA, Department of International Business, Keimyung University, Keimyung University, Daegu, South Korea Modern Economy, 2021, 12, pp. 1386–1423. https://www.scirp.org/journal/me.

© The Editor(s) (if applicable) and The Author(s), under exclusive license to Springer Nature Switzerland AG 2024

E. Löw and R. Heyd, *The Audit Failures of the Wirecard Scandal*,
https://doi.org/10.1007/978-3-031-59854-8

BLZ (Berliner Zeitung), & Reuters. (July 16, 2020): Wirecard: Manager will auspacken (B. Zeitung, ed.); retrieved on February 27, 2024 from https://www.berliner-zeitung.de/wirtschaft-verantwortung/wirecard-manager-will-auspacken-li.93575.

Committee of Inquiry: Wirecard Investigation Committee, Report on the results of the investigation mandate to support the work of the 3rd Parliamentary Investigation Committee (of the 19th electoral term) of the German Bundestag. (Deutscher Bundestag, Beschlussempfehlung und Bericht des 3. Untersuchungsausschusses der 19. Wahlperiode gemäß Artikel 44 des Grundgesetzes, June, 22, 2021, printed matter 19/30900).

Conceptual Framework for Financial Reporting issued by the International Accounting Standards Board in September 2010: revised in March 2018; cited as Conceptual Framework.

Deutscher Bundestag: Beschlussempfehlung und Bericht des 3. Untersuchungsausschusses der 19. Wahlperiode gemäß Artikel 44 des Grundgesetzes, June 22, 2021, printed matter 19/30900 (cited as Committee of Inquiry).

dpa-AFX. (November 20, 2019): Wirecard-Aktie sackt ab: Kein Testat für singapurische Wirecard-Tochter - Wirecard sieht keine Unregelmäßigkeiten; (finanzen.net, Hrsg.) Düsseldorf; retrieved on February 27, 2024 from https://www.finanzen.net/nachricht/aktien/jahresabschluss-2017-wirecard-aktie-sackt-ab-kein-testat-fuer-singapurische-wirecard-tochter-wirecard-sieht-keine-unregelmaessigkeiten-8240195.

ESMA European Securities and Market Authority (November 2020): Fast track Peer Review on the Enforcement of Financial Information (ESMA 2014/1293) by BaFin and FREP in the context of Wirecard—Peer Review Report, ESMA 42-111-5349, cited as ESMA.

ESMA SMSG European Securities and Markets Stakeholder Group (February 2021): Advice to ESMA—Own initiative overviews report on the Wirecard case; ESMA22-106-3194, cited as SMSG.

Farr: Wirecard und seine Folgen für die Abschlussprüfung, Aufdeckung doloser Handlungen nach ISA (DE) 240; Die Wirtschaftsprüfung (WPg) 2021 S. 66–74.

Führungskräfte, W. a. (March 31, 2017): Receivables Q2 2017. Financial Times; retrieved on February 27, 2024 from https://www.ft.com/content/19c6be2a-ee67-11e9-bfa4-b25f11f42901.

Führungkräfte, W. b. (July–September 2016): Report WCUK-Ireland. Financial Times; retrieved on February 27, 2024 from https://www.ft.com/content/19c6be2a-ee67-11e9-bfa4-b25f11f42901.

Führungskräfte, W. c. (October 17, 2016): WUKI Payplugger, Financial Times; retrieved on February 24, 2024 from https://www.ft.com/content/19c6be2a-ee67-11e9-bfa4-b25f11f42901.

Golod (July 11, 2020): So hat Dan McCrum den Wirecard-Skandal aufgedeckt (Z. Rundfunk, Hrsg.); retrieved on February 27, 2020 from https://www.ndr.de/fernsehen/sendungen/zapp/So-hat-Dan-McCrum-Wirecard-Skandal-aufgedeckt,wirecard110.html.

GoMoPa.net. (October 26, 2012): Staatsanwalt stellt Wirecard-Ermittlung gegen GoMoPa-Chefs ein. Press Release (G. -G. Partners, ed.); retrieved on July 7, 2020 from https://www.gomopa.net/Pressemitteilungen.html?id=1052&meldung=Staatsanwalt-stellt-Wirecard-Ermittlung-gegen-GoMoPa-Chefs-ein&__cf_chl_jschl_tk__=38a6b6b538be7b1e4e220b017ee212d260b55b1f-1595325949-0-ASbKuF4TqxEa04XiU6PRJwWTGjoYaVpqaTlgtsJMMwVzgUNR48dWjol.

Graumann: Wirtschaftliches Prüfungswesen, 6. edition revised, Herne 2020, 7. edition Herne 2023.

Großeastroth/Koch: The Wirecard scandal—Does the loss of auditor reputation cross borders? Working paper Johannes Gutenberg University Mainz (Germany) Draft Date: December 2023.

Gschrei (May 15, 2020): Kurskapriolen der Wirecard-Aktie und die EY-Testate 2017 und 2018; Wirtschaftsprüfung in den Medien (w. e.-V. Wirtschaftsprüfung, ed.). Munich; retrieved on February 27, 2024 from https://www.wp-net.com/Pressemitteilungen.html.

Hammer (November 21, 2008): Streit um Wirecard: Aktionärsschützer im Zwielicht (Zeit online, ed.); retrieved on July 25, 2020 from https://www.zeit.de/online/2008/30/querdax-wirecard/komplettansicht#comments.

Handelsblatt Online (February 22, 2017): Aktien von Wirecard brechen ein. Nach „Manager Magazin"-Bericht (WirtschaftsWoche, ed.); retrieved on February 27, 2024 from https://www.wiwo.de/unternehmen/it/nach-manager-magazin-bericht-aktien-von-wirecard-brechen-ein/19429738.html.

Hennrichs: Finanzmarktintegritätsstärkungsgesetz (FISG) – die „richtigen Antworten auf Wirecard"? Der Betrieb (DB), 2021, pp. 368–279.

Hesse (April 30, 2016): Finanzmärkte: Die Schlacht um Wirecard - Wette auf den Absturz (D. Spiegel, ed.); Der Spiegel (18/2016), pp. 65–67.

Hoefer/Engemann (April 28, 2020): Sonderprüfung bei Wirecard lässt Fragen unbeantwortet (General-Anzeiger, ed.); retrieved on July 27, 2020 from https://ga.de/news/wirtschaft/ueberregional/sonderpruefung-bei-wirecard-laesst-fragen-unbeantwortet_aid-50283803.

IDW (ed.), WP-Handbuch, 17. edition, Düsseldorf 2020. 18. edition Düsseldorf 2023.

IDW: Stellungnahme des Hauptfachausschusses des Instituts der Wirtschaftsprüfer in Deutschland e.V., Die Kapitalflußrechnung als Ergänzung des Jahres- und Konzernabschlusses (SG/HFA 1/1995); Die Wirtschaftsprüfung (WPg), 1995, pp. 210–213.

IDW (ed.), Prüfungspraxis, Leitfaden für Prüfungsmitarbeiter, 2. revised edition, Düsseldorf 2020. 3. edition Düsseldorf 2023.

Jaffe Rechtsanwälte: Referenzverfahren Wirecard AG; retrieved on March 6, 2024 from https://www.jaffe-rae.de/referenzverfahren/detail/wirecard-ag/.

Jahn (July 21, 2008): Anlegerschützer unter Verdacht (F.A.Z., ed.); retrieved on February 27, 2024 from https://www.faz.net/aktuell/finanzen/aktien/kursmanipulation-anlegerschuetzer-unter-verdacht-1665356.html#void.

Jakubeit: The Wirecard scandal and the role of BaFin, A case for unifying capital markets supervision in the European Union; working paper 5/2021, Luiss School of European Political Economy Rome, March 22, 2021.

JCapitalresearch: https://www.jcapitalresearch.com/uploads/2/0/0/3/20032477/2015_10_30_wirecard_initiation_global_shorts.pdf.

Jo/Hsu/Llanos-Popolizio/Vergara-Vega: Corporate Governance and Financial Fraud of Wirecard; European Journal of Business and Management Research www.ejbmr.org Issue 2 | March 2021.

Justenhoven/Meyer: § 246; Beck'scher Bilanzkommentar, 13. Edition, Munich 2022, 14. Edition 2024.

Karami (ed.): Skandalfall Wirecard: Eine wissenschaftlich-fundierte interdisziplinäre Analyse, Wiesbaden 2022.

Karami: Das kollektive Kontrollversagen - ein Fall für die Lehrbücher; Karami (ed.): Skandalfall Wirecard: Eine wissenschaftlich-fundierte interdisziplinäre Analyse, Wiesbaden 2022, pp. 1–85.

Kirchner (July 14, 2020): Bafin führte bei Wirecard Bank große Sonderprüfung durch. Exklusiv (finanz-szene.de, ed.); retrieved on February 27, 2024 from https://finanz-szene.de/payments/bafin-fuehrte-bei-der-wirecard-bank-grosse-sonderpruefung-durch/.

KPMG AG. (2020): Bericht über die unabhängige Sonderuntersuchung - Wirecard AG, München. Prüfungsgutachten vom 27. April 2020, Wirtschaftsprüfung; retrieved on February 27, 2024 from https://www.wirecard.com/uploads/Bericht_Sonderpruefung_KPMG.pdf cited as KPMG Report.

KPMG Report: KPMG AG. (2020): Bericht über die unabhängige Sonderuntersuchung - Wirecard AG, München. Prüfungsgutachten vom 27. April 2020, Wirtschaftsprüfung; retrieved on February 27, 2024 from https://www.wirecard.com/uploads/Bericht_Sonderpruefung_KPMG.pdf.

Krüger (July 23, 2020): EY, was soll das? FAQ zum Wirecard-Skandal (t. V. GmbH, Hrsg.); retrieved on February 29, 2024 from https://taz.de/FAQ-zum-Wirecard-Skandal/!5695456/?goMobile2=1594080000000.

Langenbucher/Leuz/Krahnen/Jan/Pelizzon: What are the wider supervisory implications of the Wirecard case? SAFE White Paper, No. 74, ISBN 978-92-846-7442-8, 2020. Leibniz Institute for Financial Research SAFE, Frankfurt a. M., https://doi.org/10.2861/936827, this Version is available at http://hdl.handle.net/10419/226215.

Lenz: Die Verantwortung des Abschlussprüfers zur Aufdeckung von Bilanzdelikten (Täuschungen, Vermögensschädigungen), Das Fallbeispiel Wirecard AG; Zeitschrift für internationale und kapitalmarktorientierte Rechnungslegung (KoR) 2020, pp. 546–552.

Lenz: Die Prüfung von Treuhandkonten – das Fallbeispiel Wirecard AG, Erwiderung auf Marten; Der Betrieb (DB) 2020, pp. 1465–1469, 2085–2089.

Löw/Kunzweiler: Wirecard – Bilanzierungsgerüchte, BaFin-Meldungen und Niederschlag in den Konzernabschlüssen, Berlin 2021.

Marten: Die Prüfung von Treuhandkonten im Rahmen der Abschlussprüfung; Der Betrieb (DB) 2020, pp. 1465–1469.

Marten/Quick/Ruhnke: Wirtschaftsprüfung, 6. edition revised, Stuttgart 2020.

McCrum (November 12, 2015): Rupee do: What is Wirecard buying? House of Wirecard series (F. Times, ed.); retrieved on July 28, 2020 from https://ftalphaville.ft.com/2015/11/12/2144182/rupee-do-what-is-wirecard-buying/.

McCrum (April 27, 2015): The House of Wirecard. House of Wirecard series (F. Times, ed.); retrieved on July 28, 2020 from https://ftalphaville.ft.com/2015/04/27/2127427/the-house-of-wirecard/.

McCrum: House of Wirecard, London/Berlin 2022.

McCrum (May 5, 2015): The strange case of Ashazi: Wirecard in Bahrain, via Singapore. House of Wirecard series (F. Times, ed.); retrieved on July 28, 2020 from https://ftalphaville.ft.com/2015/05/05/2127886/the-strange-case-of-ashazi-wirecard-in-bahrain-via-singapore/.

McCrum (July 23, 2015): Wirecard: Adjust your perspective (part 1). House of Wirecard series (F. Times, ed.); retrieved on July 28, 2020 from https://ftalphaville.ft.com/2015/07/23/2131270/wirecard-adjust-your-perspective-part-1/.

McCrum (July 23, 2015): Wirecard: Adjust your perspective (part 2). House of Wirecard series (F. Times, ed.); retrieved on July 28, 2020 from https://ftalphaville.ft.com/2015/07/23/2134015/wirecard-adjust-your-perspective-part-2/.

McCrum (February 25, 2016): Shares in fintech darling plunge on critical report (F. Times, ed.); retrieved on July 28, 2020 from https://www.ft.com/content/0706763a-dadf-11e5-a72f-1e7744c66818.

McCrum (March 26, 2019): Wirecard says some Singapore employees may face criminal liability (F. Times, ed.). London; retrieved on July 28, 2020 from https://www.ft.com/content/2d8baf22-4fd1-11e9-b401-8d9ef1626294.

McCrum (May 17, 2019): What are the Wirecard allegations? (F. Times, ed.); retrieved on July 28, 2020 from https://www.ft.com/content/12d751e8-6c0c-11e9-80c7-60ee53e6681d.

McCrum (October 15, 2019): The Wirecard documents, explained. House of Wirecard series (F. Times, ed.); retrieved on July 28, 2020 from https://ftalphaville.ft.com/2019/10/14/1571059326000/The-Wirecard-documents--explained/.

McCrum (October 15, 2019): Wirecard's suspect accounting practices revealed (T. F. Times, ed.). London; retrieved on February 27, 2024 from https://www.ft.com/content/19c6be2a-ee67-11e9-bfa4-b25f11f42901.

McCrum (December 19, 2019): Middleman's profits draw India deal into Wirecard scandal (F. Times, ed.). London; retrieved on July 28, 2020 from https://www.ft.com/content/b3672388-200a-11ea-b8a1-584213ee7b2b.

McCrum (June 25, 2020): Wirecard: The timeline (T. F. Times, ed.); retrieved on July 23, 2020 from https://www.ft.com/content/284fb1ad-ddc0-45df-a075-0709b36868db.

McCrum/Palma (January 30, 2019): Executive at Wirecard suspected of using forged contracts (F. Times, ed.). Singapur; retrieved on February 27, 2024 from https://www.ft.com/content/03a5e318-2479-11e9-8ce6-5db4543da632.

McCrum/Palma (February 7, 2019): Wirecard: Inside an accounting scandal, Singapur; retrieved on February 27, 2024 from https://www.ft.com/content/d51a012e-1d6f-11e9-b126-46fc3ad87c65.

McCrum/Palma (October 18, 2019): Wirecard: The unanswered questions (F. Times, ed.). London-Singapur; retrieved on July 28, 2020 from https://www.ft.com/content/f4a89186-f0eb-11e9-ad1e-4367d8281195.

McCrum/Palma (February 1, 2019): Wirecard's law firm found evidence of forgery and false accounts (F. Times, ed.). Singapur; retrieved on February 27, 2024 from https://www.ft.com/content/79f23db0-260d-11e9-8ce6-5db4543da632.

McCrum/Storbeck (October 16, 2019): Wirecard faces calls from analysts for information on its accounting (F. Times, ed.). London-Frankfurt; retrieved on July 27, 2020 from https://www.ft.com/content/04706e68-f029-11e9-ad1e-4367d8281195.

McCrum/Storbeck (May 5, 2020): How the paper trail went cold in KPMG's special audit of Wirecard; Wirecard AG (F. Times, ed.). London-Frankfurt; retrieved on July 28, 2020 from https://www.ft.com/content/cc64ac71-9232-4815-b2df-41c46a73a5f0.

mm-newsdesk. (February 24, 2016): Aktie bricht nach dubioser Studie ein - Short-Attacke gegen Wirecard? (m. magazin, editor & rei/Reuters, director); retrieved on February 27, 2024 from https://www.manager-magazin.de/finanzen/artikel/wirecard-dubiose-studie-reisst-aktie-in-die-tiefe-a-1079111.html.

Möllers: The Wirecard accounting scandal in Germany, and how the financial industry failed to spot it; The International Lawyer, vol. 54, no. 3, 2021, pp. 325–360.

Möllers: Marktmanipulationen durch Leerverkaufsattacken und irreführende Finanzanalysen; Neue Zeitschrift für Gesellschaftsrecht (NGZ) 2018, pp. 649–658.

Mülbert: Rechtsschutzlücken bei Short Seller-Attacken – und wenn ja, welche?: Zeitschrift für das gesamte Handelsrecht und Wirtschaftsrecht (ZHR) 2018, pp. 105–113.

Mülbert/Sajnovits: Short-Seller-Attacken 2.0: der Fall Wirecard; Zeitschrift für Bank und Kapitalmarktrecht (BKR) 2019, pp. 313–323.

Murphy, P. (December 11, 2019): Wirecard critics targeted in London spy operation (F. Times, ed.); retrieved on July 28, 2020 from https://www.ft.com/content/d94c938e-1a84-11ea-97df-cc63de1d73f4.

Navaretti/Calzolari/Pozzolo: What are wider supervisory implications of the Wirecard case? Study Requested by the ECON committee, Economic Governance Support Unit (EGOV), Directorate-General for Internal Policies, PE 651.384—October 2020. http://www.europarl.europa.eu/supporting-analyses

Niedersachsen, N. 1. (July 2, 2020): OLB gab Wirecard-Chef offenbar Millionen-Kredit (Norddeutscher Rundfunk, ed.). Oldenburg; retrieved on August 11, 2020 from https://www.ndr.de/nachrichten/niedersachsen/oldenburg_ostfriesland/OLB-gab-Wirecard-Chef-offenbar-Millionen-Kredit,wirecard104.html.

Nienhaus (February 21, 2019): Warum schützt die Finanzaufsicht das Unternehmen? (D. Zeit, ed.) Die Zeit (Nr. 9/2019); retrieved on February 27,

2024 from https://www.zeit.de/2019/09/wirecard-finanzaufsicht-bafin-schutz-unternehmen-kursschwankungen?print.

Nietsch: Abschlussprüferhaftung nach Wirecard – Uwe Schneider zum 80. Geburtstag; Wertpapier-Mitteilungen (WM) 2021, pp. 158–168.

None. (July 24, 2008): Straub stolpert über Insidergeschäfte. Wirecard-Affäre (Z. Online, ed.); retrieved on February 27, 2024 from https://www.zeit.de/online/2008/31/sdk-ruecktritt-straub.

Orlandi: The Wirecard case: Challenges for German and European supervision, working paper Luiss University Rome, Department of Economics and Finance, Chair of Market Law and Regulation, Coordinator Prof. Paola Lucantoni, Advisor Prof. Mirella Pellegrini, Academic Year 2020/2021.

Peemöller: Bilanzanalytische Aufarbeitung des Wirecard-Bilanzbetrugs, Fallstudie zur Bilanzfälschung und Erklärungsansätze zu deren Nichterkennung; Zeitschrift für internationale und kapitalmarktorientierte Rechnungslegung (KoR) 2021, pp. 89–94.

Poelzig: Shortseller-Attacken im Aufsichts- und Zivilrecht, Zeitschrift für das gesamte Handelsrecht und Wirtschaftsrecht (ZHR) 2020, pp. 697–760.

Poltz, J. (December 10, 2018): Ermittler sehen Manipulation mit Wirecard-Aktien als erwiesen an (R. -i. Nachrichtenagentur, ed.). Munich; retrieved on July 20, 2020 from https://de.reuters.com/article/deutschland-wirecard-zatarra-idDEKBN1O91TG.

Quick: Kritische Würdigung der geplanten wesentlichen Änderungen bei handelsrechtlichen Jahresabschlussprüfungen nach dem RegE eines Gesetzes zur Stärkung der Finanzmarktintegrität; Der Betrieb (DB), 2021, pp. 125–129.

Rinker: Bilanzpolitik, Bilanzkosmetik, Bilanzfälschung, Munich 2022.

Rinker/Müller/Münker: Accounting Fraud, Wiesbaden, 2022.

Rinker: Vorwürfe wegen Bilanzmanipulationen gegen Wirecard, Darstellung ausgewählter Sachverhalte aus dem KPMG-Untersuchungsbericht; WP Praxis 2020, pp. 293–297.

Rödl & Partner, Wirecard Investigation Committee, Report on the results of the investigation mandate to support the work of the 3rd Parliamentary Investigation Committee (of the 19th electoral term) of the German Bundestag (cited as Wambach Report).

Schüttler: Prüfung von Treuhandkonten auf Vorhandensein; Der Betrieb (DB) 2020, pp. 1862–1863.

Schüttler: Die Treuhand im HGB-Abschluss, Weder Treugeber noch Abschlussprüfer müssen über Treuhandverhältnisse berichten – das muss sich nach Wirecard ändern! Unternehmenssteuern und Bilanzen (StuB) 2020, pp. 671–672.

Seidenstuecker/Uhlig (May 12, 2020): BaFin nimmt Wirecard an mehreren Fronten ins Visier. Unternehmensnachrichten (Reuters, ed.). Frankfurt; retrieved on August 1, 2020 from https://de.reuters.com/article/deutschland-bafin-wirecard-idDEKBN22O14D.

Sellhorn: Wirecard – der Weckruf, Skandal zeigt dringenden Bedarf nach mehr Transparenz und evidenzbasierter Regulierung auf; Der Betrieb (DB) 2020, M4-M5.

SMSG European Securities and Markets Stakeholder Group (February 2021): Advice to ESMA—Own initiative overviews report on the Wirecard case. ESMA22-106-3194; cited as SMSG.

Stenzel (July 6, 2020): Wie ein Journalist Wirecard auffliegen ließ. Hintergrund (Augsburger Allgemeine, ed.); retrieved on February 27, 2024 from https://www.augsburger-allgemeine.de/wirtschaft/Wie-ein-Journalist-Wirecard-auffliegen-liess-id57684581.html.

Storbeck/McCrum (April 25, 2019): Wirecard seeks to put scandal behind it with results (F. Times, ed.). Frankfurt-London; retrieved on July 28, 2020 from https://www.ft.com/content/9f6b4f70-671f-11e9-9adc-98bf1d35a056.

Storbeck/McCrum (October 3, 2018): Wirecard's meteoric rise prompts questions (F. Times, ed.). Aschheim-London; retrieved on July 28, 2020 from https://www.ft.com/content/d080c3fc-c561-11e8-8670-c5353379f7c2.

Storbeck/McCrum (October 18, 2019): Wirecard chairman dismisses calls for independent audit (F. Times, ed.). Frankfurt-London; retrieved on July 27, 2020 from https://www.ft.com/content/224cfe3a-f1bc-11e9-ad1e-4367d8281195.

Storbeck/McCrum (October 21, 2019): Wirecard appoints KPMG for independent review of accounting (F. Times, ed.). Frankfurt-London; retrieved on July 28, 2020 from https://www.ft.com/content/eeb18c70-f3ce-11e9-a79c-bc9acae3b654.

Storbeck/McCrum (November 6, 2019): KPMG widens review of Wirecard accounting (F. Times, ed.). Frankfurt-London; retrieved on July 28, 2020 from https://www.ft.com/content/e132cb98-0073-11ea-b7bc-f3fa4e77dd47.

Strunz (July 2, 2020): Bilanzen über Jahre aufgebläht? Wirecard-Skandal (A.-a. /. tagesschau.de, ed.); retrieved on July 27, 2020 from https://www.tagesschau.de/investigativ/ndr/wirecard-149.html.

Untersuchungsausschuss, Deutscher Bundestag: Beschlussempfehlung und Bericht des 3. Untersuchungsausschusses der 19. Wahlperiode gemäß Artikel 44 des Grundgesetzes, 22 June 2021, Drucksache 19/30900 (cited as Investigation Committee Committee of Inquiry).

Wambach-Report: Rödl & Partner, Wirecard Investigation Committee, Report on the results of the investigation mandate to support the work of the 3rd Parliamentary Investigation Committee (of the 19th electoral term) of the German Bundestag.

Wirecard (July 18, 2008): Yumpu (Wirecard AG, ed.); retrieved on February 27, 2024 from https://www.yumpu.com/de/document/read/281724/pressemitteilung-des-vorstands-und-des-aufsichtsrats-der-wirecard-ag.

Wirecard AG (May 3, 2020): Kernaspekte des KPMG-Berichts über die unabhängige Sonderuntersuchung der Wirecard AG (Wirecard. AG, ed.); retrieved on February 27, 2024 from https://www.wirecard.com/uploads/statement_2020_05_03_DE_KPMG_Kernaspekte.pdf.

Wirecard AG cited at Dow Jones & Company, Inc. (October 9, 2008): Wirecard sieht sich nach Prüfung durch Ernst & Young bestätigt (I. B. GmbH, ed.). Grasbrunn; retrieved on February 27, 2024 from https://www.channelpartner.de/a/wirecard-sieht-sich-nach-pruefung-durch-ernst-und-young-bestaetigt,267105.

Wirecard AG, a. (March 12, 2020): Wirecard AG: Sonderuntersuchung von KPMG; DGAP-News (Wirecard AG, ed.); retrieved on July 22, 2020 from https://ir.wirecard.de/websites/wirecard/German/5110/nachrichtendetail.html?newsID=1923071&fromID=5000.

Wirecard AG, b. (April 22, 2020): Wirecard AG: Sonderuntersuchung von KPMG dauert bis 27. April 2020 an. Untersuchung liefert bislang keine Belege für Bilanzmanipulation; DGAP-News (Wirecard AG, ed.); retrieved on July 22, 2020 from https://ir.wirecard.de/websites/wirecard/German/5110/nachrichtendetail.html?newsID=1949979&fromID=5000.

Wirecard AG, c. (April 28 2020): Wirecard AG: KPMG legt Bericht über Sonderuntersuchung vor; DGAP-News (Wirecard AG, ed.); retrieved on July 22, 2020 from https://ir.wirecard.de/websites/wirecard/German/5110/nachrichtendetail.html?newsID=1952849&fromID=5000.

Wirecard AG, d. (May 25, 2020): Wirecard AG: Veröffentlichung des Konzernabschlusses am 18. Juni 2020; DGAP-News (Wirecard AG, ed.); retrieved on July 22, 2020 from https://ir.wirecard.de/websites/wirecard/German/5110/nachrichtendetail.html?newsID=1970157&fromID=5000.

Wirecard AG, e. (March 26, 2019): Wirecard AG: Externe Untersuchung stellt keine wesentlichen Auswirkungen auf die Abschlüsse von Wirecard fest; DGAP-News; retrieved on July 22, 2020 from https://ir.wirecard.de/websites/wirecard/German/5110/nachrichtendetail.html?newsID=1763447&fromID=5000.

Wirecard AG, f. (January 31, 2019): Wirecard Statement zum Artikel der Financial Times. Statement gegenüber den Aktionären; retrieved on July 25, 2020 from https://ir.wirecard.de/websites/wirecard/German/5110/nachrichtendetail.html?newsID=1750985&fromID=5000.

Wirecard AG Annual Report (2015): Stay in the flow of your success—Synchronise your Business with Wirecard—Annual Report 2015, Aschheim, Wirecard AG; retrieved on August 14, 2020 from https://ir.wirecard.com/download/companies/wirecard/Hauptversammlung/160_DE0007472060-JA-2015-EQ-D-01.pdf, cited Wirecard Annual Report 2015.

Wirecard AG Annual Report (2016): Connected Commerce—Annual Report 2016, Aschheim, Wirecard AG; retrieved on August 14, 2020 from https://ir.wirecard.com/download/companies/wirecard/Annual%20Reports/DE0007472060-JA-2016-EQ-E-03.pdf, cited Wirecard Annual Report 2016

Wirecard AG, Annual Report (2017): Digitise Now—Annual Report 2017, Aschheim Wirecard AG; retrieved on August 14, 2020 from https://ir.wirecard.de/download/companies/wirecard/Hauptversammlung/08_DE0007472060-JA-2017-EQ-D-00.pdf, cited Wirecard Annual Report 2017

Wirecard AG, Annual Report (2018): Transition to Tomorrow—Annual Report 2018, Aschheim Wirecard AG; retrieved on August 14, 2020 from https://ir.wirecard.com/download/companies/wirecard/Annual%20Reports/DE0007472060-JA-2018-EQ-D-02.pdf, cited Wirecard Annual Report 2018.

Wirecard AG, g./Stöckl (February 1, 2019): Wirecard Statement zum Artikel der Financial Times; retrieved on July 25, 2020 from https://ir.wirecard.de/websites/wirecard/German/5110/nachrichtendetail.html?newsID=1751411&fromID=5000.

Wirecard AG, h. (February 4, 2019): Wirecard Statement February 4, 2019; DGAP-News: Statement zu den Vorwürfen; retrieved on July 25, 2020 from https://ir.wirecard.de/websites/wirecard/German/5110/nachrichtendetail.html?newsID=1751503&fromID=5000.

Wirecard AG, i./Stöckl (February 7, 2019): Wirecard Statement February 7, 2019, Folgestatement zur Stellungnahme vom 04. Februar 2019; retrieved on July 25, 2020 from https://ir.wirecard.de/websites/wirecard/German/5110/nachrichtendetail.html?newsID=1752577&fromID=5000.

Wirecard AG, j./Stöckl (February 8, 2019): Wirecard Statement February 8, 2019. Stellungnahme; retrieved on July 25, 2020 from https://ir.wirecard.de/websites/wirecard/German/5110/nachrichtendetail.html?newsID=1752749&fromID=5000.

Wirecard AG, l. (March 26, 2019): Wirecard AG: Externe Untersuchung von Rajah & Tann ergibt keine wesentlichen Auswirkungen auf die Abschlüsse von Wirecard; DGAP-News Stellungnahme (Wirecard AG, ed.); retrieved on July 25, 2020 from https://ir.wirecard.de/websites/wirecard/German/5110/nachrichtendetail.html?newsID=1763461&fromID=5000.

Wirecard AG, m./Stöckl (March 29, 2019): Wirecard Statement March 29, 2019, Statement zur Financial Times (Wirecard AG, ed.); retrieved on July 25, 2020 from https://ir.wirecard.de/websites/wirecard/German/5110/nachrichtendetail.html?newsID=1764635&fromID=5000.

Wirecard AG, n. (October 15, 2019): Wirecard Statement October 15, 2019, Statement zur Financial Times (Wirecard AG, ed.); retrieved on July 25, 2020 from https://ir.wirecard.de/websites/wirecard/German/5110/nachrichtendetail.html?newsID=1836799&fromID=5000.

Wirecard AG, o. (October 16, 2019): Wirecard AG: Statement zum Artikel der Financial Times; DGAP-News Statement zu Al Alam (Wirecard AG, ed.) Aschheim (München); retrieved on July 25, 2020 from https://ir.wirecard.de/websites/wirecard/German/5110/nachrichtendetail.html?newsID=1836741&fromID=5000.

Wirecard AG, p. (October 21, 2019): Wirecard AG beauftragt unabhängige Prüfung; DGAP-News (Wirecard AG, ed.); retrieved on July 25, 2020 from https://ir.wirecard.de/websites/wirecard/German/5110/nachrichtendetail.html?newsID=1838277&fromID=5000.

Wirecard AG, q. (November 20, 2019): Wirecard Statement November 20, 2019, Statement (Wirecard AG, ed.); retrieved on July 25, 2020 from https://ir.wirecard.de/websites/wirecard/German/5110/nachrichtendetail.html?newsID=1857619&fromID=5000.

Wirecard AG, r. (December 12, 2019): Wirecard AG Statement December 12, 2019, Statement zur Financial Times vom 11. Dezember 2019 (Wirecard AG, ed.); retrieved on July 25, 2020 from https://ir.wirecard.de/websites/wirecard/German/5110/nachrichtendetail.html?newsID=1871847&fromID=5000.

Wirecard AG, s. (December 17, 2019): Wirecard AG Statement December 17, 2019, Statement zu den zitierten Excel Dokumenten von Al Alam (Wirecard AG, ed.); retrieved on July 25, 2020 from https://ir.wirecard.de/websites/wirecard/German/5110/nachrichtendetail.html?newsID=1874757&fromID=5000.

Wirecard AG, t. (March 16, 2016): Wirecard Stellungnahme (Wirecard AG, ed.); retrieved on July 25, 2020 from https://ir.wirecard.de/websites/wirecard/German/5110/nachrichtendetail.html?newsID=1642675&fromID=5000.

Wirecard (2020): Application for opening of insolvency proceedings; retrieved on July 27, 2020 from https://ir.wirecard.com/websites/wirecard/English/5110/news-detail.html?newsID=1988247&fromID=1000.

Wirecard AG, u. (June 3, 2020): Wirecard AG zur aktuellen Situation des Unternehmens (Wirecard AG, ed.); retrieved on February 27, 2024 from https://www.wirecard.com/uploads/2020_06_03_DE_Statement-zur-aktuellen-Situation-des-Unternehmens.pdf.

Wirecard AG, v. (July 18, 2008): Yumpu (V. u. AG, ed.); retrieved on July 29 2020 from Yumpu.com: https://www.yumpu.com/de/document/read/281724/pressemitteilung-des-vorstands-und-des-aufsichtsrats-der-wirecard-Wirecard AG, w. (December 31, 2016).

Wirecard AG: Monitoring Customer Relationships, Tabellenkalkulation; Financial Times; retrieved on February 27, 2024 from https://www.ft.com/content/19c6be2a-ee67-11e9-bfa4-b25f11f42901

Wirecard AG, w. (2020): Statement of the Management Board about the current situation of the Company; retrieved on July 27, 2020 from https://ir.wirecard.com/websites/wirecard/English/5110/news-detail.html?newsID=1985593&fromID=5000.

Wirecard AG, x. (December 31, 2017): Q4 2017 Monitoring CR_intern. Financial Times; retrieved on February 27, 2024 from https://www.ft.com/content/19c6be2a-ee67-11e9-bfa4-b25f11f42901.

Wirecard AG, y. (July 20, 2017): Übersicht Dritt-Acquirer, Tabellenkalkulation (F. Times, ed.); retrieved on February 27 2024 from https://www.ft.com/content/19c6be2a-ee67-11e9-bfa4-b25f11f42901.

Wysocki von: Grundlagen, nationale und internationale Stellungnahmen zur Kapitalflussrechnung; Wysocki von (ed.): Kapitalflussrechnung, Stuttgart 1998, S. 1–33.

Zapp (producer), & NDR (director) (2020): So hat Dan McCrum den Wirecard-Skandal aufgedeckt [movie]; retrieved on July 27, 2020 from https://www.ndr.de/fernsehen/sendungen/zapp/So-hat-Dan-McCrum-Wirecard-Skandal-aufgedeckt,wirecard110.html.

Zeranski/Sancak: Does the 'Wirecard AG' Case Address FinTech Crises?, working paper, ZWIRN Zentrum für wissenschaftliches, interdisziplinäres Risikomanagement und Nachhaltigkeit, working paper ZWP/2020/2, October 17, 2020.

Index

© The Editor(s) (if applicable) and The Author(s), under exclusive license to Springer Nature Switzerland AG 2024
E. Löw and R. Heyd, *The Audit Failures of the Wirecard Scandal*,
https://doi.org/10.1007/978-3-031-59854-8

F

G

H

I

SPRINGER NATURE

GPSR Compliance

The European Union's (EU) General Product Safety Regulation (GPSR) is a set of rules that requires consumer products to be safe and our obligations to ensure this.

If you have any concerns about our products, you can contact us on ProductSafety@springernature.com

In case Publisher is established outside the EU, the EU authorized representative is:

Springer Nature Customer Service Center GmbH
Europaplatz 3
69115 Heidelberg, Germany

FSC
www.fsc.org
MIX
Papier | Fördert gute Waldnutzung
FSC® C083411

Kolibri 360 GmbH
Ferdinand-Jühlke-Straße 7
99095 Erfurt, Deutschland
produktsicherheit@kolibri360.de